For Donna,

Remember to

brEAThe

Blessings,

Muriel Brakefield

MURIEL BRAKEFIELD

PRAISE FOR brEAThe:

"Muriel determined she would see the truth about her life, and, tell what she saw. In the midst of the telling she uncovers moments of grace and light in a journey that was at times dark and difficult. Her words bear testimony to the mystery of faith that sustains her life. This is a story of great courage."

Christopher Page,
rector of St Philip's Anglican Church, Archdeacon of Tolmie in the Diocese of British Columbia and author of five books including: The Way of Courage, Mark's Gospel, Christ Wisdom, Shadow Dancing and Spirit Life.

———∞∞∞———

"As medical professionals, 'labelling' the patient may make us think that we have understood. Muriel's beautifully written, insightful memoir, has shown me how little I sometimes know about what is really going on and what it feels like to be on the receiving end of medical diagnoses and treatment. Her story moved me to tears and has challenged me to listen more carefully to the hidden story, the one that even the patient may not yet fully know. brEAThe inspires belief that against all odds healing is possible."

Dr. Juliette Eberhard MD,
has been practicing medicine as a family physician for over 30 years.

———∞∞∞———

"Muriel takes you on a journey to the darkest and most desolate realms. You find yourself torn by such devastation and then cheering her on as she astonishingly finds her way back to a place filled with hope and promise. A must read for every woman who needs a hero".

Liz Haslam,
mother of five and avid reader.

brEAThe

Forgiveness to Freedom,
A Memoir of Hope

MURIEL BRAKEFIELD

WESTBOW
PRESS
A DIVISION OF THOMAS NELSON

WestBow Press books may be ordered through booksellers or by contacting:

WestBow Press
A Division of Thomas Nelson
1663 Liberty Drive
Bloomington, IN 47403
www.westbowpress.com
1-(866) 928-1240

The names and identifying details of some characters in this book have been changed.

Cover Design Idea: Lisa Gray and Pat Rankin
Cover Photograph: Cindy Pakulak

ISBN: 978-1-4497-9066-0 (sc)
ISBN: 978-1-4497-9065-3 (hc)
ISBN: 978-1-4497-9067-7 (e)

Library of Congress Control Number: 2013906046

Printed in the United States of America.

WestBow Press rev. date: 04/09/2013

For Alan: in whom I found refuge during the darkest days and deepest nights. Who held me in his arms and heart until I could find myself hidden in Christ.

Strength for today bright hope for tomorrow...
Great is Thy Faithfulness.

Thomas O. Chisholm

Contents

REBUILDING

Forward by Mark Buchanan

"Taste and see that the Lord is good."

Thus exuded King David, with joyful playful child-like trust.

"My God, my God, why have you forsaken me?"

Thus lamented David, with sorrowful miserable cynic-like grief.

Will the real David please stand up?

Well, he is. He is both men: the one who dances with all his might, throwing himself with reckless abandon on God's wild lavish mercy; the man who skulks with resentful wariness, angry at God's inexplicable absences and strange caprices.

I think of David when I think of Muriel, and I think of his psalms when I think of her book—the one you're holding now.

Muriel, like David, has been in both places. She has tasted and seen that the Lord is good, and she has felt the terrifying emptiness of God's abandonment. She has exuded, and she has lamented, and sometimes nearly in the same breath.

All is to say, hers is a story both unique and deeply human. She tells of the capacity of good people to sometimes act very badly, and for bad people to sometimes change, and for good people to sometimes rise to the fullness of their goodness. She tells of betrayals and reconciliations, of dissolutions and restorations, of appalling hypocrisy and radical faithfulness. Hers is a story to break your heart and to heal it, just as her heart has been broken and healed.

This is a story of darkness and light, of madness and beauty. And the light and the beauty are all the greater because the darkness and the madness seem so all-consuming.

Muriel has a metaphor pulsing through this book—two, in fact. The first is eating—or, more to the point, her refusal to eat. She speaks candidly, painfully, at times humorously about her bulimia and anorexia, and the attempts of a whole phalanx of family members, friends, doctors, counsellors to get food into her.

The second metaphor is breathing. In and out. Deep, deeper.

It's in learning the art of breathing—literally, figuratively, spiritually— that Muriel at last learns the art of eating—literally, figuratively, spiritually. Herein is good news for all of us.

But I'll leave you now to the story itself.

Taste and see that the Lord is good.

Mark Buchanan is a pastor and award winning author of six books including: Your God is Too Safe, Things Unseen, The Holy Wild, The Rest of God, Hidden in Plain Sight and Your Church is Too Safe.

A Note to you from the Author

*E*veryone has a story. You are your story as I am mine. In sharing them we tell the truth of who we believe we are. Speaking our truth allows us to trace the hand of God, discovering and then declaring His faithfulness, as he interfaces with us in our fragile human experience.

I was asked to share my story at a Women's conference a couple of years ago. To pack 50 years into 50 minutes is a challenge; this book is the expanded version. My story is one of being lost and found, wounded and healed. It is an ordinary tale of redemption yet redemption is never anything less than extraordinarily miraculous.

I had a typical life in many ways. I was born into a Christian home. From the moment I drew my first breath, I was immersed in the life of the church: faith has always been part of my life. I gave my heart to the Lord when I was four years old and made a public declaration at fourteen. After high school, I went to college for a couple of years then joined a Christian ministry where I met my husband. Alan and I have been happily married for thirty years and were blessed with four sons. We raised our boys in a vibrant church and homeschooled them when they were small. After they were in school full time, I worked supporting children with special needs in a Christian preschool. Alan and I are enjoying this season of our lives as empty nesters and are involved in our church. I share my life as a peer mentor, work and volunteer part time at a therapeutic community and spend hours reading, writing and gardening. I am surrounded with lots of wild and wonderful friends.

That is the true story of my life, the neat and tidy version. But in between each sentence are cracks. Beneath them lay huge chasms where the real story is wedged, hidden, out of sight.

A few years ago, I witnessed a crime and had to go to court. After taking the stand, and placing my hand on the Bible the clerk said, "Do you promise to tell the truth, the whole truth, and nothing but the truth, so help you God?"

It struck me that when we are called to give our testimony the first part is simple: we tell the truth, we don't lie. The last part is equally straight forward: we don't add on or elaborate. But by far the most challenging piece is being faithful to the middle: telling the whole truth. And to tell the truth even half right we need God's help.

But why bother to tell the truth of our lives at all, especially the messy parts?

"You shall know the truth and the truth will set you free". These ancient words attributed to Jesus echo through the ages and resound in our hearts. Sharing my truth with you allows me to live more fully in that freedom and opens the possibility that you too will be set free to do a bit of storytelling of your own, if only to yourself.

Telling truthful stories can be tricky. One difficulty we have when we set out to tell our story is we all come into awareness about our lives part way through. Even those with typical family experiences rely heavily on others to frame their early life. Our formative years—the critical period where our young soul is shaped, our beliefs are indelibly etched on our hearts and our genetic code is being tweaked—begin long before we are able to use words to create a tale.

Children record pictures in their mind and store experiences in their bodies as feelings. They are taught to interpret those images and sensations by those around them. The stories we believe to be true shape us and become the narrative we live out of.

As children, our stories are often captured as photographs. Both literally and figuratively, our parents take snapshots through their lens, frame it from their perspective and then hand us a photoshopped version telling us the story. Their reality, our family's version of the story, is the one we are taught to believe is true. What becomes challenging is when our memories—the movies in our mind, the emotions embedded in our cells—don't match the still frame sitting upon the mantle in our childhood home, and the rhetoric accompanying that shot caught on canvas.

Telling the truth, our truth, our account of the story can be risky. If, as a child, our tale fails to match the family story, we are often corrected. Sometimes we are immediately edited so our version is more in keeping with the prevailing one. We are told we have it all wrong and are retold the accepted story. "No honey that's not the way it happened. You may not remember because you were quite small but...". If we persist on giving our rendition, we are said to be confused, lying or completely crazy. As children, we often stop telling our story altogether. As adults, we continue to force ourselves to live another's version of our experience. Living in untruth keeps us bound and gagged, squishing out life. We can't breathe.

Coming to understand my family of origin and how growing up within it shaped my life has been much like gathering a handful of confetti after it has been tossed in the air and blown by wind then trying to tidily arrange those tiny round circles and fit them into the sheets of paper from which they were cut. If I were to take those million little pieces and make them into a perfect square, creating a story with a smooth narrative arc, I most certainly would be accused of writing fiction rather than a memoir. It would require tampering with truth, something I am not prepared to do. I have tried to tell my story truthfully. Some of the tales have jagged edges and hang awkwardly in my book because they remain perched unsupported in my child's mind.

But perhaps neither my story nor the one first told by my family is most important. The real story, the one that matters, the tale I need to learn to tell, is the truest, most freedom-filled story of all, a God-breathed story, the story of who He says I am.

Fool, fool can you not put together the puzzle?
Is it too difficult for your mortal brain to discover?
Can you not see how the pieces fit?
Are you still confused by my wit?

I find it difficult to believe you do not understand,
all the tricks I have played, control I have on demand.
Is it by glass, mere separation
you lose full comprehension?
Or is it your inadequacy to see
on two levels through one dimension
to take knowledge learned,
wisdom of a realization?

I laugh but somehow cry for you
pity overwhelms my view
I remember how once so inseparably we shared
now you don't remember, don't even care.

Then pain to you, sorrow and shame
caught in a world once childish game
Person divided, person not whole
I give you the body but I keep our soul

MURIEL RUTH
MARION ROSE
age 15

The Formation of Faults

Fault

1: obsolete: lack

2: a: weakness, failing; *especially: a moral weakness less serious than a vice*

   b: a physical or intellectual imperfection or impairment: defect

   c: an error especially in service in a net or racket game

3: a: misdemeanor

   b: mistake

4: responsibility for wrongdoing or failure <the accident was the driver's fault>

5: a fracture *in the crust of a planet (as the earth) or moon accompanied by* **a displacement of one side of the fracture with respect to the other usually in a direction parallel to the fracture**

Jarred awake, instantly freezing, strong rhythmic waves send ice surging through my veins. My tongue glued to the roof of my mouth, my lips stuck together, I swallow hard and breathe—In then out.

I open my eyes. It is dark.

Lying on my back, my left arm strapped to a board. Steep steel rails engulf me. Out of the corner of my right eye, an outline of a door with a window in the upper half and a dim light shining beyond it takes shape.

I hear a noise. Inhaling sharply, I hold my breath.

My heart, hammering in my chest, thrusts its way up into my throat until it takes over all the space in my head.

My eyes dart left.

There are three other beds in the room and in the far corner a shadow by the window comes into focus.

A woman, hovering over the side of one of them, is hanging a glass bottle in the air.

Then I remember: I am in the hospital.

Gasping in, exhaling deeply, the fear slips out with my breath.

Breathe, just breathe.

Epicentre

I was fifteen when I ran away from home. I ran away for the same reasons most kids do: because I was hurt and angry but most of all sad. It was dark and pouring with rain as I turned the corner of the street where I lived—a busy corridor that runs east to west in the High Park area of Toronto—and headed up Laws Street toward Dundas Avenue. I really didn't know where I was going, just away, as far away as I could run. The pulsing of my heart grew stronger in my head, the rhythmic thumping drowning all noise, inside and out. The faster I ran, the less I could think, the less I could feel. I struggled forward, hunched over by the ache in my side, staccato gasps sucking in icy air, stinging my lungs.

I was picked up by a police officer who flashed his lights, whirled the siren and demanded I get into his cruiser. At first, when he asked my name, I didn't answer. Instead, looking straight ahead, I watched the windshield wipers go back and forth, cradling my thoughts, lulling them asleep. Twisting my fist into my side, I tried to work out the knot in my tight gut. Then, inhaling deeply, I held my breath to keep the tears inside where they belonged.

He probably wasn't used to being ignored, especially by a scrawny teenage girl who had taken off just before midnight. He told me if I didn't tell him my name and address he would have to take me to juvenile hall. I turned and looked at him. I don't know if I was more mad or sad but I was definitely scared. It frightened me enough to tell him who I was and when I told him where I lived, he laughed.

It really wasn't funny. I did live at a boys' Group Home. It was the same one he and many of his cronies had paid countless visits to over the previous months. My mom and dad were the Group Home parents and that is where I lived—me and eight juvenile delinquent boys: just one big unhappy family.

He took me home and when my mom finally answered the door it was obvious she had been asleep. Oh, she knew I had gone out all right. She had tried to stop me, grabbing the back of my jacket as I slithered out of it to break free, bolting into the cold October night. I guess she was tired because she had just returned that evening from a six-week vacation. Calling a trip to visit my brother and his wife in Michigan a vacation may be harsh, but she did vacate. The Group Home, where we lived and where she had worked that last year, had taken its toll. She was exhausted. So one day, weary of it all, my mom booked a flight. She told me she was off to see Wayne and didn't know when she would return but it would be after my birthday, which hurt my feelings. By then my feelings were getting hurt on such a regular basis and I was sick of hearing how sensitive I was so I pretended not to feel, especially not to feel hurt. I secretly thought she wasn't coming home. I knew that if I were her and had a one-way ticket to anywhere in the world I wouldn't come back. I would vacate permanently. And that's what I did. I disappeared inside. I became vacant.

Fractures

I hated the Group Home from the beginning. It was the latest in a long list of places my family had lived as my parents found different ways to serve the Lord. Moving had always been part of our life because when I was little my parents had been Majors in the Salvation Army.

My dad had always been a Salvationist like his mom and dad before him. His parents had been soldiers, so in all the old black-and-white family photographs they wore their uniforms proudly. When Dad was a young man, just out of Normal School—the words they used for Teacher's College back when he was twenty—he felt called to the ministry and went through the Officers Training College in Toronto and was commissioned as a Lieutenant.

My mom had grown up in the Salvation Army too. I know even less about her family and nothing of my parents' younger years other than that they were, as they said, "posted all over the map". They met at Congress, an annual gathering of officers from all across Canada and the only place single officers were able get to know one another. After writing letters for a year they decided to get married and start a family. Dad was thirty-two and Mom twenty-eight when one Monday evening in 1948, surrounded by a small gathering of friends, wearing their dress uniforms, my parents were wed. My brother Wayne was born nine months and nine days later and Margaret arrived two years after, right on schedule. I didn't show up until the fall my sister started grade one.

Being the baby of the family has some advantages to be sure, but it can be lonely as well. By the time I was old enough to play, there was no one to play with. Each morning when Wayne and Margaret left for school I'd stand at the window waving goodbye. Through my tears, I would watch as they walked down Lount Street, turn the corner, then vanish.

Most often I spent the long mornings at the Hall with my parents. They were busy. There was always a lot for my mom and dad to do: preparing sermons, organizing music, meeting with people and the endless sorting of clothes in the Thrift Store where I was not allowed to go. The smell from the mothballs made my eyes burn and nose itch and once I started sneezing, it continued until I was certain my head would blow off. So, instead, I played downstairs in the Sunday School room. I had tons of toys: puzzles, books, dollies and even a play kitchen with a pretend tea set. I would line up the plastic children, sitting them in chairs and sing to them at the top of my lungs, teaching them all the songs I learned in Sunday School, and then I'd preach to them. But I was lonely.

I often asked Mom if I could, "please, pretty please, with sugar on top" have a baby sister so I would have a friend to play with, but she said that she was too old to have another child and it was probably true. Mom turned thirty-eight the year I was born and did not want another kid. She told me once she had always thought she would have four children but she said, "it hadn't been the Lord's will". I asked what she would have named this other child and she said his name would have been Murray James, the one chosen for me had I been a boy rather than a girl. I didn't want a brother. I wanted a sister to play with so when pressed she said if I had had a twin she would have named her Marian Rose. I liked that, Muriel Ruth and Marian Rose. From that day on Marian, my twin sister, and I were inseparable friends. I finally had someone to talk to.

Having an imaginary friend was fun but it helped with more than the loneliness. When things didn't go well it was never my fault. I could blame bad things, like the thoughts in my head or stuff I didn't want happening, on her and pretend we were separate. Although she mostly lived on the other side of the mirror, she could pop out and be right there with me when I needed her most, but sometimes it was hard to remember where she began and I ended.

I was born with a cold, or so it was thought, before the tests I had at the age of four revealed I was allergic to almost everything in the world. The doctor stuck my arms up and down with little pricks that hurt like bee stings and, instantly, those tiny bumps joined hands and made my arms swell to the size of two overripe zucchinis, proving I was allergic to life. From then on, everything from cats to grass, wool to varnish, along with all the pretty flowers that made me sneeze and caused my eyes to swell up tight, were off limits.

The soft bedside mat in my room had to be removed and the hardwood floors needed to be damp-mopped daily, making lots of extra work for Mom. All my stuffed animals had to be given away because they were ridden with dust mites. Even my Sam Sam the Bedo Man, a sock monkey with ridiculously long arms and legs whom I loved, was put in a box and taken down to the Thrift Store behind our Hall. I never really understood until I was much older why my big brother laughed so hard when I said my monkey's name since I was just copying him. He called him Sam Sam the B.O. Man. Years later, Wayne had to painstakingly walk me through the humour, explaining B.O. was short for body odour. I was mad when I finally got the joke but I was really more sad that Sam had to be sent off in a box.

My allergies were not just a nuisance; I got really sick. Each Friday afternoon, my dad would take me to Dr. Kristov's office for my injection. I would pretend Marian was getting the shot, not me. It was easier to be brave when the doctor put that huge needle in her arm rather than mine. But after dinner each Friday night, there was no mistaking it: I felt sick. I would lie on the couch with a big bag of frozen peas pressed to my upper arm which was a swollen tight knot as big as my fist and burning hot to the touch. I didn't feel well Saturday either but usually by the time Hockey Night in Canada came on I was all better and would climb up on my dad's knee and we would cheer for the Toronto Maple Leafs.

It wasn't just things outside that made me sick. There were too many foods on the off-limits list, including oatmeal, which I had had nearly every morning of my life and continued to be served, because it was, as my mom said, "good for what ails you". With a twinkle in his eye and the best Scottish accent he could muster, my dad would tell me I should eat my porridge because it put hair on your chest, which seemed a strange reason to eat anything. It was breakfast, as simple as that. It always had been and always would be even if it made my throat itch and nose pour. Complaining was not allowed in our family, so I learned to keep my thoughts and feelings tucked tightly inside.

My favorite part of the day was teatime. When I was tiny, I would awaken from my afternoon nap and call downstairs, "Is tea ready yet mommy?" and come paddling down to find my Bunnykins cup and saucer sitting alongside one of her very fancy teacups on the dining room table. She would pour the milk in first—because that was the proper way to do it—then from the big teapot, which had been steeping for just the right amount of time, she filled our cups, but not too full. Mine was mostly milk and Mom referred to it as "poothsue". It was good that mine was "water bewitched and tea begrudged", another name she had for the weak brew. If someone poured my mom a cup and she called it by either name, I knew she thought it was a pretty poor cup of tea.

Growing up there was always one thing I could count on: change. Each spring, the week after Congress—the Salvation Army's annual meeting—a big manila envelope would arrive in our mailbox. The typed one-page letter gave us our ministry assignment and every two years it would tell us where we would live; they were our Marching Orders. Once we received this letter, things happened fast. The following Sunday, we had our farewell service and the next week our family was welcomed into the new corps. We often moved clear across the country. It was Army policy that we couldn't even write to the soldiers in the old corps for a complete year so we had a crisp clean break, a fresh start.

Moving was pretty easy because almost everything belonged to the Army. The houses where we lived were called the quarters and they came fully furnished, right down to sheets and cutlery. The only things we had to pack and take with us were a few gifts Mom had received as wedding presents, china we used for Christmas dinners, some pictures, our clothing and books. A couple of favorite toys were sometimes transferred with us. Moving within the same town was all but unheard of. We arrived in a new city at the beginning of July, moved into a new house that was completely different from the one before, began again at a new corps and started over in a new school in the fall.

I loved the Salvation Army: the uniforms, the big brass band, the deep sound of the bass drum and the flag emblazoned with the words "Blood and Fire" that led the procession down the main aisle of the Hall where we met each Sunday morning and evening. It wasn't a church, but rather a corps; to speak of anything within the Salvation Army in anything other than militaristic terms was sacrilege. Standing on tippy-toes atop my chair, belting out all five verses of *Onward Christian Soldiers* marching as to war, is what I remember most from those young years. I may not have looked much like a soldier then in my frilly cotton dress poofed out by an itchy crinoline, with white ankle socks, black patent-leather shoes and fine hair falling unnaturally in ringlets due to sleeping in curlers each Saturday night, but I dreamed I was one. I couldn't wait for the day when I was old enough to wear a uniform, join the Songsters and learn the drills of the tambourine troop making ribbons fly through the air with such precision.

It would never happen. I was eight years old when my parents got kicked out of the Salvation Army. They had been officers for twenty-five years. It all had to do with speaking in tongues. My parents, well my mom anyway, had just been baptized in the Holy Spirit and had started praying in a weird language that sounded something like Chinese. In their dismissal papers, the Colonel formally charged my parents with insubordination. He went on to say that speaking in tongues was dispensational and the gifts of the Holy Spirit, recorded in the *Book of Acts*, were just for the disciples and people in biblical times, not for modern day Christians. My mom said she was being persecuted and we were dismissed. Leaving the Army was not like quitting any old church where you could pop down the street and join another denomination you liked better; it was more like being banished from your life. We had to move into a new life and start all over. After that, there were lots of changes, ones I couldn't predict. There was little I could count on.

Dad didn't have a job. He was fifty years old and had been an Army officer forever. He had become a teacher in his early twenties but had never actually taught school. He was good with numbers, so he began doing taxes for people and selling life insurance. He worked from early in the morning and took courses at night school so he was rarely home before I went to bed. In three years, he graduated with his degree from the University of Toronto and started teaching accounting at George Brown Community College.

Things changed for my mom too, but I don't think she liked being at home cooking and cleaning all the time. She had relished the busy-ness of Army life and especially loved being with people. She was such an organized person that, by the time I left for school, she would have all the daily chores done and then have empty hours to fill. That first year, she spent lots of time praying and writing in her Bible. When I came home for lunch, I could tell she had been crying. She cried a lot when she prayed but because she was speaking in her secret prayer language I didn't know what she was saying or what she was crying about. When I asked her, she said she wasn't sad—but she looked sad to me.

Mom liked to write and paint and made beautiful pictures using copper-tooling. She constantly had new projects on the go. She had always made our clothes and that became even more important after leaving the Army because we must not have had a lot of money, although no one would have ever known by looking at us. She made me beautiful dresses from scraps of material or remade them from the ones my sister had before me. She embroidered my name on some of them because Muriel was unusual, unlike Debbie or Cathy. No one could ever pronounce—let alone spell—my name and you certainly could never buy anything with Muriel written on it, so Mom would make a fancy M and then, with tiny stitches, craft the other letters onto the upper corner of my jumpers. She always made hair bands to match and even designed clothes for my dollies out of the same fabric, which really impressed my friends. Until my sister, who worked at Reitman's the summer I was turning eleven, bought me five beautiful store-bought dresses with unfinished seams, made out of cheap material, I always wore clothing designed and sewn by my mother.

Mom continued to do a lot of preaching after we left the Salvation Army. She was very involved in Women's Aglow. My brother nicknamed the group The Neon Ladies. When asked, my mother would always say that it was a charismatic Christian organization. I didn't know what that meant. I did know, besides having big retreats where my mother was often the guest speaker, that these women sat squeezed tightly together in our tiny living room each week. When I came home from school I would peek in and see them gathered there, glued to my mom's every word as she taught them from the Bible. People loved to hear my mom talk. She was gifted with words. Whenever she spoke in churches, she drew big crowds and after she finished her sermon people responded with long, loud prayer meetings. At home she was on fire for God too and started answering our telephone by saying, "Praise the Lord" which always made Margaret roll her eyes.

When I was nine my mom decided she wanted to be a nurse. She told me she had always dreamed of being an RN and this was the perfect time for her to go into training. I was used to having my mom around so I didn't know what to think about that change. She was gone all day and I had to buy tickets in the morning to have hot lunches at school and in the evening she had to study. Dad was studying too. Reading and studying became part of our evening routine.

I liked the sameness of routine. It made me feel safe. In public school, I liked the certainty that each morning we started by singing God Save the Queen and O Canada followed by reciting The Lord's Prayer. Of course, every year was a little different but I knew teachers liked schedules too, so by the end of the first few days I could pretty much count on what was going to happen next. I liked routine so much that, once I could write, I made my own to-do list for the mornings before school and one for after I got home as well. Saturday was a free day but I secretly followed the same schedule as much as possible. Sunday, although entirely different, had a rhythm all its own.

Sunday came early in our household; it was orderly, fast-paced and actually started the evening before. Saturday night after my bath, I sat on the floor in the living room in front of Mom and tried not to wiggle while she parted my wet hair into tiny sections with a pointy comb. Each piece had to be rolled tightly into black curlers that had prickly white barbs sticking through them before being secured in place with sharp pink pins. I listened as Wayne practiced the piano. He always started with scales and triads then went on to studies. He finished by polishing up the new piece he had been working on all week, the metronome keeping time, keeping him in line. Margaret sat to the side in the dining room polishing the silver while Dad, in the mudroom, polished all our shoes.

By morning, my beautiful black shoes with the shiny silver buckle shone so brightly I could almost see my reflection in the smooth leather if I looked closely. They were set squarely on the floor by my closet with my frilly lace ankle socks tucked inside. At the end of my bed, there was a chair where Mom hung my Sunday dress the night before. On the seat, my panties, slip, and crinoline lay neatly beside each other. My little white Bible that had my name etched in gold on the bottom right-hand corner and the card with the week's memory verse were placed together under my purse.

My curlers which scratched my scalp making sleep almost impossible had to come out, but not until after breakfast. When I heard the house begin to stir, I would put on my slippers and buttoning up my housecoat carefully, paddle downstairs. Dad, whose job it was to stir the porridge, would ask me how his Little Scotch Bluebell slept. I would stand up on a chair beside him and watch as he plopped hot cereal into our bowls before sprinkling brown sugar on top which Mom said was done too generously. We always ate together so while Mom was calling Wayne and Margaret, who were tired teenagers, I would sit at the table swinging my legs and practice being patient.

After breakfast dishes were cleared away and the table was set for Sunday dinner, I went upstairs to wash and start the dressing process. When I was really little, I needed help. Remembering to put the slip on first was important and the crinoline was tricky. Getting it to poof out my dress just so always took time. Because my dress had tiny buttons in the back, it was impossible to do on my own. As I grew older and my dresses didn't have to be quite as fancy, I was able to manage myself. I don't know if the styles changed or whether my mother just grew tired of the fuss but eventually that part of Sunday was scratched from the routine.

Having my hair done was the last thing I needed to do, so after getting fully dressed I headed downstairs and climbed onto the high stool in the kitchen to wait for the blue brush to appear. I had to sit completely still while my mom took out each curler and I had to try not to wince even when she had to tug and pull. She brushed then twirled every piece around her finger until each ringlet hung just right. Then I waited until my tight headband with the tiny pearls was set in place. In the end, Mom's smile made me know it had been worth it. We walked out the door looking like the perfect family.

We always had Sunday School before the service in the Salvation Army and in the new Pentecostal church we had started attending. I liked Sunday School, singing songs with action choruses, hearing familiar Bible stories that the teacher acted out on the flannel-graph board and reciting our memory verse. I always knew mine because we practiced at home, so I usually went first and got my sticker that was shaped like a Bible.

I liked church too but I definitely liked the Salvation Army's version better than the Pentecostal one. Both started the same way, singing hymns that felt as solid as my bones, but once it came to the prayer time, anything could happen at Glad Tidings. I was always scared because people cried so much. They cried and shouted and spoke a language I didn't know. When someone had the presence of mind to give an interpretation they often said scary things were going to happen—and then I never knew when the wailing would stop. Amen was said so often but it didn't mean the prayer had ended so I had to keep my eyes closed until I guessed it was over. I always wished we could go back to the Salvation Army where I knew what to expect.

The good part about Glad Tidings was that, after the first prayer part and the offering had been taken up, the children were dismissed to go to Junior Church. It was just like Sunday School all over again except all the kids were together instead of grouped by grades. Sunday morning was definitely long at the Pentecostal church. As soon as we heard the organ's deep chords begin to bellow from the adult service, we had to scramble. Quickly taking the chairs used in Junior Church, we lined them up neatly in rows and transformed the upstairs back into a prayer room. People would start pouring in through both doors just off the exit from the upper balcony and find a chair. Kneeling down and facing the wall, they would cry and pray. It could go on for a long time and I always had a headache; I was hungry.

After church, we went home and had the most delicious meal of the week: roast beef with all the trimmings. Mom would slip that hunk of meat, surrounded by carrots and onions, into the oven right before we left for church so the savory aroma would rise up to meet us when we walked through the door of our house. My mouth would instantly begin filling with water, my jaw ached from hunger, and my hollow tummy grumbled loudly.

We often invited a family from church or strangers visiting from out of town to share this meal with us. The timing of this part was really important but we all knew what to do. The table, which had been set before we left for church, always had enough extra places for our guests. When we got home, Dad took everyone's coats and Wayne hung them neatly in the hall closet. Our guests were shown to the living room where my brother played the piano and sang while my mom, Margaret and I headed to the kitchen and put our aprons on. The potatoes, which had been peeled the night before and left to soak in cold saltwater, were started in the pressure cooker—which I was not allowed to touch. My job was to take all the little glass bowls holding pickles, aspic and pretty preserves from the fridge and place them neatly on the table. While my mom was mashing potatoes, my dad took his long carving knife out of the blue box and, after sharpening the blade, with a sound that made my teeth hurt, he cut the meat into perfect thin slices and arranged them in a fan on the big platter. Dinner was ready to be served.

After gathering everyone to the table, Mom let our guests know where they were to sit. My chair, where I sat on top of the Yellow Pages so I could see my plate, was to the left of Mom who was closest to the kitchen. Dad sat at the opposite end with Margaret on his right and Wayne across from her on his left so the visitors were scattered evenly in between. My mother called on Dad to say grace. He always started with the words, "Our Gracious and Eternal Heavenly Father" and ended with "for these and all Thy tender mercies we give Thee thanks." We all said a hearty Amen. My father's prayers were never particularly long and I liked them because they were spoken slowly, softly and sincerely.

All dinners were important and practicing manners was part of each one, but on Sunday there could be no mistakes. If I watched Mom carefully, I knew exactly what to do. The serviette, always tucked under the forks, needed to be carefully slipped out, shaken gently and placed on my lap. Food was passed from the left to the right and, after taking a spoonful from each dish, I was to pass it to the person beside me. It didn't matter if I didn't like what was in the bowl, I always had to take at least a small helping and my comments stayed inside my head. The main meal was eaten with the big fork. The small one was there as a reminder that if I ate everything on my plate the lemon meringue pies cooling on the kitchen counter were waiting for me. Cutting the roast beef took a lot of persistence, not because the meat was tough—it would actually melt in my mouth—but rather because Mom thought it was impolite to put a knife down. Remembering that rule took time. Mom never had to say a word; her eyes talked loudly.

Sunday dinner was full of talking, usually about the sermon. My attention was focussed on keeping my knife in my right hand and taking small bites from my fork in my left, balancing it between my fingers the way Mom had taught me, poised like a pencil not scooped as a shovel. When everyone had been offered seconds and we were almost completely full, knives and forks were neatly brought together and placed dead centre on the plate to let everyone know the meal was finished. When we all had done so, Mom would glance my way and Margaret and I would begin clearing the table.

I was glad to be in the kitchen. Margaret and I knew exactly what to do. I scraped the plates saving the little scraps of meat for our dog, Penny, while Margaret scrubbed pots. It didn't take long and singing together helped make the time go by faster. I wasn't particularly interested in listening to a rehashing of the sermon and hearing what people thought Pastor Peterson had said all over again anyway. With the dishes washed, dried and stacked on the kitchen table, the hot water warming the teapot and the kettle freshly brought to a full-rolling-boil, my mom would come into the kitchen to make tea. It was time for pie.

Mom had a way of making the meringue, piled so high, dipping in soft curls and then toasted to golden perfection, look so beautiful that it was always rather sad to see her begin to cut into it. But it tasted so good. Everyone always commented on Mom's baking. She would say thank you but shrug it off. I don't think she ever thought being a good cook, housekeeper or baker was anything other than meeting the bare requirements of being a woman.

After Sunday Dinner, my parents and their guests sat in the living room and talked. Sometimes people stayed right through the afternoon and went to church with us in the evening but I always took a nap; there was really nothing else to do because Sunday was a day of rest. We weren't allowed to play outside or talk on the phone, although sometimes I saw Margaret with the cord stretched around the corner huddling in the kitchen whispering. Her wide icy blue eyes screamed for me to be quiet and keep her secret. She thought rules were dumb and often said so right out loud. Wayne and I knew better.

I liked rules because they helped me know what to expect. There were lots of rules in our house, so many that it was hard to keep track of them all. I didn't mind the ones about meals or bedtime and all the other things that had to happen like brushing teeth and saying prayers. The rules I found tricky had to do with what was allowed and what was not permitted because of our religion. All the rules were there to help you know if you were acting like a real Christian but no one ever sat me down and explained how the whole thing worked so I always felt a bit scared. I wanted to go to heaven when I died. I didn't want to be left behind. Sin was wrong and had to be punished. I wanted to follow the rules so I wouldn't get into trouble.

That's one reason I liked the Salvation Army. In the Army, what you should wear was clear. When you were old enough to join the Band or the

Songsters, you had a uniform. My parents had always worn theirs when they went out of the house. At home my mom dressed in a simple smock that buttoned up the front. It wasn't really a uniform but she wore it so faithfully I always thought it was.

There was only one time during those early years I ever remember my mom dressed differently. I was about six. It was late in the evening and my dad was not home, which wasn't unusual, but what made that night different was Margaret and Wayne were arguing and Mom was mad. I didn't know what was happening, but as their voices grew bigger and louder, I shrunk down into the corner of the chesterfield and crouched beneath the deep cushions, becoming as small and quiet as I could. Mom stormed up to her room, slamming the door behind her, and moments later came strutting down the stairs, hand gliding down the banister, with her hair piled loosely on top of her head rather than tightly in a bun. She was wearing a short black skirt, her long legs showing off stockings with a criss-cross pattern and frilly holes. Her cheeks had pink circles painted on them and with her bright red lips she said, "You have driven me to the streets," as she headed out the door. I started crying and begged her not to go out into the cold, dark night and through my sobs I promised to be good. Wayne stood staring straight ahead; Margaret laughed out loud. I waited up for her but in the morning I awoke in my bed. When no one talked about what had happened that night, I thought perhaps it had been a just bad dream. I knew my mother didn't own makeup; it, too, was against the rules.

In the Pentecostal church, they didn't allow lipstick either and, although they didn't have uniforms, the rules about what you should and should not wear were still there. Dresses could not be too short or sleeveless or come with a neckline too low; that was against the rules. But you never knew, unless you broke the rule, what was unacceptable. Then you would be told, not necessarily with words but with looks, that what you had on was bad.

I always wished I could wear a uniform and even begged my mom to send me to St. Cecilia's so I could go to school dressed in a navy blue tunic and white blouse like the Johnston girls. They were from a Catholic family of eight kids, four boys and four girls, who lived down the street. Mom said it wasn't possible for me to go to St. Cecilia's because it was for a different religion but when I talked to Michelle's mother she told me they were Christians and believed in Jesus too. I found all of it very confusing. I secretly wanted to become a nun when I grew up. I saw the Sisters who lived in the nearby convent with their long, black and white habits flowing in the wind and thought that was smart, it would take the guessing part out of what to wear, making life easier.

Following the rules about what to wear and how to have good manners was pretty easy. But there were so many rules I didn't know and many I found hard to understand. When I was seven, there was a girl in my grade two class who wore blue-framed glasses. Her name was Yolanda. Each morning during Opening Exercises she had to stand outside in the hall and one day I asked why. She said it was because of her religion—I was sure glad I wasn't a Jehovah's Witness like her. She told me it was against her religion to sing the national anthem and real Christians shouldn't pray or read the Bible with others who were not. I told her I was a real Christian. The next day during recess, while we were eating raisins by the chain-link fence, she informed me, after talking with her mother, that she was sure I wasn't a real Christian, which made me mad. But although we belonged to different religions, sometimes we had the same rules to follow. She wasn't allowed to go to dances either and when they were held at our school, both of us, along with Cathy and Carol, the Moorhouse twins, would have to stay in a classroom and do extra arithmetic because dancing was against all of our religions.

Movie theatres were definitely bad at one time but the rules around them changed one day. I didn't know why watching a movie on TV was okay but seeing the same thing in a theatre was not allowed. After listening to my sister and Mom squabble about it, I thought there must be something about the building itself that was evil. I was really upset when Mom told me she was taking me to see *The Ten Commandments*. I told her I didn't want to go to the "devil's playground," as she had called it when I overheard her scolding Margaret, but she assured me that because it was a Christian movie, it was fine. I was scared throughout the whole thing and was glad when finally we got out of there. I decided I didn't want to go to movies, just to be safe.

Music was another part of being a Christian I didn't understand. Secular music was of the devil and hymns were holy. Everyone knew that. And even though I didn't understand what a *Rock of Ages Cleft for Me* was, the way the organ thundered out those cords and everyone sang along in three-part harmony, it just felt right. I preferred the hymns with their five verses that told a complete story using old language with Thees and Thous which made them seem more mysterious. It always made me wince when they would omit verses three and four or only sing the even ones; it was like ripping chapters out of a book and expecting it to make sense. The newer choruses we started singing at the Pentecostal church, with upbeat music and words that were repeated over and over, requiring everyone to raise their hands and sway back and forth or clap on the offbeat, made Dad's face go tight but Mom sang them out loudly. I didn't know what I should think about them.

The rule about Sunday was clear. There was a commandment about it: remember the Sabbath Day to keep it holy. So we never went shopping or talked on the phone or played outside. It was better to just take a nap to be sure.

After my Sunday afternoon sleep we went back to church. The evening service was long. We did have Junior Church at Glad Tidings but as soon as I was old enough, I helped in the nursery. I liked holding babies; that's what girls over eleven did. It wasn't even the service that went on forever, but the prayer meeting afterwards certainly did. It was louder than the morning one and people cried even more. I felt sorry for them that they were so sad but it scared me as well.

I tried praying at church sometimes. I sort of wanted to be baptized in the Holy Ghost and learn to speak in tongues. By repeating the words being shouted in my ear, I even started a few times but it never really worked. It always felt stiff and I certainly couldn't pray like that for hours. I did pray at home though. I always had.

There were the formal prayers, said at night before climbing into bed.

> Now I lay me down to sleep
> I pray the Lord my soul to keep
> If fushadie before I wake
> I pray the Lord my soul to take.
> God bless mommy and daddy, Wayne and Margie
> and make me a good girl for Jesus' sake
> Amen.

It was the prayer I said almost every evening, kneeling with my mom beside my bed, hands folded, head bowed and eyes shut tightly. The words had been framed and hung on the wall at the foot of my bed alongside the pictures of Wynken, Blynken and Nod that Mom had made out of copper-tooling and given me as gift for my third birthday.

When I was finally able to make the black sticks and circles with spaces in-between burst into words, I was delighted: I could read. A whole new world opened up. But lying in bed one night, I looked at the words mounted on the wall that had been there as long as I could remember, and read the third line to that prayer. I got scared. "If I should die before I wake"? I had never known what a "fushadie" was but there were lots of things I didn't know and not all my questions were welcomed, so I kept most of them inside my head. It had never occurred to me I might die while I slept. I tried to stay awake from then on but as in the poem, Wynken, Blynken and Nod, my two little eyes and my little head would finally drift off and see the wonderful sights that be and I would sail into my dreams. But I never liked that prayer after I knew dying in my sleep was a possibility.

I prayed at other times too. Not just the required grace before meals and my nightly prayers—I prayed for forgiveness a lot. I don't know when I became conscious of sin but it was pretty early. I must have been between four and five years old when one Sunday evening Dad was preaching and I was listening. There was no such thing as Junior Church in the Salvation Army so I sat with Wayne and Margaret in the third row on the right-hand side and tried not to wiggle too much. Mom was on the platform and from there her eyes kept me pinned to my seat. If Dad was preaching that meant she led the other part of the service, they just switched back and forth.

Dad had preached for a while. I don't remember what he said but he was getting ready to finish, which I could always tell because my mom started playing the piano softly as he spoke, the same tune every time. I knew the words by heart. The hymn started slowly, "Softly and tenderly Jesus is calling, calling for you and for me". It went on to say Jesus was calling for the sinner to come home and the chorus came to a grand crescendo with the plea "Come Home, Come Home, Ye who are weary Come Home" and finished with "Earnestly, tenderly, Jesus is calling, Calling, O sinner, come home!".

That night, I listened to the story Dad told during the altar call. He said Jesus was a shepherd—I'd heard that before, we even had a picture hanging in the hallway of our house showing Jesus with a lamb wrapped around his neck. Dad went on to say that in the olden days when a shepherd had a little sheep who went astray he would go and search for it—I knew that story too, how the Good Shepherd would leave the ninety and nine and go and look for the one lost sheep. I had heard it many times in Sunday School—I knew most of the stories. But then he told a part I had never heard before. He said if a little sheep kept getting lost the shepherd would take the lamb, break his leg and put it up on his shoulder carrying him while his leg healed. I could almost hear the bone snap as I scrunched up in my chair. Dad continued saying we didn't have to wait for the Lord to break our leg; we could simply come now, pray and ask Jesus into our hearts. I started to cry. I didn't want my leg broken. Moments later, along with a man who smelled poor, I walked down the aisle and knelt at the Mercy Seat. Dad got down on his knee beside me and we said the sinner's prayer together. I got saved. From then on I was a born-again believer.

Since that night, I had known how important it was to pray and ask Jesus to cleanse my heart. I prayed when bad things happened to me or when I said mean things, even if it was only under my breath, because I knew God could see and hear everything, even the terrible thoughts inside my head. I had many things to ask forgiveness for, so I prayed a lot.

Displacement

My big brother Wayne, eight years older than me, left home shortly after our family's exile from the Salvation Army. I was nine when he joined a gospel quartet where he played piano and sang harmony. He was a Christian rock-star, writing songs and cutting records, touring around, rolling into big cities, singing in huge churches, then signing autographs after the concerts. He had his glossy picture on his first solo album and sometimes when he took me on tour with him I was allowed to sit at the back and help sell records after the concerts. When he introduced me as his baby sister, I felt proud.

After Wayne left home, Mom was sad. She missed him because the music that had filled our house went out the door with him. Although my mom played piano and sang, my brother had a gift that soothed her soul.

He had been gone only a few weeks when her sadness turned to fury. I came home from school one chilly winter afternoon to find my brother's picture, which sat framed upon the mantle, covered with a piece of black cloth. I didn't know what that meant but knew better than to ask. I looked at Mom, who had obviously been crying, and asked if she wanted a cup of tea. She said no but I put the kettle on anyway because sometimes no means yes but is too hard to say when you feel sad or mad. I made the tea carefully. By nine years old I knew all the rules: water brought to a full-rolling boil, steeping for the perfect amount of time and carefully covering the pot with the tea-cosy. Putting the milk in first, I filled our cups and put them on a tray, carefully brought it into the living room and gently placed it on the coffee table.

Mom sat on the couch facing the hearth where a fire might be blazing if it had been a happier afternoon. I sat down beside her, our eyes staring straight ahead, as we sipped our tea in silence. Through her tears, Mom finally blurted out how sad she was. She said it hurt when children break your heart. I knew her heart was fragile from having rheumatic fever as a baby and anything could set off a spell and make her sick. Margaret had, on many occasions, broken her heart. I could never understand why my sister disobeyed the rules and made my mom sick. But this time, my mom's sadness had to do with my brother. Pointing to the frame, shrouded in black velvet, she said if Wayne didn't care enough to write, "he was as good as dead". I whispered I was sorry and vowed then and there when I grew up and had to move away from home I would send her a letter in the mail every week. I would not break her heart. If Wayne, whom I knew she treasured, could be blotted out so quickly, I knew I did not stand a chance. Writing every week was a promise I intended to keep. What I didn't know was there were more ways to break her heart and many more ways to be cut off, veiled in darkness.

Wayne married Sharon when he was twenty. They met in youth group at the Pentecostal church and had dated since they were teenagers. Her gentle grey-blue eyes and wide smile were as soft and open as her heart. I thought she looked exactly like Barbie except with dark hair. Not that I had ever had a Barbie—that was not allowed. Christian girls didn't play with those kind of dolls but Sharon reminded me of the Barbies I had seen at my friend Susan's house in that Sharon was beautiful and wasn't a girl but, rather, a woman. She sang in the front row of the choir and her folks had been missionaries. My parents were happy about that. My brother had made a wise choice and they were proud of him. We all were.

My sister Margaret was six years older than me. She was always in trouble. Mom worried about her because, although she got good grades, she hung out with the wrong crowd and smoked. Dad said she was a hippie and would grow out of it but Mom, certain she wouldn't, closed her eyes and shook her head. I learned a lot from watching Margaret; I learned what not to do, what didn't work in our family.

When Margaret was twelve, she had had a boyfriend who was eighteen.

I never liked him. He was a geeky guy with greasy black hair that he slicked back with Brylcreem. His upper teeth were fake and when he slipped them out, he could touch the tip of his tongue to his nose. He reeked of Brut aftershave and Juicy Fruit gum that he chewed constantly to cover-up the smell of his cigarette-breath.

When they were dating, I was six. Driving around in his big blue convertible with the top down was scary because he always went very fast and played music so loud I could feel it in my chest. Dad didn't approve of the music they listened to and when he heard me singing some of the words to a song I had heard on the radio (they keep their boyfriends warm at night), his thin white face grew red and the blue veins near his temple bulged out. I overheard my dad talking to Mom in the kitchen that evening. He was saying The Beach Boys and Beatles were not good bands and CHUM was not a station we should be listening to. But my mom told him he was old-fashioned and, besides, she was glad my sister finally had a boyfriend.

The summer I was eleven, men were landing on the moon and Margaret was on the other side of the planet. That was the last summer we were sisters living together in the same house and I missed her. She was chosen to play her French horn in the All Ontario Youth Concert Band and they went to Europe for a whole month of July. She turned eighteen in Germany and bought lederhosen which she wore to the embarrassment of our mother.

Because both my parents were working I was sent to stay with family friends. They weren't exactly friends. The man was that guy my sister used to date when she was twelve. He had married a tiny little woman who didn't like me very much and I had to stay with them for the whole month. I hated being there and was relieved when Margaret came home and I could spend the rest of my summer just being a kid.

On weekends, I spent the long hot days at our cottage sitting for hours propped under the shade of the big weeping willow tree, reading books or catching snakes that slithered through the tall grass in the back field by the train tracks. When I had to stay in the hot sticky city I got up early, packed a lunch and walked to High Park where Susan Smyslo and I swam in the big outdoor pool.

Susan was my best friend. We had met in grade three and from the time we were eight years old we went everywhere together. We laughed and talked and shared secrets. We even tried to dress alike, although with her dark brown hair and olive shaped chocolate eyes, I'm sure no one ever really mixed us up. She wasn't a Christian, or so my mom said, but she was Czechoslovakian.

Susan lived just a few blocks away. Almost every day after school, we went to her house to play. The bell rang at 3:10 and if we ran as fast as we could we'd touch her door within five minutes. We would stand on the front porch, throw our heads back and laugh really hard. Placing our hands on each other's chest we could feel our hearts banging as we caught our breath. After unlocking the door with a key that was hidden under the flower pot, we would go inside and I'd watch Susan bolt it tightly again. We never locked the doors in our house. After picking up the mail that had spilled onto the floor and placing it neatly on the telephone table, Susan and I would go into her kitchen. In the fridge, there were two tall glasses of milk her mother had poured for us before she left for work in the morning.

I liked afterschool time with Susan. After drinking our milk, we headed up the long windy oak staircase that was polished so brightly that the smell made my nose sting and the smoothness made my hands slip. Susan's grandmother lived on the second floor and from her kitchen the smell of fresh-baked things with strange names drifted through the air. Her grandma spoke to her in Czech and, although Susan said she couldn't speak it, she understood what she was saying. But even I knew what Baba meant when she put platefuls of pudhe, the Czechoslovakian name for perogies, in front of us and said, "sníst". Eat. As simple as that and then, "Eat, eat, and eat some more". And we would, devouring platefuls of the hot, steaming, slippery half-moons of dough that had been crammed full of mashed potatoes, boiled then fried and then slathered with heaping spoonfuls of sour cream. They were delicious. Then we played, sometimes even with her Barbies. I wasn't allowed to play with them and never really did touch them exactly but sat and watched as Susan dressed those breasted dolls in modern outfits, combing their hair with a minuscule brush. I don't know where Susan's mom worked but when she came home at five o'clock sharp and took off her fancy coat with a real fur collar and hung it in the hallway closet, it would be time for me to be on my way.

I had loved the Salvation Army because it was uniformed and predictable, a small pocket of time when everything still made sense. Even though moving had been part of our lives in the Army—the changes swift, clear-cut, no questions asked—they always happened on schedule at the end of June. One day in February the year I was twelve, my mom excitedly announced to Dad during dinner that she had sold our house and bought what she called, "the cutest little place" and we had only a month to move. The new house, she said, was in a brand-new section of Barrie, which was then a tiny town an hour north of Toronto. Our family had been stationed there when I was little, so going back was to be a homecoming of sorts, a chance to settle in and start over. I looked up from my plate of meatloaf and mixed vegetables and watched Dad's face. He nodded. I didn't remember living in Barrie; Toronto was where my friends were, the only place that felt like home. But, as usual, no questions were asked and we began packing. It probably hadn't occurred to my mom that Army days were over and Marching Orders were a thing of the past.

Dad had a job teaching in Toronto and packing up on a whim in the middle of the school year wasn't the best idea. He had to continue working in the city during the week, so he rented a tiny upstairs room in somebody's house. It was so small he could barely turn around in it. There was a desk with a chair that overlooked a busy street and beside his bed on a night stand was a hotplate where he cooked his meals. I only saw it once. It made me sad he had to live there all by himself and I only got to see him on weekends.

We moved and I started going to a new school in April of my grade seven year. I didn't know anybody in my class. I was an outsider inside a small school where everybody knew everyone and, by the time I got there, all the friends had been taken. It was crowded in all the wrong ways so when the end of June burst open those heavy school doors to the soft summer wind I could finally stretch again. I was able to breathe.

That year we went to the cottage for the whole summer so I had lots of friends. Mom got a job nursing at the hospital in town and I was free to do whatever I pleased, which was usually sitting on the back deck reading during the long afternoons and playing hide-and-seek outside with all the kids once it was dark.

Our church had a campground right on Lake Ontario. A few years earlier, we had purchased a rundown little shack that Mom transformed into one of the most beautiful places on the property. I think we were one of the first to have indoor plumbing. The curtains between the beds were taken down and traded for real walls and the living room was extended and finished with sliding glass doors that opened onto a large deck overlooking the lake. Once glass windows replaced the old wooden shutters and white vinyl siding covered the old clapboard, it looked like a real house. I loved the cottage, not because of how it looked, I liked the way it made me feel. Being there every summer was the closest feeling I had to belonging after we left the Army.

During the month of July, the place was swarming with children. The first week was Kids' Camp and even those of us who were cottagers stayed in cabins, four bunks to a room, and ate our meals in the dining hall. Most of the morning activities were held in the Big Tabernacle. We learned new songs, had Bible stories and lessons about our faith. But sword drills where my favourite part. The leader would stand on the platform and bellow, "Swords drawn". With our Bible held straight in the air, the address to a scripture would be given—"John 3:16". It would be repeated, followed by the word, "charge". The first to find the scripture passage and stand up reading the correct verse would gain a point for their team. It usually came down to me and Sharon's little brother Edward and I won for the girls most often.

The afternoons were filled with arts and crafts, sports and swimming at Flat Rock. The boys and girls had separate times for bathing; those were the rules. But it was always at Flat Rock we would gather when we snuck out of our cabins late at night after the counsellors did room checks. We would huddle there and laugh and talk because right from the very first day, the week was always almost over. The lump in my throat would start then with vows to write letters over the winter, which never happened, but it would turn into a tickle in my tummy while packing for camp the following year and promises would be made all over again.

The last two weeks of July were Family Camp. People who didn't own cottages came with trailers and tents and set them up in a big open field. The children had their own Tabernacle near the dining hall and the bell rang out for all to attend the morning services. In the afternoons, there was a list of activities for everyone to choose from. Sometimes we did crafts, played miniature golf or other sports.

Wayne was helping out with the kids one afternoon. Everyone was gathered down at the boat ramp taking turns learning to waterski, the bravest going first. Huddling on the bank, I watched as the boat took off, sending kids flying, often tumbling in the air before crashing into the icy cold lake. Wayne said it was my turn. I was scared and said I didn't really want to go but he convinced me to at least give it a try. As the boat idled noisily, Wayne got me organized. After strapping thick boards to my feet he told me to lie back in his arms. Steadying my legs as they were sticking straight into the air, he told me to hold tightly to the rope, relax and let the boat do the work of pulling me up. Moments later, I was flying around Lake Ontario. After circling around for what seemed an eternity, I realized I didn't know how to get off. Exhausted, I finally had to let go of the rope and sunk gently into the water. Wayne swam out to where I was bobbing in the water, laughed and said I was a natural. I was so happy that my big brother was proud of me.

After we had dinner it was time for the revival meeting. The Big Tabernacle was in full glory during those evenings. The singing and preaching went on for hours. Wailing from the prayer room often continued until long after the moon climbed up high and sent diamonds scattering over the surface of the lake. People were filled with the Holy Ghost, slain in the spirit and would pray out loud speaking in tongues. You would have thought I would have gotten used to it, but I never did. I was, according to my dad, "a dyed-in-the-wool Salvationist through and through".

The summer I was twelve, I was really happy to be at camp. It was my last year of Kids' Camp and I wanted to be the Queen. Each year a Royal Family was chosen on the final day, a prince and princess from each age group, the oldest pair crowned King and Queen. Points were given for Bible memory, sword drill, cabin inspection and who knows what else. Every year I had been beaten out by just one demerit, usually by Martha Peterson, the pastor's daughter. So when I was given the title of Queen of the Camp this year, I was filled with regal pride. The winners, with our tinfoil-covered cardboard crowns securely fastened to our heads, were driven around on the hoods of the counsellors' cars while the horns beeped. Then the entire Royal Family was paraded in front of the kids that didn't win as they stood outside the Big Tabernacle waving and cheering. It was a real honour to win and a terrible way for those who didn't to end their week at camp.

I was still too young to go to Teen Camp, which was always the second week in July, but because I was a cottager, I hung out down at the Tuck Shop eating Lucky Elephant, the pink candied popcorn that came with a prize in each box. I had my first boyfriend the summer I was twelve. His name was Richard. He was eighteen and the son of one of the most prominent preachers in our denomination. I sort of liked him but he just wanted to kiss all the time and I was more interested in skipping rocks. Mom told me it was time I grew up and more or less insisted I go out on dates with him. After I got home, she had our tea ready and we would sit and talk. She always asked me what we did and was interested in every detail.

After Labour Day weekend we closed up the cottage for the season and drove back to Barrie. I started grade eight and did my best to make friends at my new school. Wayne and Sharon had just been married and were living in Ann Arbor, Michigan so we didn't see them often. Margaret was at nursing school in the little town of Orillia, half an hour away. Mom set up a room for her downstairs in our new house. Her bed, yellow basket chair and desk, laminated with a map of the world, sat there neat and tidy because she never came home, not even to visit. Dad was working in Toronto so during the week it was just Mom and me.

The house was nice enough but it was never a home. Mom said she loved it because it was newly constructed and in the suburbs, not like the cramped old brick houses in Toronto. I think she liked it because it was fancy and had all the latest fashions. The red wall-to-wall carpeting in the living room and new black vinyl furniture with the glass coffee table looked like something on the cover of a magazine at the A&P grocery store checkout stand. The kitchen appliances were avocado green and we bought new melamine dishes to match. Everything about the place looked and felt new. It didn't smell like a home. It was strange, just the two of us alone in a new life together.

One day in September, my mom got sick. I came home from school to find a note on the kitchen table telling me to call the hospital. With hands trembling, I could barely dial the numbers and when the lady on the other end asked my name I forgot to answer at first. I was told my mom had been taken to the hospital by ambulance and she was very sick. When I heard that, I stopped listening, her words became muddled and my brain went blank. After she said good-bye I hung up the receiver, crumpled to the floor and cradled my dog Boo on my lap. She licked the tears away. I was sure glad she was there. That night I sat on the edge of my bed and, staring straight into the mirror, asked the girl inside the glass right out loud what we should do.

She was disgusted by my tears. Here I was, thirteen, and sniffling like a sissy. I wandered out to the kitchen, made a peanut butter sandwich and, after washing it down with water, climbed into bed. I gathered Boo into my arms and snuggled into her softness. I felt her heartbeat and her even breathing soothed me to sleep.

Through the years, migraine headaches kept Mom in a darkened room for days on end, rocking back and forth, throwing up. This was different. Something was wrong with her heart. She had had rheumatic fever as a child and the doctor said the illness had created a heart murmur. It had caused problems before and kept her from going to the mission field. When my sister was a baby, my folks had felt called overseas and filed all the necessary papers to work within the Salvation Army's Foreign Missions Program but when it came down to the physical examination, my mom failed. She had never failed at anything in her life before, so she took it hard. She decided if she couldn't go to the mission field she would have another baby. At least that's the story always hastily told when people commented on the space between my sister and me.

That damaged mitral valve had made my mom's blood pressure go whacky and landed her in the hospital. I was home alone during that whole long week and, if it hadn't been for Boo, I would have been totally by myself. On the weekend, my dad came home and we drove to the hospital. Mom didn't move when we walked into the room. I stood staring at her stony face, all pasty white and blending into the sheets. When she opened her eyes, she told me she wasn't going to die. I was sure glad she said so because it looked to me like she was dying with all those tubes hanging like spaghetti and the box beside her bed keeping track of her every heartbeat.

When she came home several days later, Mom's face was still the colour of plaster and just as stiff. She stayed in her bed a lot and when she got up she moved slowly. It was important that things were quiet so we drank tea by the potful and played Scrabble or Rook during the long evenings.

We had always played Rook at home. It was a card game I loved. I had learned to play when I was little while sitting on my mother's lap. By watching carefully I could see how she thought.

We played partners most often and, once I was old enough to have a hand of my own, when Mom and I paired up, no one could beat us. I could tell by the way she bid whether she had a decent hand or whether I was expected to take it. When she put her first card on the table she would look at me and then I knew how the game was going to go. There were lots of tricks to winning; my mom's favourite was called "bleeding". She would take control of the game and make everyone play all their trump cards so there could be no surprises. Mom and I were great partners. People said I could read her mind. I didn't have to, I knew how to watch. Someone once jokingly said that Rook was "Baptist Bridge" or "Pentecostal Poker". I watched as my mother's face turned fiery red. I thought she was going to explode. She didn't think that was the least bit funny.

That year in Barrie, there was only two of us so we had to play with a dummy hand. It wasn't nearly as fun as sitting around the table at the cottage with friends but it did make the evenings go faster. I loved playing Rook and learning new tricks. Watching and paying attention were becoming even more important.

The vibrant autumn leaves, that made the whole town look as if it were on fire, surrendered quickly to the icy grip of winter. The snow in Barrie was bountiful and beautiful, the way it looks in pictures on Christmas cards. There were no streetcars busily taking people to important places or turning the pure white snow into a brown slushy mess. The whole town went to sleep in the winter. It was cold outside and inside too.

I fell more in love with words that winter and sat for hours at my father's empty desk in the office courting them. I discovered writing was almost more fun than reading. By turning words on their heads you could make sentences come alive and tell a story that was true or completely make-believe and no one would know the difference.

At school, we were given an assignment to write a modern-day fairy tale, so I retold the story of Hansel and Gretel. My teacher loved it and sent a copy to the local paper. Before they printed it, a man came to our house and talked to me and took my picture. When the story ran my name was followed by the caption, "promising talent as a writer" but when I read the short biography attached at the end, I was stunned. The editor had turned my words completely over making up a story of his own. I had been asked questions about what I liked to do and things that interested me and then a fairy tale was created which made it sound like I was a snob from the big city. It didn't go over well or help making friends at my new school any easier.

All the kids in Barrie picked on each other. Ricky, the biggest bully at school, lived next door so he pestered me at home as well. He called me Gumby because I was thin and tall for my age. I pretended to ignore him, but when I got home and talked to Boo, I cried.

One day during recess, Ricky pushed me. I fell on the ice and broke my face. Laying on a gurney in the Emergency Room, trying to be brave, I asked the doctor who was holding my x-rays to the light if he thought my nose was broken. He chuckled and told me he hadn't taken them to see if it was broken but rather to determine how many pieces there were to the jigsaw puzzle. My nose and both cheekbones had been shattered. I had to have surgery and was in the hospital for ten days. After I got home, I had to go to school with my purple and green puffy eyes peeking out from behind the stiff white plaster cast. I was thirteen.

Susan came to visit once. Her dad brought her to see me the winter I broke my face. I had just had the cast taken off and Susan looked it over, gently touching the ridges of my nose and cheekbones and told me it looked just fine. We had our picture taken together sitting in the backyard of that house. It is one of the few things I kept from that year. We laughed and talked and shared secrets. I told her about the mean kid who lived next-door who pushed me on the ice when I wasn't even looking. She told me her parents got a divorce and her dad had to move out. I began to wonder if my parents had gotten a divorce and that was the real reason Dad was living in Toronto. Mom said it was nonsense to think such a thing, Christians didn't get divorced. I guess Czechoslovakians did.

That spring, when Ricky swallowed a hat pin on a dare and they thought he might die, I wasn't the least bit sad. He would have deserved it; I had had enough of him. But the day he picked on David, I got mad. The teacher had left the room and Ricky thought it would be funny to dump David, who had Muscular Dystrophy, out of his wheelchair and watch him squirm on the floor. He was a tangle of twisted, limp limbs and had no way of getting up. Everyone was laughing because Ricky thought it was hilarious and the kids knew if they didn't join in they would likely be the brunt of his next joke. My face was burning as I bolted from my seat. I picked David up in my arms and settled him in his wheelchair. He glared at me. He was embarrassed by being picked up by a girl but I didn't know what else to do.

I put on my coat and walked out the door of that school almost a year to the day I had entered it. I marched home and told my mom I was never going back. She must have taken me seriously because that afternoon we drove to Toronto and rented an apartment. I think my dad was relieved. He hadn't been able to get a job in Barrie and living in a one-room boarding house with only a hotplate must have been hard on him too.

As quickly as we had moved to Barrie, we sold the house, packed up and headed back to Toronto in time for me to finish the year and graduate from public school with my friends. I was glad to be back in my old neighbourhood surrounded by the comfortable kids I had grown up with. Even though we had to live in a cramped basement apartment, it felt more like home. But that summer, Mom found a tired old house only a few blocks away that she worked on feverishly to restore. We moved into that huge eight bedroom house a week before I started high school.

Shortly before my fourteenth birthday, my parents told me they wanted to talk to me after dinner. It seemed strange they had called me into the living room. That night we sat, side by side, on stiff chairs, with formal faces and there was a long heavy pause before Mom began to talk.

I knew it was going to be a serious conversation. Mom said we should open with prayer, a sure sign something was up. My mother did most of the talking, which was the way of most conversations in our house. She said that they—meaning my dad and her—had been praying and the Lord had spoken to them. "They" and "them" were just words. Pretty much anyone who knew anything about our family at all knew that what my dad thought made little difference when it came to decisions that were made. She continued by telling me how much they missed being in the ministry and how, since leaving the Salvation Army six years before, their hearts had felt empty. They had been patiently waiting on the Lord to give them their next ministry assignment. After our whirlwind trip to Barrie, which Mom said was a "necessary preparatory season in the wilderness," the Lord had directed them to buy this big house so we could share our lives with others.

Mom told me she had walked by the house and the Lord had spoken directly to her heart. She had clearly seen in her mind's eye the house filled with troubled young boys who needed the love and security of a family. She was made keenly aware how, in her words, their "broken lives would be mended", "their addictions healed" and how they would become "strong men of God" after experiencing His love. She told me they had been led to speak with others which had set off a miraculous chain of events resulting in timely meetings with people who had similar ideas, which was real confirmation to her that this was the Lord's will. She told me they had just received word that their application to start a Group Home for young juvenile delinquents coming out of reform school had been approved and we would be receiving our first boys within the week. Her excitement was palpable, the room abuzz with enthusiasm. She looked at me expectantly with her deep brown eyes and wide smile, nodding her head hypnotically then said, "Well honey, what do you think?"

I don't remember exactly what I said but when I did speak I told her in no uncertain terms I thought it was a really bad idea. She was stunned. Mostly I think she was taken aback because it was highly unlike me to voice thoughts not neatly measured and aligned, or to have an opinion that opposed hers. She didn't say much more and nothing to me directly, instead said we should close in prayer. Then there were lots of words, most of which I didn't hear or can't recall but I specifically remember her asking the Lord to take my selfish heart and exchange it for a more generous spirit. I said "Amen" out loud because that's what you are supposed to say when a prayer is ended. It means "so be it" or "I agree" but I didn't and secretly prayed it would not be so.

The boys did come, two at first and within months our home had been invaded by eight. Even though it was a huge house, the noise made it feel tiny. The main floor had a large formal living room and a separate dining room, each with big bay windows. My parents' bedroom and office were near the kitchen that was constantly turning out massive volumes of food to fill the hollow legs attached to big mouths, always clamoring to be stuffed. My bedroom was upstairs where the boys' slept. Because I was a girl, I didn't have to share a room but that never stopped them from barging into mine and bugging me.

I didn't like the boys: they were loud, mean and so unpredictable; anything could set them off. It was never quiet but things could be normal and then for reasons I could never quite figure out there would be an explosion. Two guys would pass each other in the hall and one would decide he had been looked at the wrong way and then it would start. The bigger one always pushed his chest out and if the smaller kid was too dumb to back down immediately, punches would be thrown. They would flail and crash around, fists flying, pounding each other in the face and at the end there were usually fat lips and holes in the walls.

I learned to keep my eyes down while walking from my bedroom to the bathroom. I knew if I didn't, I could get myself slammed to the wall and pinned tightly until they felt like letting go. They usually just held me there and laughed because they could see I was scared, which made them smile. Even Boo, who had slept with me every night since she was a puppy, refused to come upstairs and took to quivering in the corner in the office downstairs beside my parents' bedroom.

Dinner time was always a disaster. The boys didn't know any of the rules. They crammed food in their faces, chewed with their mouths open and threw things instead of passing them properly. I sat staring straight ahead, wishing they would all go away but then immediately felt bad because, of course, they had no other home to go to; we were their only family.

Fortunately, they didn't go to my school. They didn't like to study and even Western Tech School was reluctant to take them because of their "juvie" records. I was always embarrassed to be around them because they told rude jokes, spit everywhere, said bad words and then laughed because they knew it made me mad.

The year I was turning fifteen, just before school started, my mom told me she was going to visit Wayne. We had been running the Group Home for a whole year and she needed a rest. I asked when she was coming back. She said she didn't know. I pleaded to go with her but she told me missing school wasn't an option. I was sad that she would be away for my birthday but I could see she was exhausted and I was pretty sure she wanted to get away from me too.

While my mom was gone, I thought my safest bet was to keep focused at school where I still felt safe and comfortable. Early each morning, I got up, dressed and silently made my way down the back stairs and slipped out the side door. I don't know why I thought I needed to be quiet. Dad was deaf in one ear but what made him most hard of hearing had more to do with his busy-ness, I suspect. He was working full time teaching math at the local community college and in the evenings he sat stiffly at his big desk biting his nails, poring over ledgers doing taxes and accounting side jobs to keep our books balanced. Chips—my mom's kooky friend who wore beaded hippie clothes, let her long grey hair go wild and whacky and plastered her face with bright red rouge and matching lipstick—had been roped into doing the laundry and cooking while Mom was gone. She was so bleary-eyed and had such a hard time keeping track of what needed to be done that I don't think she could possibly have noticed I was never around.

I walked to school each morning and, as I opened those heavy doors, I entered a world that was light and free and easy to understand. The routine and the rigidity made sense and had a rhythm that was reliable. I liked the learning part too, the interesting classes and the way the teachers treated us almost like grownups because we were in high school. I had signed up for many extracurricular activities. Before classes began, I had band, orchestra, wind ensemble and either girls' choir or chamber choir and after the day was done there were sectionals and scales to practice. I did my homework in the school library and after it was done, recopied all my notes from each class and made study cards for upcoming tests in the teensiest print possible. At five o'clock when the janitor came to lock the doors, I'd gather my stuff, head down the street to the public library and finish up there. Just before 9:00pm the librarian would tap me on the shoulder and, after making her final rounds, put on her coat, turn out all the lights and we would walk out together. I'd stand there on those huge stone steps and watch as she locked the door. I could have lived in the quietness of the library, surrounded by walls of books absorbed in their many words, if that were possible.

With all the doors to the safe places in my life locked up tightly, I slowly walked the six city blocks back to the Group Home. As I rounded the corner, the huge three-story brick building, standing brazenly against the night, came into sight. Scanning each window carefully to see which lights were still on, I quietly snuck in the side door, tiptoed up the back stairs, passed the boys' bedrooms and slipped into mine, closing the door carefully. Because it did not have a lock, I jammed a chair tightly under the door knob and, after stacking my books neatly on my desk, took off my jacket and began lighting candles. I liked the way the flames danced off the mirror and caught the night from the window pane and made shadows play tag with one another. In minutes, my room was transformed into a space that was mysterious, perhaps even holy, a place where I could pretend to live. After gently lifting my guitar, I sat on the edge of my bed and began to strum softly. I only knew a few chords but I could sing and write poetry and weave the music and words into a song.

Mom returned home unexpectedly one night but I didn't know she was back. After school, I had gone to the library to study and when I got home I snuck up to my room as usual. I was sitting on my bed struggling to make my fingers transition from an A cord to an E minor when the door was flung open, sending the chair flying. Mom stormed right into the middle of my bedroom. She looked mad. I have since learned that fear and anger look similar on the face. It was late, almost bedtime. She told me to go downstairs and eat the dinner she had saved for me in the kitchen.

Later that night, I was again playing my guitar. The boys were banging on the wall and telling me to shut up but I had learned to not hear anything on the outside of my own head. Dad barged in. He was angry. He told me if I didn't put my guitar away, he would break it. I was stunned. Dad never got mad, at least on the outside. He always spoke quietly, especially to me. I don't know whether it was the shock of seeing my father's fury and having him speak harshly or whether I was just strung so tightly that anything could have set me off, but something inside me snapped. I put on my coat and went barrelling down the back stairs. I was heading out the door when Mom tried to stop me. She grabbed my jacket but I wiggled out of it and then took off running.

I guess my mom went to bed figuring I would come to my senses and, realizing mid-October in the pouring rain was not an ideal time for a run, I'd come home. Or maybe she was just too jet-lagged from her long plane trip home to think. But when a policeman rapped loudly on the back door and it took several minutes for the kitchen lights to go on and for my mom to finally open the door just a crack, it was pretty clear, she had been asleep. Her fiery eyes darted from me to the policeman then back again. Our eyes locked for a brief moment before mine were sent looping down and lodged themselves in the labyrinth of the linoleum.

The policeman had lectured me on the dangers of running around in the middle of the night and so when he brought me home I was not only soaking wet but sodden with shame. I had never been in trouble before. I had only once seen the inside of the principal's office and only then because I had witnessed a scuffle in the school yard and was called upon to give my account. But that night, standing in the kitchen with the policeman towering over me and Mom's eyes piercing me through, I knew I was in big trouble. It was my fault.

As the police officer was leaving, his huge hand firmly grasping the door knob, he stopped, turned abruptly and faced my mother. He looked her in the eye and said, "This is great. You save everybody else's kid but lose your own. Not smart." Leaving that statement reverberating off the walls, he pivoted on his heel and stomped down the back stairs. I heard the powerful engine of his cruiser as he drove into the stormy night. I was standing in the kitchen, freezing cold, soaked to the bone and shaking uncontrollably. Mom told me to get to my room.

I tiptoed up the back stairs and slid silently down the long hallway, holding my breath as I passed the boys' bedrooms. Opening the door to my room, I saw some of my candles were still flickering. A few had only wisps of smoke trailing in the air but most had gone out. I climbed into bed and curled into a tight ball. Tears began gushing out. Clutching my pillow, I pulled the covers over my head and held my breath to still the sobs. The thoughts pounding my brain were the usual barrage of accusations, the inside voice badgering me. "How could you be so stupid?" "You have wrecked everything." "It's all your fault." The chaos which had been building finally erupted, exploding outside. I was sure everyone would see, everyone would know the truth: I was bad.

The worst part was that I had always vowed to be good and, until that night, managed skilfully to keep everything organized. My mind, like my room was neat and tidy; thoughts and words inside my head, tightly, precisely measured, were all lined up, carefully arranged and in their places. I knew what was expected of me and always tried to say and do the right things. I wasn't like my sister, who tangled with Mom, said whatever she thought and let her room become a pigsty evoking our mother's rage. But that night, everything came crashing down and tumbling out.

I lay huddled in a heap, hugging my pillow, shaking with deep, long quivers surging through my bones. I heard Mom climbing the stairs. She entered my room and placed a tray on my desk. On it there was a teapot, a creamer filled with milk and a sugar bowl with the special silver spoon with curlicues on the handle and two cups ready to be filled. Mom sat on the edge of the bed and put her hand on my back. She told me to sit up and we would "have a cuppa and get all warmed up". As she turned away, I watched her pour the milk first and then the steaming hot tea into our cups. She whisked in a little sugar, although I hadn't used sugar since I was a little girl, but sometimes she forgot.

Having tea together had been our ritual, our time to connect throughout the years. The question, "Would you like a cup of tea?" was not at all about tea but rather a call to talk, an invitation to intimacy. A cup of tea could warm an otherwise bone chilling conversation.

When my mom handed me my cup and realized I had crawled into bed with wet clothes on, she bit her lower lip and told me in her slow, steady voice to get out of my soggy jeans and sweatshirt and get into pyjamas. She helped me pull my shirt over my head. Even though the only light in the room was a soft glow from one remaining candle that had been burning for hours, I could see her eyes widen and face drop. "You are nothing but skin and bones. What has happened to you?" I quickly put on my pyjama top and fumbled with the buttons. Yanking up my pants, pulling on socks, I bundled up tightly in my housecoat and sat on the edge of my bed quivering. I wrapped my hands around the cup to soak in warmth. I took a sip. It felt good going down. Another larger gulp soothed my insides. And then I began to vomit.

Foreshock

I vomited for hours with a deep retching that turned my stomach inside out. My parents talked in hushed angry tones before Mom left my room abruptly. I didn't know if she was just mad at me for running away or furious with my dad because I was sick when she got home from her trip. Mom's anger was always difficult to gauge. Usually the quieter her voice, the more fury there was to follow. Outside my room, I could hear her whispering to someone on the phone, describing in detail the events of the evening.

I was hustled down the back stairs, out the side door and into the dark night. Dad was sitting in the car, sheets of rain slicing through the head lights, plumes of smoke from the exhaust gathering up wind. The engine was humming loudly and the heater blowing full blast. I climbed in and was sandwiched between my parents in the front seat of our old Dodge Monaco. It was a long drive through the gloomy night. The lights from oncoming head beams, the sudden stops, the quick turns and the windshield wipers going a million miles a minute made my head spin. I was holding a dishpan on my lap, letting the drool from my mouth run down into it and then the churning and the deep, long heaving would start again.

Finally, we stopped in front of a great gray building. In big, bold, red letters the word "Emergency" was burned into the night sky. Dad gathered me in his arms and carried me into The Hospital for Sick Children. There, a nurse motioned for him to put me on a gurney and a heavy white curtain was drawn between us, my parents outside and me alone inside a tiny icy cubicle. I lay there shivering.

A group of doctors came in and a nurse stood beside them answering their questions. The old doctor began examining me while younger ones looked on. A glass thermometer was stuck into my bottom. A big grey band was tied around my upper arm and then a ball, pumped up by the doctor, made it squeeze my arm so tightly I thought it would burst and then the air eked out slowly. The doctor opened my shirt so everyone could see. A cold round piece of metal, the size of a silver dollar, was put on my chest then moved all over my tummy as he listened to the sounds of my insides. I was told to breathe slowly, to breathe in then out. I was wishing I was not breathing at all. A bright penlight pierced every opening of my body, first my eyes, nose, throat, ears and then down below, a place never meant to be seen in the light.

I could only understand a few words they said. The doctors spoke in dull voices amongst themselves in a language that was largely unfamiliar. My head hurt, my stomach ached. I was freezing. They took blood from my veins, saliva from my mouth and even gathered stuff from my—whatever it is called down there—where no one should be looking or touching. I knew the only thing to do was to be quiet, hold my breath and pretend to be asleep. It would be over soon.

Then the interrogation began. They asked dozens of questions, none of which I seemed to have the right answers to. "How old are you?" "When did you first start losing weight?" "How long have you been nauseous?" "When did your menses begin?" "When was your last period?" I was still shaking, my teeth chattering loudly. The cold was like nothing I had ever known. It was as if my bones themselves were made of ice, the doctors' sharp questions, shattering and splintering me inside. Then it was over. The group of doctors disappeared as quickly as they had arrived.

A lady came into the cubicle where I lay shivering. She told me to take a deep breath. I watched as she stuck a huge needle in the back of my hand. She cursed under her breath. But I heard her. She looked up and when our eyes met she said she was sorry. It took several tries but eventually, with the long needle in place, my left arm was taped to a board. I watched clear liquid drip from the bottle that hung directly above my head and begin snaking its way along the plastic tube until it disappeared inside my body.

A nurse brought warm blankets and bundled me up. The side rails were raised and locked. I was rolled down a long corridor, into an elevator and, after the bell signalled our arrival to the sixth floor, the gurney came to a stop in a four-bed room. A nurse, who introduced herself as Irene, told me she would be taking care of me and if I needed anything I could push the grey button that was pinned to my pillow.

That first night, I felt deeply cold, sad and ashamed. It was more than their questions, it was the way the doctors looked at me, the disbelief in their eyes, the nodding amongst themselves, as if they thought my answers were lies. It wasn't that I didn't know at least some of the answers to their questions. I did. I knew my first period had started shortly before my twelfth birthday; it came as a surprise as I'm sure it always does for young girls. I read the thin pink booklet they gave us in gym class when I was in grade five, the one with diagrams showing a girl's body, describing the changes that would happen during adolescence. I guess I had hoped it would never happen to me like it did to Monica Pratt, whose breasts grew, bulging out of her blouse, bursting buttons. She had to wear a bra that the boys got great pleasure out of snapping when the teacher wasn't looking. But it had happened to me. I had matured, which is a kind way of saying my body betrayed me, shoving me into an uncomfortable way of being in the world.

I didn't mean to lie when the doctor asked when my period had started. First of all, I had to translate the word menses; it was part of the language they spoke that I didn't know. I came to understand that if a long word could be substituted for a short one, doctors would use it first and if they got a blank stare they would quickly search the thesaurus of their mind and come up with a simpler word. What I didn't know was why he was asking me that question in front of so many people. So instead of being truthful, the first thing that blurted out of my mouth was, "I don't know," which became the answer to almost every question that followed.

Laying on the hard bed with high metal bars that looked and felt more like a prison, I turned over the other questions, which in my panic, I had just blurted "I don't know" to. When was my last period? It had been awhile. I used to write it down, in code of course, in my diary, the little blue book with gilded edges that had a matching golden miniature lock and tiny key, where I had hidden my secrets. It had been given to me as a gift for my birthday the year I turned twelve. I liked to write and liked the idea of putting words to thoughts but my secrets all needed so many encryptions to keep them safe that writing became something I did only when I could burn the pages in my candle's flame and watch memories crumble into ash. I would count the days and, just like my teacher said, on the twenty-eighth day or there about, my period would arrive and give me an excuse not to have to swim or take showers in gym class. But they had been so regular, I lost interest after about a year. I would feel a slight cramping just under my belly button that would let me know it was about to begin and, after a few days of inconvenience, it would disappear for another month. So I really didn't know when my last period had been. I didn't see the importance of it anyway. I thought it had been rude that they looked down at my—whatever you call it down there— and although it didn't hurt, it made me feel really stupid.

They asked me if I had a boyfriend. I think I remembered to say, "No!" to that question. That was the last thing I wanted. It made me sick to even think about it. I hated boys. They were obnoxious.

That first night in the hospital, goosebumps covered my whole body and I couldn't stop shaking. When the nurse came to my bedside she popped a thermometer in my mouth, gently held my wrist and looked intently at her watch. She told me she was going to take my blood pressure, then carefully wrapped the cuff around my arm and pumped it up until it squeezed tightly and, together, we watched the silver blob drop as the air oozed out with a hiss. She took the thermometer from my mouth and, after shaking it with a quick rhythmic flick of her wrist, she jotted down numbers on a clipboard. Her soft eyes met mine. She asked if I was still cold and I said I was. She left the room and deposited her stack of clipboards in a clear plastic holder outside the door. Moments later, she returned with warm flannel sheets and tucked them snugly around me. I fell back to sleep.

I was jolted awake by ice coursing through my veins. It was weeks before I figured out the sudden gush of cold in the middle of the night was due to changing the IV bottle, stored on the window sill taking on the winter's cold, rather than something pathologically wrong with my body. After taking a deep breath and holding it in for a moment my heart moved down from my head, back into my chest, giving my brain room to think.

I was awakened several times during that first night. With the constant clatter and chatter seeping in from the world outside my door, the nurse coming and going, the taking of blood pressures, the clank of IV bottles, the moans rising and falling from the bed across from me and the intermittent cries of the toddler whose cot was kitty-corner to mine, it was difficult to sleep. When morning finally did arrive, it was with a quick flick of a light switch and the brisk pulling of curtains to acknowledge the grey, rainy, October dawn, the start of a new day.

A different nurse was busy cranking beds to upright positions, adjusting brown bedside tables that swung overtop and saying good morning to each of us in an annoying, well-practiced, sing-song voice. The nurse rolled a big steel cart into the middle of the room and took trays from the shelves and placed them uniformly on each table. My eyes followed her. She was in a hurry, her movements sharp and quick. In just moments, she was out the door wheeling the cart to the next room, I guessed.

My tray held a metal bowl, the lid concealing thick gloopy oatmeal. I hated porridge. We had had it for breakfast every morning during the winter growing up and it still made my throat itch. At home it always had a vitamin C pill plopped dead centre sending orange squiggles spiralling out of it, my mom's clever idea to make us remember to take our vitamins to fortify our immune system. It was better than the cod-liver oil and fresh squeezed orange juice she made us gulp back while plugging our nose if she suspected we were catching a cold which, because of my allergies, I always seemed to have.

I wasn't hungry that first morning in the hospital. I was still nauseous and the smell made my stomach turn and my mouth begin to fill with water again. I tried sucking and swallowing hard but it didn't work. I turned my head to find the little steel kidney basin Irene had given me the night before. My stomach began to contract, slowly at first and then with deep, long retching. Nothing came out except green stuff that tasted awful. I wiped my mouth and slid down toward the bottom of my bed where it was flat, curled into a ball and closed my eyes tightly to keep the tears inside. My brain finally stopped rolling and I drifted back to sleep again.

A muffled sound of mumbling made me peel the covers from around my head and listen. Then the voices grew louder and became more distinct. Moments later, the group of doctors who had been standing outside the door came bustling in and clustered around each bed in turn. This was called rounds. It happened every weekday morning.

The doctor with the longest coat, Dr. Williams, was in charge. The others were a mixture of interns and residents, all in different years in their medical studies. Each morning, they burst in and talked to each other about every kid in the room, asking tricky questions they already knew the answers to. While it was something I never got used to, I learned to pay attention. By listening, I found out things about each kid, stuff that was none of my business just as I'm sure they learned things about me that was none of theirs, things we all would have preferred to remain private. The Hospital for Sick Children was a teaching hospital and the education of young doctors was most important, so having each case discussed in everyday rounds or Grand Rounds, where they filled a lecture theatre with hundreds of people and talked about me, was part of the price I paid for receiving the best care Canada offered.

They started with Joanne. Her bed was across from mine. She was a nine year old girl who had the blackest skin I had ever seen in my life. She had Sickle Cell Anemia. Tubes were snaking all around her and she breathed through an oxygen mask that made a hissing sound. Her frail body was mostly still but sometimes she rocked her head as she moaned day and night. The doctors discussed the importance of pain control and tossed the names of medications in the air before deciding on her cocktail. They deliberated about her blood levels and used all sorts of words I had never heard. They talked about her palliative care regime and platelet count. I heard them say she had only days to live; she was going to die.

She did die. She died before I understood what all the words that described her illness meant. She died before I got to know her. She died in the middle of the night and left her mom and aunties sobbing beside her bed. When the nurse finally came and put her arms around their shoulders and led them into the hallway, Joanne was left there in the room with me. I sat up and stared across at her silent ebony skin. It was so sad. I cried too. She was too little to die.

They moved on to Debbie who was two. She had blond curls, big blue eyes and she cried constantly. She had CF, Cystic Fibrosis; a nasty and all-too-common disease that seemed to plague the kids on 6C. She had to have her lungs clapped by the physiotherapists several times each day. They would cup their hands and pound so hard on her little back it was surprising she didn't break. She had an oxygen mask too. It was taped to her head in an ongoing, feeble attempt to keep her from ripping it off, which she did all the time anyway. They even tried wrapping her tiny arms snugly at her side but wiggling and tugging she'd work them lose and then yank the mask from her face and fling it over the side of her crib. At night, she would climb into bed with me. She would giggle and touch my face, then snuggle in and finally fall asleep. Her breath smelled funny, almost sweet but not quite right. The nurse would come in and take her back to her crib, which had bars over the top to keep her safe, but the little Houdini would somehow escape and paddle over and crawl in with me again. I didn't mind. Her crying drove me nuts, so there were actually times I would go over and get her and carry her back to bed with me just so I could sleep. Sometimes I got into trouble but usually the nurse just let us be. It was the only thing that kept Debbie quiet.

The doctors moved across and began discussing the weird little four year old boy who had a braid popping out of the top of his head. He had bandages wrapped around his entire face covering his eyes. The old doctor spoke in low disapproving tones when he discussed his case. Apparently this was his second admission for the same injury. He had again burned his eyes with mustard in the Krishna temple and when asked why, he simply said it tasted yummy. He was an annoying little kid who jumped up and down on his bed and more than once he sent his IV bottle crashing to the tile floor. I was happy when he finally went home.

Then the crowd of doctors came and huddled around my bed that first morning. I wanted to run away, or at least disappear. I tried holding my breath to see if that would help but my heart was pounding so hard I thought my head was going to explode, so I finally had to inhale. They talked about me as if I wasn't there. "We have a fifteen year old female who presented to the emergency room last night." the old doctor began, "Pulse and blood pressure—unremarkable. Temperature—low, moderate hypothermia. Blood work came back showing severe dehydration with decreased potassium levels. According to her parents, she was picked up by the police after running away from her home; they said this was unusual behaviour for their daughter. Upon physical examination it was noted she is quite emaciated and she was vomiting throughout the exam." He paused, and I caught him look at the group of young doctors. As he continued giving his report it was obvious, at least to me, by the change of tone and pace of his speech he was now going to talk about the important stuff. "She said she doesn't know when her menses commenced or when her last menstrual period was." They probably went on to say many more unspeakable things but I was so horrified I tried not to listen. I had practiced not hearing the same way I had practiced not feeling.

They were talking, right out loud, about my private stuff and asked all the same questions the doctors had the night before. But this time I knew the answers. Well, at least, I knew the answer I was going to give to every question, "I don't know!" "I DON'T KNOW!" I said, "I don't know" even to the easy questions: "What's your name?" "How old are you?" What kind of questions were they? The doctor had just told everyone I was fifteen a minute ago; did he seriously not think I knew how old I was? Then I realized I wasn't saying anything. It was just that voice inside my head screaming. I tried not to look at any of them. It was easier not to hear and definitely easier not to feel when I looked straight ahead and held my breath. It was only when they turned to talk amongst themselves that I looked around at all.

There must have been eight or nine of them, only one of the whole bunch, a woman. She glanced at me, a faint smile crossing her lips. It was more a look of pity or embarrassment, I thought. As they were walking out of the room, I heard the old doctor say, "I want a repeat on that pregnancy test." My heart began banging in my head again. A pregnancy test! What kind of a girl did they think I was? I pulled the covers over my head and held my breath but the tears wouldn't stay inside.

There wasn't much time to cry. There were important things that needed doing. The nurse with the quick, jerky movements came back into the room pulling the steel cart behind her. She began collecting trays from the bedside tables. Joanne never touched hers. She hardly ever moved. She hadn't even opened her eyes while the doctors were talking about her dying. Debbie just played with her food. She had managed to open the grape jelly and was busily painting the steel rails of her crib and sheets the most vibrant shade of purple, her oxygen mask flung to the floor as always. I have no idea if the annoying little boy with the braid ate his breakfast. I only know I didn't. As the nurse quickly gathered trays, she glanced over mine, then, staring right at me said, "If you don't eat you can't go home". With that curt statement she left the room, yanking the steel cart behind her.

I felt slightly less nauseous. I had discovered if I lay on my right side, kept my head still and looked straight ahead I could keep my stomach from moving. Anything that made my eyes shift could cause the heaving to begin and once started it only stopped after I threw up. Even though there was nothing other than green slime left, once I got that out I'd feel better for a while. Then I could start all over again, laying still and keeping my eyes fixed on the door knob.

There wasn't much time to lay still. The nurse with the jerky movements came back into the room. She was busy. She started with Debbie because she was a mess of grape jelly. She gave her a sponge bath. Then it was Joanne's turn. I don't think she noticed. The little boy, whom I never bothered to attach a name to, was next. He jumped up and down while he was cleaned up and then the nurse came over to me. I looked straight ahead and tried not to breathe as I was wiped down like a kitchen counter. I felt her eyes look at my body; I hated both my body and her looking at it.

I thought she would leave the room and give me a chance to sleep but this was morning at the Hospital for Sick Children. Doctors were being paged over the PA, their name always called twice, "Dr. Mustard party on line, Dr. Mustard party on line". Porters and therapists were bustling in and out of rooms, calling names from their lists, checking wrist bands to make sure they had the right kid before taking them for various tests and treatments. Physio came for Debbie. She screamed as soon as they walked through the door. I didn't know how she could tell. It could be a completely different woman each time but she wasn't too little to know it was time for her treatment to begin. They clapped her little back, she cried, sputtered, coughed and coughed some more. I knew it was for her own good they did this therapy every few hours but I don't think she ever did. Ladies from the lab, the IV team, were always taking vials of blood from everyone. It seemed chaotic but once I had been there awhile, I learned it had a definite routine, one I could count on.

A nurse came in with a wheelchair and unlocked and lowered the bars to my bed. She helped me get into a sitting position then swung my legs around letting them dangle over the side. She tugged little white slippers on my feet. I watched as she unhooked the IV from its place and attached it to a portable pole on wheels. She told me to slide off the bed and get into the wheelchair. My head was spinning. I felt as if I was going to start heaving again. She told me she didn't have all day. From the sharpness in her voice, I knew I had better pay attention and do as I was told. She wheeled me down the hall past the nurses' station. I learned it was command central for both wards 6C and 6D. The nurses, when they weren't taking vitals, giving sponge baths, making beds and keeping order of the children on their list, would sit behind the desk and write notes in charts. The doctors, after their rounds, would also scrawl in those steel clipboards. It was always a source of curiosity, at least to me, what was being scribbled in those ever growing volumes.

I was wheeled around the corner and the nurse opened a door with the words "TREATMENT ROOM" in all-cap black letters boldly stamped on it. In it, there was a gurney like the one I had first been put on in the Emergency room. Cupboards with glass doors were mounted on the wall by the windows. Through them, bandages and scary looking tools were lined neatly in rows. To the left, there was a sink and beyond it a huge black and white contraption with cables and weights. I was told to stand on the scale. It was different from the little one Mom had tucked in the bottom cupboard in our bathroom at home. I stood facing the blank wall and waited. It creaked and crunched as the nurse teased the bar up, up and up before clunking the weight down another notch. Then I watched as she pushed it down, down and down some more. When it came to rest and she was satisfied she had measured just right, the numbers were jotted in my chart. I was told to sit in the wheelchair and was rolled back to my room.

After I was settled in bed, a lady wearing a dress with a short white coat overtop walked into my room. I remembered her from the early morning gang of doctors who clustered around my bed asking all those tricky questions. She had looked at me kindly and seemed as embarrassed as I did by everything the old doctor was talking about. She walked over to my bed and in a crisp French Canadian accent said, "I am Dr. Lefebvre from psychiatry. Come with me." She turned and started walking out the door. I was glad the nurse, in her hurry, had left my slippers on and my IV was still attached to the pole with wheels. Grabbing it, I started in the direction of the door. My head was whirling.

I caught up to the doctor who was marching ahead, clutching my chart to her chest. I was grasping the back of my gown which was flying open while awkwardly trying to manoeuvre my IV pole that, like an errant shopping cart, had a mind of its own. I followed her down the corridor through a set of doors and onto an elevator. She pushed a button and the number two lit up. Moments later, we got off the elevator, turned a corner, walked down a short hallway and entered her small windowless office.

She sat in the big chair near her desk. I was told I could sit in either of the other two that were available. I chose the one closest to the door. Sitting on its edge, eyes fixed firmly on the floor and my back teeth cemented together, I waited.

She wheeled her chair over to face me. For a long time we sat, my heart racing, banging loudly in my ears, forcing my face to feel numb. I was freezing. Slowly I inhaled. From the time I was four years old I had learned when I held my breath and paid more attention to what was happening inside my own head, it was easier to not notice what was happening on the outside of it. My chest burning, head bursting and ready to explode, I couldn't stay any longer. I needed to get out, to vacate.

There was a mat on the floor in Dr. Lefebvre's office. The mat had stripes, twenty-three to be exact. I counted them inside my head saying the numbers slowly and deliberately with my inside voice "one, two, three" until I reached the end, "twenty-one, twenty-two, twenty-three" then started all over again. I found if I stared at the mat, counted loudly in my head and breathed, in then out slowly, keeping perfectly still, I could make all her words run nonsensically together, the noise inside my head scrambling sentences apart. She droned on for what seemed an eternity and continued to ask questions, I think. She may have just been talking but I was practicing not hearing, the way I had practiced not feeling. Once focused in the centre, the noise of her voice was drowned out altogether.

With the steel chart lying squarely on her lap she began asking questions. Some of them were ridiculous: "What is your name?", "How old are you?" I listened without lifting my eyes. I reasoned that if she really didn't know my name, which was clearly written in big letters on the masking tape stuck to the side of the chart, we were in big trouble. I had already decided I didn't like answering questions, especially stupid ones. She'd ask a question then pause. I could feel her staring. Then she'd ask another even dumber question. I panicked for a moment and wondered whether the reason the doctor was asking my name was she could see Marian Rose, the brave one, was sitting in the chair while Muriel, once again, cowardly crouched deep inside herself. But I knew that was ridiculous. It was our secret game, one we had learned to play to make life bearable. There was a long pause.

The silence shattered, her voice breaking through emptiness. Startled, I glanced to the side, my heart racing, thumping in my ears again. Dr. Lefebvre was sitting, facing the desk, arranging books, shuffling papers. She told me I was going to be with her for an hour and, if I decided not to talk, it was my choice but I wouldn't be going back to the ward any sooner. I drew in a deep breath. I thought this must be what a detention was like, although I had never had one because I always did my school work and had never been in trouble before.

She opened my chart and started to write. When I was certain she wasn't looking, I breathed in, then out slowly and watched. From the side, I could see she was tall and thin. Her dark brown shoulder-length hair, parted on the side was neatly tucked behind her right ear. She had big eyes, dark and bright. Her lips were thin and her face serious but not hard. She was beautiful, I thought. She looked intently at the chart, pausing frequently, index finger to lips. Then she would begin scribbling again. I wondered what she writing about me, what secrets she knew, what she was believed was true. I felt stupid. I wanted to talk but I didn't know what I was supposed to say.

I didn't know what I was supposed to do either. With my head still low, holding perfectly still, my eyes scanned the room. It was full of toys. Beside me on a small table, there was a game. Four marbles were poised at a starting gate leading to varying tracks that looped up and down and twisted around each other. There was a finish line at the bottom. Across from my chair were shelves lined with books and puzzles. In the corner, there was a box of stuffed animals and puppets spilling lifelessly over the sides: button-eyes, dead as doornails. I knew how they felt. I wondered if she expected me to play with them. I had read a book for a school project called *Dibs in search of Self* by Virginia Mae Axine. It was about a little boy who wouldn't talk and the doctor used play therapy to connect with him. I wasn't going to play with any toys and I wasn't going to talk.

Then it was over, my first appointment with a psychiatrist. It would become a daily ritual while I was in hospital. After I was discharged I'd continue to see her twice a week as an outpatient until I was too old to see a child psychiatrist any longer. She said our time was up. I followed her down the hallway and we got on to the elevator, my eyes remaining motionless on the moving floor, my stomach falling, tumbling down on the way up. We stopped on the sixth floor. Dr. Lefebvre said she would see me at the same time the next morning and I watched as she headed toward the nursing station.

I made my way down the long corridor pushing my IV. I was finally getting the hang of it. Little did I know that in a few months I would be able to run down the hall, jump on and pop wheelies like I saw others doing. It could have disastrous consequences when two kids came careening around a corner at the same time, sending glass shattering and saline spewing everywhere. It made the nurses mad and we were sent to our rooms for sure, but kids, even sick kids, like to have fun.

That first morning as I was heading down the hallway, I peeked in all the rooms. I saw children sitting in beds, lined up like little soldiers, watching TV, eating their lunch. I found my room and was pleased when I saw my little cubicle all neat and tidy with crisp white sheets and a pretty blue bedspread. I put my IV pole near the headboard and, being careful not to get tangled, climbed into bed.

My brown bedside table had a new tray on it. There was tapioca pudding in a small glass dish. I guessed it was dessert. Those beady little fish eyes I had to squish between my teeth didn't look like anything I wanted to eat. There was a tuna sandwich cut on a diagonal sitting alone on a plate. I imagined the carcass of the dead fish whose eyes lay piled in the dish beside. It made me wince, sending shivers tingling through my spine. Lifting the lid to the steel bowl, I smelled the aroma of beef and barley soup as it wafted into the air. My mouth started to water. It actually smelled good, but I decided it was too risky; I didn't want to start throwing up again. Two crackers lay stranded on the tray. I picked one up, turned it over and began licking the salt off. I liked the taste but didn't want to eat it. I wasn't sure what I was supposed to do. Tired, I rolled over, closed my heavy eyes, breathed deeply and drifted off. I guess sleeping was the right thing to do because moments later the nurse came crashing in, collecting trays and closing thick curtains. It was quiet time.

The quietness was really loud in the dark. I was thinking about my time with Dr. Lefebvre, all her questions, the toys in her room and wondering what she was writing about me in that book. I decided she must think I was crazy. I had never met anyone who had seen a psychiatrist. I had only heard of such a thing and always as a joke. When my mom became exasperated she'd throw her hands in the air and say, "If I wasn't of a sound-minded race of people, I would end up in Ponoka." I didn't know Ponoka was the name of a town in Alberta that had a mental hospital but

I guessed it was a place you ended up when you went nuts. I figured that was exactly what everyone thought had happened to me; they thought I had lost my marbles.

I must have fallen asleep because the next thing I knew lights were flicked on and curtains were being opened. There was a different nurse changing my IV bottle, taking my temperature and blood pressure and counting out the beats of my heart, then recording the numbers in a little book that slipped into her pocket. If she told me her name I don't remember it. I only remember Irene who had been there the first night. She was my favourite nurse.

When Irene was on day shift she let me help her. We made beds together. She was impressed that I knew all about hospital corners. I told her my mom was a RN too and when she had gone to nursing school the year I was nine she taught me how to make beds properly, folding the sheets precisely the way you wrap the ends of a birthday gift when you want it to look like a work of art. I liked Irene. She moved slowly and talked quietly and never asked questions I didn't know the answers to. Sometimes she brought me tea in the middle of the night and we talked about her favorite books and sometimes she just sat beside my bed and didn't use words to speak at all.

That first afternoon in the hospital, I sat up in my bed with so many words crashing around inside my brain that I thought my head would blow off. I tried to remember what day it was, what classes I was missing at school and which tests I needed to be studying for. I knew I didn't have time to be sitting in a hospital bed doing nothing.

Luckily I found out The Hospital for Sick Children knew all about how important school was. Across from the Treatment Room, there was a door with the words "Toronto Board of Education" on it. There was a teacher who helped kids with their work. I could either study at a desk in the school room or in my bed. I liked to go down each morning and work in the classroom because it was easier to block out the noise of the ward. That first week, the guidance counsellor from my high school, Miss Mather, came with her arms loaded. She brought all my books and gave the teacher at the hospital an outline of my courses, complete with homework assignments, projects due and tests from each class. I was glad about that. My two friends Susan and Cheryl came to visit and both promised to take good notes and let me copy them.

Cheryl had been my friend since public school. She played flute in the band and we sang alto side by side in Miss Ashworth's choir. One year, we got a perfect score at The Kiwanis Festival, which had never happened before, and we were invited to sing at city hall. Cheryl and I were excited and when our choir recorded an album, we were standing together on the front cover, smiling our big eleven year old grins. We had been good friends for a long time but Susan Smyslo was always my best friend.

When I had moved back to Toronto, Susan and I picked up where we left off being best friends although it was never the same. After we started the Group Home, she wasn't allowed to come to my house—even once—and see my room, which was upstairs with the boys. Her mom wouldn't give her a reason but I liked going to her house better anyway. High school changed lots of things. Susan and I walked to school together most mornings. We met at the corner because she wasn't even permitted to come on the side of the street where I lived. We had some classes together and she played clarinet in the band and orchestra but didn't join the choir.

Susan visited me that first week I was in hospital and kept her promise to take notes that she allowed me to copy. We never talked about The Hospital for Sick Children. It was as if my being there never happened, a secret we silently agreed to keep from one another. After I came home, I never told her that every Tuesday and Thursday afternoon at 4:00pm I had to go to the hospital and talk to a psychiatrist. I didn't know what to say. Soon there was nothing to talk about. We stayed friends but not the kind that share secrets.

When quiet time was over and the nurse was done taking my temperature and blood pressure, a girl about my age, called a Candy Striper, came into the room with a trolley filled with books. I loved books and even though they were mostly ones for little kids I found a couple I thought I might like to read. Books were great. They took me on trips to places I may never travel to but would see just as clearly in my mind's eye. Reading let me live in a world filled with people who I may never meet but could be as close to as any old friend. I loved the way they felt in my hands and would run my fingers over the bumpy spine where the title was etched surrendering a hint of what adventure was bound together in that volume. I loved even the smell of books as I fanned the pages with my thumb; the way the breeze tickled my nose made me feel alive. I loved books, even my textbooks from school. I couldn't imagine a world without them.

The first week went by, quickly at times, yet sometimes so slowly that I thought the hands on the clock hanging on the wall between the two beds across from me were glued to its face. There was a routine and from it I made a schedule. I took a piece of three-ring binder paper that had come with my school books and turned it sideways. With the holes at the top, I divided it evenly into seven, one column for every day of the week. Down the side margin, I put the time, starting at 7:00am because between 7:00 and 7:15 the nurse always came to do vitals; those were the important blood pressure, pulse and temperature numbers. At 7:30, I was weighed. Between 7:30 and 8:00, breakfast was served and the doctors came in for rounds, sometimes before, sometimes after, so I put them together on the same line. The school room was open at 9:00am so, after the mob of doctors moved on to the next room, I would get out of bed, make it neatly with hospital corners and get cleaned up. I was allowed to go to the bathroom down the hall and have a bath on my own as long as I let the nurse know ahead of time.

The first day, I was allowed to take a bath at the hospital was on the weekend. Irene offered to help but I said I was okay on my own. As the water was running in the tub she put a plastic bag over my arm to keep my IV site dry and helped me take my off my gown but made a real effort not to look. When she left, I turned around and caught a glimpse of myself in the mirror. I didn't recognise the face staring back at me; only the blue eyes were vaguely familiar. The body did not belong to anyone I knew. I looked for only a brief moment, then quickly climbed into the water and let the warmth seep into my bones. It was the first time I hadn't felt cold in a long while.

I liked baths as long as the water didn't touch my face. I always kept a cloth nearby to make sure and never ever closed my eyes; that was one of my own rules. When I was eight years old, I almost drowned in the bathtub and had been afraid of having my head plunged under water ever since that day. When my brother baptized me in the lake the summer I was fourteen, I was terrified. I had been told beforehand that it was to symbolize dying and that when I came up out of the water I would be really alive. But when I saw my brother's face, I still felt dead inside and I was even more frightened of having my face covered with water.

That Saturday morning in the hospital, I ran more hot water and filled the tub over and over. After washing my long hair and rinsing it carefully, I stood up. Tiles surrounding the tub squeezed in tightly from the sides, creating a dark tunnel, and as my eyes were sucked into the blackness, the room collapsed. That was the last thing I remembered. Later Irene told me my blood pressure was too low and the heat from the water had done something to my blood vessels. I had had baths all my life and my blood vessels had been fine. I guessed I really was sick.

After carting me back to my room in a wheelchair and taking my blood pressure several times over the next hour, Irene decided I was going to be okay. She was a kind nurse and, even though I had just fainted, she took me up to the eleventh floor like she promised. I'd heard about it from Jan, the new girl in my room who had taken the bed across from me after Joanne died. Jan was almost eighteen and, because she was closer to my age, we talked. In the hospital, kids came and went quickly and after they were discharged they may never been seen again, so Jan and I were hospital friends. She had rheumatoid arthritis and had been sick since she was nine months old. Her hands were so misshapen she could barely hold a pen. Her knees and ankles were swollen and red and she said they were as painful as they looked. Jan was funny and friendly and we laughed together. She asked me what I was in for and when I said I didn't know, she left it at that.

On Saturday afternoon, Irene put me in a wheelchair and we got on the elevator with Jan. Jan could have gone on her own because she had an Independence Badge. An Independence Badge was a rectangular card with green swirls covered in plastic that could be pinned to your shirt. It had the word Independence at the top, your name and ward written underneath and was signed and dated by the head nurse. It did just what it said: it gave patients their independence. If we had one, the man who ran the elevator would let us on and take us to different floors; without it, we were left stranded on our own ward. Jan had her badge but that afternoon she came with me and Irene to the eleventh floor.

As we got off the elevator, we entered the large playroom filled with toys, puzzles, books, art supplies and a large TV. There was a boy lying on a stretcher with his casted leg hoisted in the air with pulleys. He was playing checkers with another kid, who was bald. There was a group of young children sitting in a circle with a lady who rolled a ball to each one in turn, singing out their names. Some kids were colouring at tables and others were being read to. The TV was on and a group of boys were watching.

Jan said, "Hi" to a woman who came and gave her a big hug and then introduced herself as a volunteer. Irene pushed me over to a room tucked around the corner. The sign on the door said Teen Lounge and below, in smaller letters, it stated clearly that patients must be thirteen years old to enter. It was a small room with a couple of comfortable couches and a table with chairs where three girls were playing cards. Jan said, "Hi" to them and one asked when she had been admitted. She told them she had been in only a day and was on 6C. They obviously knew each other. Irene introduced me and said she would leave for about an hour and then be back. She told me I was not, under any circumstance, to get out of the wheelchair and if I needed help I could call one of the volunteers by pulling the cord in the corner of the room near the bathroom.

After Irene left, the girls asked Jan if she wanted to play cards. I could tell she wanted to but felt bad because there was only room for one other player. I told her to go ahead because I wanted to check out the stash of books on the shelves. I wouldn't have wanted to play anyway. They were using real cards. I didn't know why I wasn't allowed to play with cards that had pictures of Kings and Queens and Jokers, those were just the rules. I had seen them before and even watched Margaret and her friends play games with them when my parents weren't looking, but I never touched them. I heard Mom say something one time about satanic symbols and that was a good enough reason for me to stay away from them.

I was lost in a book when one of the girls asked what my name was. I was used to having to repeat it several times because it was unusual. She asked what I was in for. Her words stopped me short and, with my heart pounding loudly, I quietly said I didn't know. She asked what my diagnosis was and when I said I didn't know that either, she started firing lots of questions. She asked whether the onset of my weight loss was gradual or sudden and whether the vomiting was projectile or not. I didn't like her questions any better than I liked them when the doctors asked and I think Jan knew I felt uncomfortable. When the girl asked who my doctor was, Jan called her "a nosey-parker" and told her it was none of her business. They got into an argument and the girl said she was only trying to help. She got mad and stormed out the door but not before telling me it was it was very important to know your diagnosis because without one you couldn't know your prognosis. I was relieved when Irene came and took me back down to the sixth floor.

When I got back to the ward, I sat on my bed and went over my schedule, colouring in all the boxes with my pencil crayons. Sometimes there wasn't really anything to put in the block but I filled up each square anyway. I had times for studying Biology and French and even though I didn't enjoy it, Math had its own slot along with the other important things. At 11:00am, I saw Dr. Lefebvre each weekday. I coloured that square grey.

I started talking to her by accident one day. I had been in her office several times and was counting stripes on the carpet, ignoring her questions as usual. After she grew tired and started writing in my chart, I looked around. Without thinking, I flicked the switch to the game on the table beside me sending four marbles, red, green, yellow and blue, flying down a race track doing loopety-loops, tumbling this way and that until finally they came crashing to a halt. It startled me and I said right out loud, "The blue won", to which she responded, "And you're winning with me." So our conversation began with me defending myself, telling her I wasn't playing a game.

She said that it must feel awful to have to see a shrink and it was understandable that I was really mad and very sad. When she said those words, my throat got tight. I tried holding my breath and swallowing hard but when I finally had to breathe the sadness had sounds, not words, but little gasps. The tears slipped down my face. At first, I stared straight ahead and tried to force them to stop but when I couldn't, I crumpled forward, burying my face in my hands. She silently slipped a Kleenex between my fingers. I could feel her gentleness holding me even though we weren't touching. She stopped asking questions after that and instead sat with me in the stillness. We didn't talk much. There was nothing to say. I looked forward to my hour with her. Mostly we sat and counted stripes together.

Mom and dad came to see me after church Sunday afternoon. It was impossible for them to come downtown during the week because there was so much work at the Group Home and they never got a break. I understood clearly that, by being in the hospital, I was making their lives even more complicated. I felt bad. When I saw my parents walking down the hallway towards my room, I was relieved, happy and scared at the same time. When my mom came through the door, it was hard to look at her. She breezed in, surveyed the room and went over to my IV bottle and read the word "Potassium" out loud. She asked if I was still throwing up. I told her I was feeling much better. She said she was glad to hear it but that she was a little confused because someone had called and told her I was going to be in the hospital for quite a while and had suggested she bring in clothing and a few other things I may need. She told me she had dropped off a bag at the nurses' station and then asked what all this was about. I swallowed hard. Her presence was scorching. My mouth instantly became a desert. My words evaporated. I said I didn't know. She briskly asked about my school work and so, fumbling to say the right thing, I explained I was keeping up and there was a teacher and a school room and I had all my books. I showed her my schedule.

She snatched the paper from my hand. Her eyes, darting back and forth like a typewriter, quickly scanned the page. Placing it firmly on the table, she twirled it around to face me then tapping the gray square at 11:00am asked what "Dr. Lefebvre" meant. I told her that was my doctor and I had to go into the office for the hour each day before lunch. Mom said it seemed strange I would see a doctor for an hour and asked what tests he was doing. I told her Dr. Lefebvre was a woman who just talked to me. There was silence, like black velvet covering my face. There may have been more words but the conversation ended. The rest of our visit was stone cold. I tried several times to catch my mom's eye but she wouldn't look at me. Dad stood at the end of the bed with his hands behind his back. They were only there a few minutes longer before my mom announced they had to get going. As she was walking out the door, she turned and, looking right at me, she asked if this Dr. Lefebvre was a Christian. When I said I didn't know, she closed her eyes and shook her head. I knew what she meant. After my parents left, I curled up in bed. I was shaking again but it was a different kind of cold. I knew what it felt like to be veiled in darkness, cut off. I was breaking my mother's heart.

Ground Rupture

As the days dragged on, I started getting more used to everything. Having my schedule helped. I knew what to expect but there were always annoying things that messed up my routine. One morning when I was supposed to be studying for Science, I was taken for a test where I had to drink a milkshake that tasted like chalk and then x-rays were taken of my stomach. I didn't want to drink it but the lady who gave it to me didn't seem like the kind of person anyone should argue with.

Mrs. Stokes, the dietician, came in each day but never at a predictable time. We filled out menus and I was allowed to choose what I wanted from the list because I was on a special diet. Sometimes we went to her office. She had charts on the wall with pictures of fruit and vegetables and on her desk she had stacks of the Canadian Food Guide which she encouraged me to borrow. In the corner by the window, she had a tray like the one that came to my room each meal time and on it were empty dishes. She asked me to put pretend food on the plates that I thought made up a healthy meal. Because she was an older lady, I didn't want to hurt her feelings and say I thought what she was doing was silly, so I played along. But she did tell me some things I didn't know. I had never been on a diet so when I learned all foods, even the things you drank, were made up of calories, I found it interesting. It didn't really matter though because I had decided not to eat or drink anything at all.

The first day I was in hospital, the nurse had told me if I didn't eat I couldn't go home and that seemed like a fair trade. I didn't want to go back to the Group Home, although I would never have said it out loud. Not eating was a small price to pay to be able to stay away from a house full of rude boys. There wasn't a life I wanted to go back to at all. I don't know if I thought that in the front of my mind or if it was hidden in the back corner where I stored the many stories and secrets I didn't know what to do with. But I did know one thing: I wasn't going to eat and no one could make me.

My whole schedule was thrown out the window when my face blew up one morning. I woke up to find my lips swollen, bulging out with little bubbles all over them. When I tried to open my eyes, they were sealed shut with thick green goopy glue. My tongue was twice its normal size and my whole mouth was tight and itchy. When, through tiny slits of my eyes, I saw my face in the mirror later that day, I looked like a complete freak. The doctors had a very big word for what was happening they called it "angioneurotic edema" and said it had something to do with my allergies and being anxious. They gave me a shot which did take the swelling away but even after my lips and eyelids had peeled off and returned to normal, I had to continue taking some green medicine called Atarax. I hated it. Within a few minutes of swallowing the sticky stuff it was so hard to read or do my school work because my head felt like it was made of cement yet the thoughts were like wisps of air that drifted in clouds. After that, I didn't follow any routine at all; I was too sick. All I wanted to do was sleep.

One rainy afternoon, I was told there was going to be a conference and that I would be called in. I didn't know what that meant but my stomach was in a knot. I didn't know what time the meeting was going to start but when I saw my mom and dad in the hallway and I was told to stay in my room, I was pretty sure it was about to begin. I saw lots of peoples' heads bob by the window of my room: Dr. Stevenson, the resident assigned to my case; Mrs. Stokes the dietician and her assistant; then all the doctors, young and old began drifting by. Although I didn't see her, I heard Dr. Lefebvre's voice.

It was officially quiet time on the ward, the curtains sealing out the bustling world. The emptiness was filled with the hammering of my heart and the sound of each breath as I tried to still my insides. I had heard the expression, "heart in my throat" and, until that day, thought it was a metaphor but I could feel each beat on the side of my neck pounding a fast, even rhythm. I was lying on my bed trying to read but my eyes stared at the page, the words refusing to paint pictures. I decided to sleep or escape to the centre, the place deep inside, but couldn't do that either. The hands on the clock were stuck.

Irene finally came to get me after 3:00pm. She looked me in the eye, smiled gently and told me I was going to be just fine. I was toting my IV beside me as we walked out of the room. Down the hall, I saw the back of my parents' heads getting smaller and smaller as they were sucked into the elevator. When they turned around, their eyes were on their toes. Mom looked up, she saw me, but didn't wave goodbye. The door slid shut.

Irene opened a door to a big room, filled with people sitting tightly in chairs lined up in stiff rows. In the sea of faces there were some I knew and many I didn't. I was told to sit at the end of a long narrow table. Dr. Williams, sitting across from me, began to speak. His words rolled out in slow, deep waves.

He told me I was very sick. He went on to say I had a serious illness and that 15% of people, primarily young women, with this disease died. I was staring straight at him. I kept swallowing hard. My throat and stomach were tied together, one tight knot. My face was numb. My heart, pounding fast, made it difficult to breathe and hard to hear. He continued. He said the name of this disorder was Anorexia Nervosa. I had never heard the words before. I was still stuck back at the word "died". I was certain there had been a serious misunderstanding. I knew I was sick but surely not sick enough to die like Joanne had.

He talked for quite a while. Not to me really, but more for the benefit of the students he was teaching. I don't know when I started listening again but when I did, he was explaining my treatment plan. He was standing, pointing to a complicated chart, written on a large paper that hung from an easel. I heard him say I would be weighed every morning in a hospital gown. Other than the hospital gown, that was nothing new; it was already on my schedule. He said I would be required to eat 3,500 calories each day and to gain 1.5 kilograms per week. I was wishing I had paid closer attention to Mrs. Stokes because the only calorie equivalent I could remember was that a hard-boiled egg had 73. I was terrible in math but, calculating quickly, I realized this was hopeless.

But then things turned upside down. Looking straight at me, Dr. Williams said that everything I had was a privilege. Being able to get dressed, going to the school room and even having my books, all these things I may have taken for granted, were actually privileges that needed to be earned. He told me I was lucky because they had decided I would start with all my privileges, including having an Independence Badge, which he held in the air, showing it to everyone in the room. He smiled and placed it on the table directly in front of me. He went on to explain how every time I did not eat what was agreed-upon for each meal or meet the weight requirement at the end of the week, my privileges would be taken away. The best I could hope for was that if I cooperated, I would maintain all my current privileges, gain weight rapidly and get to go home before Christmas. The worst that could happen was I would be stuck in my bed, wearing hospital pyjamas without access to TV, school or any books. He asked if I understood. I nodded that I did. He asked if I had any questions and with my eyes looking straight at the floor, I shook my head.

I don't know what they talked about after that because all I could hear was the noise inside my skull. There weren't any words in my head, or at least none that made sense; it was more like an explosion. Feelings I had never learned names to crashed around, beating at my brain. I felt like I was drowning. I wanted to run or disappear or just die right there on the spot. I wanted to scream or cry or be silent forever. I couldn't think and I guessed that even if I could, it wouldn't help, so instead I sat still and stared straight ahead. I wasn't going to cry. Dr. Williams asked again if I had any questions and when I shook my head he told me I was excused and could go back to my room. As I stood to leave he called my name, strutted over, smiled and handed me the Independence Badge. I took the plastic-covered name tag with the green swirls and set it down, sliding it to the centre of the table and looking straight at him said quietly, "I don't want it".

The meeting, at least my part in it, was over. I left the conference room and walked down the hall yanking my IV alongside me. I went into my room and got into hospital pyjamas, crammed all my stuff, books included, into a couple of bags and plunked them outside my door. I unplugged the TV and climbed into bed, curled up in a tight ball and demanded the tears stay inside where they belonged.

My life became impossibly difficult from that day on. My parents didn't visit. I wasn't sure whether it was because they were still so mad at me and I really was as good as dead to them or if it was just part of the rules I didn't know about.

I was more determined not to eat and refused to drink. I was allowed to get out of bed and probably could have even dressed and read books for the rest of the week until my weight went down and all my privileges were formally taken away but I just stayed in bed and pretended I wasn't alive.

The only thing I could count on was the nurse coming in to take my vitals at the beginning of every shift and enduring rounds each morning where Dr. Williams, his underling Dr. Stevenson and the tag-along gang talked about my lack of cooperation. Seeing Dr. Lefebvre at 11:00am was the only thing I looked forward to. I don't know what we talked about, if in fact I said anything at all, but it was an hour that I was allowed off the ward and her office was a warm place to be.

Because my weight kept tumbling down, they put in a feeding tube. One sad and scary day, Dr. Stevenson came into my room and told me he needed to reweigh me. I stood on the cold scale with the hospital gown gaping at the back, staring straight ahead. He pushed the bar up then down and when my weight finally hung before us, his face turned red and he kicked the wall. I was told to lie down on the bed in the Treatment Room. Dr. Stevenson stuck a tube up my nose. I felt it burn its way up then, hitting the hard edge near my eye, turn a sharp corner before it burrowed down my throat. I gagged and gasped as it snaked its way to the pit of my stomach. My face felt as if it were on fire. Quickly Dr. Stevenson took the other end of the tube and wound it around in a huge loop and fastened it in place across my face with adhesive tape securing it to my head then walked out the door. After laying there for a while, I quietly slipped off the gurney, went back to my room and crawled into bed.

I tried to pretend I didn't care but I was panicked because now they could make food go into my body against my will. I learned how to empty my stomach by vomiting after each feeding, which sounds a lot worse than it really was. I wasn't nauseated anymore but I had learned that if I drank warm water and pushed the muscles of my stomach tightly together I could make myself throw up. I did it over and over until there was nothing but clear water and then I was done until the next feeding time. I was glad I was able to maintain my stance and they were baffled by the continued weight loss.

Early one Saturday morning, I ripped out the feeding tube. I knew I would have at least a couple of days without it because doctors weren't around the ward on the weekends, or so I thought. Irene was my nurse and, rather than being angry, she sat beside me on my bed and we stared at the wall. Not long after, a doctor, whom I had seen around but never met, came into my room and introduced himself as Peter Harris. I thought that was strange because doctors, like teachers, never had first names. He asked me if it was a good time to talk and because I was so surprised he asked, I said yes. He casually mentioned that my room was not a private place to have a conversation and suggested we could go into an office down the hall if I would prefer, so I agreed.

We sat across from each other, a large round table separating us. With my arms folded tightly against my chest and my legs wrapped into a pretzel, I watched. He leaned back in his chair, opened my chart and after quickly scanning, then thumbing through the many pages, he began reading aloud. He started with my initial intake history. It was basically accurate although some of the details were not as I would have described them. He read snippets of progress notes and then, after placing the chart on the table, he turned it around so I could see how it was laid out. He showed me how it was divided into sections, places for the doctors to write and one for the nursing notes as well. Some were typed. He said those were often more formal consult notes the doctors had dictated. He flipped to the back where the lab results were and showed me charts with columns of numbers. He explained what all those blood tests meant and what was considered normal range for electrolytes and glycogen stores. He went into great detail telling me how decisions, like whether or not I had to have an IV or a feeding tube, were made by interpreting the results. It was interesting. I told him I wasn't good in math. He chuckled and confided in me that it had been his hardest subject in school too but he convinced me learning how to read test results was not about calculating numbers and was really pretty simple, and he taught me how to do so.

Leaning back in his chair again, he told me he didn't know me but by taking out my feeding tube, which he said must have "hurt like the dickens," I had made it clear I didn't want it. He continued by saying that from looking at me and reading the results of the most recent tests, he had a difficult decision to make.

He paused for a moment and then, looking right at me, asked a question. "What would you do if you were a doctor and had a patient who was this sick?" Without hesitating I told him I would let her die. His face looked puzzled. He cocked his head to the side and then, leaning forward, looked deep into my eyes. I could see tears in his. I tried to stare him down but his softness broke my gaze, sending my eyes slamming to the floor. Tears silently slipped down my face. I brushed them away and pinched the bridge of my nose between my thumb and index finger, squeezing tightly to trap the tears. With my eyes scrunched closed, I held my breath. We sat for a long while. Neither of us said a word. When I finally looked up, in a gentle voice, he said, "I'm sorry you feel so sad". Tears began flooding out. I tried holding my breath again but when I had to inhale my chest exploded. I started sobbing. I don't know how long we sat there; it seemed like a long time, but when he finally spoke I was able to listen.

He told me, as the doctor on call, that he really didn't have a choice but to reinsert the feeding tube. He apologized for having to make a decision against my wishes and promised he would try to come up with a better solution after talking with the other doctors on Monday morning. He said he would be around until noon and when I was ready I could come to the desk and he would put the NG-tube back in as painlessly as possible. He waited until I nodded my head.

He stood up, held the door open for me and we walked out. I watched as he moved confidently down the hall with my chart tucked under his arm and took his seat behind the nursing station. I turned and slithered back into my room and crawled into bed.

I watched time disappear on the clock and with just two minutes to spare, got up and went to the desk and said I was ready. He asked me which nurse I wanted to have come with us. I chose Irene and the three of us went into the Treatment Room.

I was shaking. Having the tube put in the first time really hurt and my right nasal passage was raw from yanking it out earlier that morning. He told me to sit on the side of the bed. I watched as he opened the cupboard and found the long silicone tube and slid it from its sterile wrapping. He moved slowly. He told me everything he was doing. I couldn't hear words but his voice was gentle. Instead of ramming the tube up my nose, he took a Q-tip and dabbed it with a numbing solution. He asked me to put the swab up my nose as far as was comfortable and then inhale deeply. The sharp cold fumes made me sneeze. Then he asked me to open my mouth as wide as I could. He sprayed the back of my throat with something that made it numb as well. He gave me a paper cup of ice chips and told me if I could chew on them and swallow evenly it would make the tube go down more easily. He said because his hands were too big he would let Irene insert it while I helped guide the tube down. After covering the tube with a slippery jelly, he told me to nod when I was ready.

And just like that it was done; it did not hurt one bit. Instead of making a big loop with the end, he pulled it taut, tucked it behind my ear and taped it out of sight. He brought my hair forward and told me you couldn't even notice it, which I knew wasn't exactly true but it made me feel better.

Before he left the ward, Peter, which is the name I always called him in private, stopped by my room and handed me a book. He said perhaps reading might make the day go by faster. He put several lozenges on my bedside table and told me if I felt like sucking on them it might help my throat feel better. He thanked me for being brave and said he would come in later in the evening and see how I was doing, which he did.

I don't know how things change in a big teaching hospital, who makes decisions about treatment protocols or who is in charge. I only know that from this time forward Dr. Harris became my paediatrician and I was given a chance to try and live again.

Gaining weight was the easy part. I began to eat and drink, small amounts at first, and tried not to throw up as often. Not disappointing Peter was the reason I was willing to do anything in the beginning but sometimes getting better has to start somewhere.

Books were what I bargained for first. Reading and doing well on my school work was all I cared about. End of term exams were looming and I had fallen behind. I was studying for my Biology final, buried under mountains of material and long lists of words I needed to memorize. Books and papers were scattered over my bed and I was busily recopying study notes when Dr. Harris stopped by my room late one afternoon. It had become part of our routine, something I looked forward to. When he sat down this evening, I buried my face in my hands and started to cry. I told him I was going to fail; I didn't have enough time to learn everything. He picked up my textbook, scanned the index, leafed through the thick volume and told me that in medical school the most important things he figured out were how to prioritize and tricks to trigger his mind to access information during tests.

He said all this stuff was interesting, fun and easy to learn. He made a list of topics to focus on and explained Krebs Cycle to me, the complicated sequence of reactions in the living organism which, until that day, was just gibberish. He taught me a mnemonic technique to remember the molecules "Can Adam Intrigue A Super Sexy Foxy Mama Ok!"; it made me laugh. As he was leaving, Peter told me brains were designed to work optimally when well-nourished and suggested before my exam the next morning I should make sure I had enough to eat and drink to give me a chance to prove how smart I was.

Dr. Harris came in early before rounds and gave me a pop quiz on what he had taught me the evening before. He said I was going to ace my exam because he was a good teacher and I was a bright student; he was sure I could do anything I set my heart on. Eating breakfast was easier that morning. I wanted to feed my brain.

It took time to get better and, even though my weight was actually lower than when I had been admitted, I was finally strong enough to be discharged after Christmas. I did not have to go back to the Group Home. My parents hired staff to work at night and had rented a two bedroom condominium for us to live in. I knew I made their life difficult. Each morning, the three of us drove in silence. Ten minutes of emptiness can feel like forever. Mom would stop at the corner and Dad and I would spill silently from the car onto the sidewalk. I headed to school while he went in the other direction towards the college. Mom drove to the Group Home where she worked all day. At 6:00pm we met and slogged our way through the rush hour traffic back to the condo. We never spoke about the Group Home or the hospital. It was as if they never existed. Sometimes I wondered if I had made them both up in my own head.

I went to high school like any regular old kid but my world was hidden deep inside myself. I continued to play my French horn in the band, orchestra and wind ensemble. I sang in mass, girls' and the chamber choir. I did well in my classes and studied a lot. I even had a few kids I remained friendly with at school but my interior life was consumed with weight and calories and making lists, endless lists. I stopped writing words with feelings and instead filled journals with menus and meal plans. Putting on paper what I intended to eat, what I actually swallowed and what I wouldn't touch made me feel less scared but the thought of anyone ever finding my stuff and knowing what I was trying not to think about forced me to destroy everything I wrote at the end of each day. I burned my secrets in my candle's flame until there was nothing but black soot, the grimy residue of my dark days.

Every Tuesday and Thursday, I went to the hospital after school. I took the Annette Street bus north to the Jane Junction then hopped on the subway that took me downtown. The Hospital for Sick Children looks a lot bigger from the outside than it had felt peering down from my window that winter. As I walked through the door into the big rotunda, the smell made me feel comfortable and safe. I took the elevator to the tenth floor. Teen Clinic was where Dr. Harris weighed me; it was more a measure of his care than anything else. It was a short visit but in that ten minutes I knew he heard more than my few scattered words.

I was on my way out, ready to race down to Dr. Lefebvre's office when the friendly nurse at the desk told me that because my weight had been stable for some time I could skip the next week's weigh-in session. Her words made my heart beat loudly in my head and instantly I felt like crying and dying. I stopped down the hall and slipped into the bathroom. I was shaking. I threw-up the apple I had eaten for my snack. From that moment on, I only ate when I absolutely had to in order to keep my mom from worrying. I didn't keep anything down.

When Dr. Harris weighed me two weeks later, I was sick again. He asked what happened but I said I didn't know, which was as close to the truth as I knew how to tell. Of course I knew my weight had tumbled because I hadn't absorbed enough calories but I couldn't for the life of me figure out why I had decided to stop eating again. After that, we pretty much stuck to our regular appointments. If my weight began to slip, Dr. Harris always tried to encourage me to eat more but there was an agreed-upon line and if I went below it I had to go back into the hospital until my weight was acceptable. I hated disappointing Peter but sometimes I hated being alive more.

After each weigh-in session in Teen Clinic, I went down to Dr. Lefebvre's office. We sat together for an hour. Some days were less awkward than others. I never knew what to say. I did know, however, that when I got home my mom always asked what we talked about. I wanted to be able to be truthful and say, "Nothing," so that is pretty much what we talked about. But it helped, I think. There was another person who was willing to sit and silently count stripes with me and, most importantly, I could count on her being there. I knew she liked me. Her office was the only place I felt warm.

The spring I was seventeen, my weight was low again. I was getting too old for Sick Kids so I was admitted to the Psychosomatic Medicine Unit at the Clarke Institute for Psychiatry. When I saw that sign on the door, I knew what I had suspected all along: I wasn't really sick—it was all in my head.

The ward was split evenly; five patients were skinny women obsessed with weight and calories and five were men with Gilles de la Tourette syndrome. I had heard bad words before but never spoken in such rapid succession. It was hard to get used to all the violent physical and vocal tics they had. There was one room I never saw until the fall. It was a tiny seclusion room on the other side of the nursing station that had a window so the nurses could watch your every move.

The eleven-bed unit on the fifth floor is where I spent the last semester of my high school years. I never told anyone where I was going. I just cleaned out my locker one day after school, walked out the side door and disappeared. I never saw any of my friends again. If Susan Smyslo was the valedictorian of the graduating class of 1975 as she had been for our public school ceremony, I have no idea. My diploma came by post in a manila envelope and was stuffed in a gray folder in the back of my father's filing cabinet.

When I was first admitted to the Eating Disorders Program, I wanted to get well. I was sick and tired. I was willing to gain weight, learn to eat properly and give up purging. It wasn't that I couldn't eat or didn't have an appetite or had trouble gaining weight. I simply was unable to convince myself not to starve. Somehow, feeling like I was dying made me feel more alive. None of my feelings made sense and because I knew my thinking was so ridiculous, I never told anyone what was whirling around inside my head.

The program was straightforward. Upon admission, all patients were given a thorough physical examination and were weighed and measured. There was an initial conference where individual goals were set for weight gain and the daily caloric requirement was determined. All meals and snacks were eaten in the dining room and supervision was continued for an hour afterward. Each day, we spoke with the resident psychiatrist assigned to our case and at the end of each week we were weighed. Those of us who met our weekly goals had our privileges awarded; if we didn't, our calories were adjusted and we had to try again the next week. The program was simple but strict.

If my mom disliked The Hospital for Sick Children, she hated The Clarke even more. She was not allowed to visit. When she phoned, she always disguised her voice saying she was a friend named Doris. She assured me it wasn't a lie because it was actually her first name although she was never called by it.

One evening, she defied the rules and had a showdown with my doctor. My mother appeared on the ward and, when the nurses told her to leave, she refused. Mom told me to go to my room and get my things because she was taking me home. She said if I didn't do it quickly, I would not have a home to come to. I packed my stuff and was in the hall when my doctor appeared on the ward. Mom was demanding I come with her while Dr. Garfinkel told me firmly to go to my room. I was stuck, standing in the middle of the two of them, crying. When Mom refused to listen, two burly men appeared and she was escorted from the building by the security guards. After that, I wasn't allowed any phone calls.

I still wanted to get better and worked hard to follow the program. I didn't want to hurt my mom any more than I already had. I hoped that if I got well she might be able to forgive me but what I wanted most was for my mind to be free. I was sick of counting calories and weighing myself a dozen times a day. I hated being trapped in the restricting/binging/purging cycle. I didn't understand my obsession with being emaciated but it made me feel more solid if I could see all my bones.

They were doing a lot of studies at The Clarke to more accurately define eating disorders and develop treatment strategies. One focus was on body image. A couple of doctors, Paul Garfinkel and Dave Garner, devised a machine that, after taking a picture of you in a two-piece bathing suit, could, at the twist of a dial, magically blow your size up or down proportionately. The premise of the study was that patients with anorexia have a distorted body image. They were curious about what these emaciated young women saw when they looked into a mirror. They guessed that, rather than seeing their concentration-camp, victim-like, frail body, their eyes saw a bloated mass of fat instead. It was a popular theory but I never believed it. I knew what I looked like. And every person I ever met with an eating disorder could guess another's weight within fractions of a kilogram just by looking. It never made sense to me that they would be oblivious only to their own body size. But, although I wanted to be free of my obsessions, it was hard to give up that solid, contained frame of my skeleton. I didn't always like the way it looked but I loved the way it made me feel: tight and numb.

I ate. I didn't throw up. I followed the program meticulously, met every goal and gained the weight. At first I hated both the program and my body but then I got more used to both. After I had been at The Clarke for several months, I was allowed to go out sometimes. I went for short walks at first and I even started nursing school at Ryerson College from the hospital in the fall. On the night before my eighteenth birthday, I was able to go home on a pass. It was the first time I had been home in five months.

I was waiting, leaning against the cold brick wall outside the front door of the hospital, when my mom's car pulled to the curb and I climbed in. The drive home through the rain and rush hour traffic was awkward. The conversation was stiff. It had always been strained but the tautness that evening made each word stretch to a breaking point. I dreaded hearing how well I looked and then the usual talk that started with how hard it had been on them that I was sick and ended with how they hoped I would stay well this time.

We pulled into the driveway of the house that had once been the Group Home. My parents had purchased another house where the boys lived and they had hired full-time staff to run it. It was just a few blocks away but I never saw it. We had moved back into the huge house a few months before I was admitted to The Clarke. We rented the upper two floors to strangers. They came and went quietly but that house always felt loud to me. I walked stiffly in the side door, through the kitchen and into my bedroom which was now on the main floor, my dad's old office. It was as I had left it, neat and tidy and empty of life. I always felt like a stranger in that house.

I only had a four-hour pass, so we had the dinner Mom had prepared right away. Although it was Saturday night, she had made a Sunday dinner, roast beef with all the trimmings. I knew exactly what I was going to eat. I didn't smell food anymore; I saw it in ½ cup portions and caloric allotments and loaded my plate accordingly. I cut my meat and vegetables into tiny pieces and chewed each bite slowly, putting my knife and fork down frequently; this was against our family's rules but was the way they taught me to eat in the program. I had learned that eating calmly helped. I ate slowly, far too slowly I know, which caused my parents' eyes to follow the fork as it made its way to my mouth, even more closely. The silence was interrupted with questions to ease the tension but, instead, the awkwardness of having no answers made the pauses even longer and louder. I declined second helpings, which made my mom's face fall. Dinner took a long time. When it was finally over, I was relieved.

Then my mom brought out dessert. It was a surprise to celebrate my birthday which she reminded me was the next day. I wasn't ready to turn eighteen. She had made my favourite, lemon meringue pie, crafted as always, like a work of art. There were no candles but Mom burst into a joyous round of "Happy Birthday" and Dad joined in. I smiled, said thank you, and then paused. Quietly I told her I was full, and I was. At the hospital, they didn't make me eat dessert as long as I ate the required calories. But this was not the hospital.

I was panicking, my mind racing trying to figure out what to do. I couldn't disappoint Mom again. I didn't want to eat any more. I didn't know how many calories were in any pie, let alone one so full of sugar. Mom carried on, oblivious to the explosion happening to her left because the war being waged was inside my own head which she couldn't possibly know about.

My eyes saw the pie being cut evenly into six slices. My heart was pounding loudly inside my head, my brain instantly swollen by its thumping. I was frozen. Think! Scrambling, I calculated: each piece of pie had to have well over 500 calories—I had only 200 left for my day's allotment—I always saved that for my evening snack, a banana and ¾ of a cup of 2% milk—this would be 300 calories over—I could cut that from my next day by not having breakfast—carrying calories over was not allowed in the program—I had to be back at the hospital before 9:00pm. My chest was tight. I was holding my breath. I knew I was going to explode.

My mother placed a thick slice of my favourite pie in front of me.

Everything became still. Time spread out. Life unfolded in frames, fragmented slow motion.

Trance-like, I picked up my fork and watched as it slowly melted through the meringue, toasted to golden perfection, then slithered through the smooth lemony filling before crumbling the flaky crust. The fork was slowly brought to my mouth. With eyes closed the sweetness swished around inside, dancing on my tongue.

It tasted so good. I swallowed. I looked over at Mom. She smiled. Then I gobbled up the whole thing. When she asked if I would like a sliver more I agreed, I could have eaten the whole pie. She was delighted and told me how she had prayed for this day when we could enjoy our meals together.

Because I only had one more hour before my mom had to take me back to the hospital, she decided to make an exception to our routine and we stacked the dishes in the kitchen. I went into my room. My mind was swirling fast, words, feelings, pulsing through my body. I couldn't think. I knew I was going to explode. I had just eaten my whole dinner and then God knows how many more calories in one and a half pieces of pie!

I went into the bathroom, turned on the fan and ran water in the sink to absorb all sound then began vomiting into the toilet. I drank glass after glass full of water and threw up again and again until I was sure my stomach was empty. It took less than a minute.

I went back to my room, standing and staring into the mirror. The face of fear and fury swelled up and swallowed me whole. I had been home for only a couple of hours and the five months' work in that stupid Eating Disorders Program had just been flushed down the toilet. I was stupid to think it would work. Of course, when you are in hospital and your food is measured out in contained portions on your plate and nurses are there to watch you afterward you can eat and not throw up but in the real world, it doesn't work! Being a child with a psychiatric illness was one thing; I didn't want to be an adult with one.

I walked into the kitchen and told my mother I needed to go look at some things stored in my trunk in the basement. I turned on the light and trudged down the stairs.

I entered the laundry room, opened a cupboard, took out a bottle of paint thinner and, noticing the warning label pictured as a skull and crossbones, drank it down.

I stand awaiting the judgment
wrenched from a horror I would have willingly escaped
yet as I try to look back the glass is too thick
only distorted figures remain and I in isolated terror stay

I look into your face and see "My god it's me"
Is it I who stand in fear of me
but then you speak independently
and I am silent hearing not words but feelings I call mine

I cannot question the punishment for shall I ask
Me or Me?

MURIEL RUTH
MARION ROSE
age 17

The Soulquake

Soul

1: the spiritual or immaterial part of a human being or animal, regarded as immortal.
2: a person's moral or emotional nature or sense of identity.

Quake

1: to shake or vibrate usually from shock or instability
2: to tremble or shudder usually from cold or fear

From a distant world, I hear my name called over and over again. My right eyelid is peeled back; hot white light pierces my brain. A moment of stillness. The other eye pried open, my mind wounded once more. I don't respond to the doctor's questions because—he already knows the answers—he can tell I'm in here. I cement my eyes shut, the thin crimson shield, the only barrier that keeps me from being engulfed by shame. Still, darkness invades. **Don't think. Don't breathe.**

The doctor leaves, pulling the curtain behind him. I part my eyes, just barely, and slam them shut again. I can't do it. I can't face another day. I hear the heart monitor bleeping, telling the world all is well—It isn't. I am alive—again—but not really. My left arm is strapped to a board. I have an intravenous, pure saline solution washing away toxins from my bloodstream. I feel a strand of hair on my face, I try to brush it away—I can't. My other wrist is bound as well, so are my ankles. Great. I swallow; my throat contracts. My tongue traces the hard edges of my soft pallet, I have an NG tube—That will hurt coming out. I begin searching the crevices of my thick brain to reconstruct time. All I find is sadness, hopelessness and the defeat of knowing I am still breathing. Maybe if I just keep my eyes closed I will fall asleep and never wake up—that is all I want, the best I can hope for. I breathe—in, then out. I hate that my lungs keep filling with air. I want to sleep forever. **Don't think. Don't breathe.**

I jolt awake. The blood pressure cuff is inflating, squeezing my right arm. They no longer need nurses to take vitals, everything is done by machine. There are fewer reasons to touch or have awkward eyes meet; I prefer it sometimes, at least today. I resent that I am alive—again. My brain scrambles against my will to make sense of my surroundings. It rarely gives me any other option unless I can take enough medication to cease the firing of neurons. There aren't enough pills on the planet to do that, at least for longer than a few hours at a time. Then I am forced again to gather information and seam together the frayed edges of a senseless life. **Don't think. Don't breathe.**

I am in Emerge. I can hear life beyond the curtain that separates me from those clinging to it and me in here grasping for the dying option. I hate myself. Not even with my eyes closed can I keep the shame at bay now. Hot tears slip down the sides of my head and pool in my ears. I can't wipe them away. My wrists are attached to the steel rails of the gurney. It's my own fault. It always has been.

Don't think. Don't breathe.

Aftershocks

I arrived in the emergency room in a coma and wobbled between two worlds for almost a week. Mom crouched in the corner of the sterile ICU room and read. The light of a goose-necked lamp scattered scary shadows all over the white walls while I pretended to sleep. I was lying on my back, the stiff gurney burrowing its way deep into my bony spine. My wrists and ankles were tethered tightly leaving me unable to even wiggle. When Mom caught me opening my eyes one night, she pushed past machines and leaned over my bed. Her face searched mine. Tears silently began slipping down the side of my face. When our eyes met I could see she was crying too. Through her gasps, she told me she had been terrified and asked how I could do such a terrible thing. I knew I was breaking her heart. I shut my eyes tightly to seal out shame.

One morning, a doctor stood at the foot of my bed rifling through and reading my chart. He looked up and said I was lucky to be alive. After checking my eyes and asking me to read words in a magazine, he told me the foolish thing I had done could have cost me my eyesight. The blood test still showed my liver was struggling but in time that might even get better. He told me the antidote for the acute methanol poisoning had been to insert an NG tube and pour alcohol into my body. He joking told me that was not an ideal way to have my first drink and celebrate becoming an adult. He said I was still very ill, my respirations remained dangerously low. I didn't want to breathe.

Once stabilized, I was taken by ambulance back to the Clarke and admitted to a huge ward filled with frightening people. Dr. Garfinkel came to see me. He asked what had made me feel so desperate and wanted to know when I had begun having suicidal thoughts. I told him I had never thought about killing myself, it just happened. One minute I was fine, at home on a pass eating dinner, the next, I couldn't stand being alive any longer. Before he left, he gently told me that as soon as a bed opened up on the fifth floor he would make sure I was moved. I was scared. I curled into a tight ball and tried to disappear, imagining myself dead.

I was transferred back to the Psychosomatic Medicine Unit days later. My room was a tiny nook on the other side of the nursing station. The windows had curtains that nurses opened and closed, monitoring my every move. I was told I was now an involuntary patient. Even if I wanted to, I could not leave. The door to the unit was locked. I was never sure whether that change was to keep me in or my mom out. I felt safe.

I had to quit nursing school and start the Eating Disorders program all over again. I spent a few more months at The Clarke and slowly began to feel well again. When it came time for my discharge planning, it was decided that going home was not a good idea. My sister lived in Victoria BC and she agreed to have me come and stay with her. She was expecting her first baby so I boarded a plane and headed 3,000 miles west for a visit.

Margaret and her husband Peterjon were running a group home for kids. It was busy and noisy but not a nasty place. The children were full of life and friendly; they didn't try to hurt one another's feelings just for fun. The two girls in their care were beautiful, natural sisters, eleven and fourteen years old. Margaret renamed them Sarah and Rebekah because I think she believed that if you changed your name you had half a chance of changing your life. Stephen, a quiet, awkward teenager who was close to sixteen and Billy Johns, a young native boy with disabilities, lived there too. They were such nice kids. I always wondered why their parents had given them away.

When I arrived in Victoria, the February I was eighteen, I had no plans. There were seven of us cramped together in a tiny townhouse on the corner of Hillside and Cook in a complex called The Cridge Centre for the Family and there was work to do. Cleaning was the most obvious. It was never my sister's forte so I busied myself with vacuuming and doing endless loads of laundry.

Margaret was in charge and ordered everyone to call me Aunt Muriel upon arrival but when my sister's baby was born a few weeks later, I knew what it felt like to be a real aunt. She named her first son Wayne after my brother. Holding him in my arms I sank into the vast blueness of his eyes and swore I could see the depth of his little soul. I knew in that moment I wanted to be a mother someday.

From the instant I arrived, I felt at home on the West Coast with mountains rising from the ocean floor and ancient forests to explore only minutes outside of town. In the spring, I enrolled at Camosun College, moved into a room near campus and signed up for life. I started my courses and became absorbed in the world of learning; I loved school, my friends and my church. I was alive, more alive than I had been since before I was born.

I met a young man at church who was visiting from Ontario soon after moving to Victoria. One afternoon, after talking for hours, Don and I went for a walk. I had never felt so full, blood coursing through my veins making my heart beat loudly in my chest, sending warmth up to my cheeks, pouring out my eyes. When we kissed the first time, I was filled with life, light and hope. My fear dissolved in his love.

We never talked about anything other than our life together in the moment. I didn't mention The Hospital for Sick Children, The Clarke or trying to kill myself only months before. Instead, we lived each day growing more and more in love with life and each other.

In his presence, I felt beautiful and free. Don loved to kiss but never minded when I just wanted to skip rocks. He didn't ask tricky questions he already knew the answers to but instead listened intently when I spoke. He thought I was funny and laughed at the little things I said that no one before had noticed were a twisting of phrases intended to cast shadows. He loved words too and we made up several of our own, creating a secret language. When we used them in casual conversation and others stared blankly, we made faces like they were the most common words anyone should know. We played silly games like hide-and-go-seek but I'm pretty sure he never knew how long I had been hiding, how desperately I needed to be sought and that being found was all I ever wished for as I counted alone in the dark. In his arms, I laughed until I cried because sometimes the happiness that allowed me to unravel and unfold in such a comfortable way made my heart burst with the newness of it all as an unexpected, sudden emerging from a chrysalis.

We cooked pancakes for breakfast and I gobbled them up with strawberries and sometimes even whipped cream. I learned to drink coffee and decided I liked it as well. When he took me to Murchie's Tea Shop, I discovered there were more varieties than Red Rose and being a tea snob had endless possibilities if I decided I wanted to be one, which Don said was entirely up to me. Before we went on one of our long Saturday afternoon adventures hiking through Goldstream Park, Cathedral Grove or skiing at Forbidden Plateau, we always stopped at a local deli. We stood, faces pressed against glass, and chose different meats and cheeses with names I had never heard, something new always required to expand our experience. With fresh bread from the bakery and a bottle of wine added to our backpack, we headed out to touch life.

We both loved to read although Don's appetite was comically insatiable. Each week, we perused old book stores and thumbed through thick tomes in tiny shops that lined the back streets and allies of downtown Victoria. He always chose seven books and read each one, most often juggling three at the same time. He always chose a good book first, a "literary classic". Biographies of famous people fascinated Don because he was certain you could glean so much from the lives and experiences of others so he hunted down titles, old and new alike. A couple of escapist trash novels or mysteries were always thrown in for fun to keep the mind intrigued and agile. And then he just had to add some how-to books to his pile: *How to Rewire an Old House, How to Build your own Canoe*. When asked if he ever planned on doing either he laughed aloud and said, "You just never know". We often read by the fire late into the evenings listening to Vivaldi's Four Seasons, stealing soft glances as we sipped wine with toes touching. I had never known such tenderness mixed with laughter. On my nineteenth birthday, when Don asked me to marry him, I cried in awe as he slipped a ring on to my finger. It had a small centre stone with two golden hearts etched on either side, each embedded with a tiny diamond. He kissed me and said he would love me forever and I believed him.

In May of 1977, five weeks before our wedding, long after the invitations had been sent out and I had had the final fitting of my dress, two police officers arrived on my front porch right before the evening news came on. They told me Don had been in a serious accident on the Malahat, a severe stretch of road carved out of the craggy mountainside north of Victoria. When I asked how he was they simply said, "I'm sorry he didn't make it".

I couldn't breathe. I didn't cry. My first thought was, "I should have known. I should have known this was too good to be true." I said and did all the usual things portrayed on movie screens in scenes where someone is told of a sudden death. I didn't believe them and showed the officers my ring as evidence we were getting married. They said they were sorry for my loss but their brave words couldn't hide the sadness they felt or the horror of being the bearer of such awful news.

The policemen refused to leave before I called someone. I could have phoned my sister who lived on the other side of town but instead I called Peter who lived on the other side of the country. He wasn't my doctor anymore but I needed to hear his voice. When I did, my tears drowned me and I was left gasping for air. The older policeman took the phone from my hand and explained what had happened then gave the receiver back to me. I sat crumpled to the floor, supported only by the hardness of the door-jamb, cradling the phone to my ear and listened. I don't know what he said. It didn't matter. It never had. Just the sound of his gentle voice was enough to make the room stand still for a second and give me hope there was a possibility I could survive the moment. Peter reminded me to breathe.

I flew back to Toronto the day after Don died. The only people I wanted to see were Dr. Harris and Dr. Lefebvre. We met at the Hospital for Sick Children and sat in the warm office with the striped mat. We cried and, through their tears, Peter and Arlette somehow convinced me my life would go on and Victoria is where I needed to live.

A few days later, I returned to Victoria with Don's mom and dad and his younger sister Lynn. We had the funeral at the Church of Saint Barnabas where our wedding was to be held the next month. Father Page performed a high Anglican mass; the liturgy was important for Don's family. But the service I wanted was separated by only a few pages in the Book of Common Prayer, The Celebration and Blessing of a Marriage not the Burial Rite of the Dead. I wanted Don alive, with me, getting married like he'd promised.

The kindest thing about grief was it only allowed me to glimpse the world through its gauzy film. My clearest memory from that day is, while standing and greeting people in the narthex after the service, the man whose logging truck Don's little car had collided with begged me to forgive him and told me through his sobs how sorry he was. Everyone was.

I didn't know what to do. My hopes and dreams were a mangled heap on the side of some road. Don was dead and I was supposedly alive. I cancelled everything, the reservations for the church, reception hall and the photographer. When I went into Miss Frith's Bridal Shop to tell them I no longer needed my wedding dress, the whole store, a blaze of dazzling white sequins, was shattered by the darkness I brought in with me. I was the only one not crying, there were no more tears left for that day. I was numb. I could barely breathe.

I went back to school to finish up the year because at least while I was in class there were some edges around my tears. The friends I made at school and church were kind but no one knew what to say. When they did speak, their words often created confusion rather than comfort. In their futile effort to fill the bottomless chasm of grief, they poured in words, words and more words. Some of them wounded so deeply it was hard to imagine a broken heart having any more ways to be fractured. It wasn't their intention but people, especially people who say they believe in God, often speak words during painful times that can be hard to hear. I was told that God had allowed this terrible tragedy to happen to draw me closer to Him. They went on to reason that because God was in control, He had done this to teach me important lessons or maybe because He had someone better for me. Those were the kinder of the messages I received. Others said that perhaps because I had sin in my life God was trying to get my attention. I didn't know what I was supposed to think about a God like that so I decided not to try. Instead, I tucked those thoughts away in the far back corner of my mind where all the other stories and secrets crowded in unsorted stacks.

I finished my year at Camosun College and enrolled at the University of Victoria in the fall. I didn't know what I wanted to study but I needed to fill my mind with something other than pain. Mornings were hardest. There was a small sliver of time between being asleep and fully awake when I felt almost normal. Then the grief, which started as a wave of fear in my gut would surge into my chest, thrust through my throat and crash into my head. Bolting upright in bed, drowning, I'd gasp for air. Each day I had to gather every strand of willpower to yank myself to my feet, wash my face and brush my teeth.

School helped. I loved learning. The days were filled with interesting classes and, once again, the library became my refuge. I could hide and seek, lose and find myself in words and I did. Living on campus in the Lansdowne dorms, I was close enough to hear joy-filled chatter echo down the hallway during long lonely evenings yet I was far enough away to silently wrap myself tightly in the cocoon created of grief and, in emptiness, wait to be reborn.

I worked hard to complete my courses and made some new friends who were single. Being with couples Don and I had known together was awkward, my very presence a stinging reminder that their relationships could be smashed up in an instant. I tried to be okay with knowing I was not getting married but sometimes it was like being encased in an airless snow drift, the sorrow so thick I thought I would suffocate. But the real cruelty of grief is, rather than getting to die, I continued to exist in a state of perpetual hibernation, numb and barely breathing. I could see the world passing by in slow motion. Leaning in, I caught a few words exchanged between friends and with real effort even participated in conversations. But, unable to touch or be touched, I remained perched on the edge peering in, straddling the brink of life and death, alone, disconnected. Survivors are the living dead.

The summer I was twenty-one, I went back to Toronto for three months for the semester break between my first and second year of university. The first glimmer of life since Don's death was beginning to stir within me. I was hired to work on the Eating Disorders unit by Dr. Paul Garfinkel, the psychiatrist who had treated me two years before.

Peter had told me during one of our many phone conversations over the winter that The Clarke was hiring summer students to help with various studies and he convinced me that working there would not only be a great opportunity but would look good on my resume should I decide to go into medicine, which is what he always hoped for me. I knew I wasn't smart enough to be a doctor. I had to work hard to get good grades but it always made me smile inside knowing at least he believed I was bright. I filled out the application Peter sent. In the early spring, when I got a letter from The Clarke Institute congratulating me for being a successful candidate, I was stunned with pride and panic.

It was odd walking onto the ward the first morning, going through the motions of being given a tour along with other nervous students, most of whom had never seen the inside of a psychiatric hospital. I was introduced to staff I already knew but smiled politely, shook hands appropriately and kept my eyes moving. Dr. Garfinkel was friendly right from the beginning and asked me to call him by his first name. Paul told me he had always known I would get better and take my experience, using what I had learned, to help others.

That summer, I sat on the other side of the desk in the nursing station and read for myself what was written in those charts and was able to hear what was said after patients were dismissed from conferences. I was surprised by what I found: compassion far outweighed criticism. Paul gently guided conversations ensuring his staff spoke respectfully of everyone in his care. He reminded us these patients were people beyond the disorder, women who grappled with pain. In the beginning, I was cautious but also curious. I imagine the staff felt the same. I was interested in knowing what they thought about eating disorders and the women who struggled with them and they were intrigued by the possibility of exploring how I perceived treatment and the unique perspective I could offer.

Paul and I talked for hours. He invited me into conferences where I was able to tell the staff: doctors, nurses, social workers and psychologists, how frightening it had been to come into a treatment program. I explained how difficult it was to be admitted into a mental hospital with tons of questions and find my only resource for answers was asking other patients who were guessing at what was going on. I told them I had felt scared, sad and hopeless, that I didn't have a clue what to expect or what was expected of me and that the weight of guilt and shame made asking questions impossible. I shared what had worked for me. I found dignity in the little things, like being given a choice to come on my own to have a feeding tube inserted, and said that small acts of kindness went a long way to elicit my compliance. When I spoke, they listened and we began to brainstorm trying to find practical solutions to gain the confidence of patients and motivate them to cooperate in their own treatment.

I was encouraged to speak with patients, to find out their concerns and, after making a list of their questions, to write about the issues openly and fairly. What I wanted was to make their stay in hospital less scary than mine had been. Because I knew some of their unspoken fears, a few even trusted me enough to talk. By the end of the summer, I had written a booklet which was ready to be given to each patient upon their admission to the unit. I was thrilled. But the part of the summer I liked best was sitting with these young women and telling them there was life after treatment, something I was still trying desperately to believe myself.

Living with my parents was difficult. Half way through the summer, I moved in with Peter and his wife. They had three little children so, in exchange for doing a bit of babysitting and helping out on the weekends, I was given free room and board. I felt so welcomed. I loved being treated as a friend rather than as a patient. But what I loved most was that Peter made me feel special. He was like a father who had fought for and protected me through my troubled teen years. I adored him and was delighted he was proud of me growing up. I knew it was because he had been my doctor that I had survived; in a real sense, I owed him my life. I wanted desperately to believe in myself the way he believed in me. As we drove into work each morning and talked, I began to share the hopes and dreams that were beginning to take root in my heart. I was starting to believe life just might be worth living. After dropping me off at The Clarke, he would head to his office at The Hospital for Sick Children. Sometimes we met for lunch but always at the end of the day we would drive home together.

On a hot and humid morning toward the end of August, I packed my things and put my suitcase in the trunk of the car. We drove to work in silence. Peter stopped unexpectedly and said he would be right back. I watched in the side mirror as he went into a small shop. Moments later, he slipped back into the car and handed me a rose. When we got to work I left the flower on the passenger's seat wilting in the morning sun. I didn't say goodbye. I never saw him again.

Near the end of the summer, I went with my parents to visit my brother and his wife. Wayne and Sharon lived almost a five hour drive from Toronto in Lansing Michigan. Sitting in the back yard snuggling my new little niece, I saw that the summer sun caught the face of my diamond ring and tiny prisms of hope were refracted into the air. Looking at Bethany, I wondered what it would be like to have children of my own.

My brother was no longer touring and singing. After getting married, he settled down and became a pastor but he still liked to travel and treasured adventure. Wayne loved the freedom of being on the water and had bought a boat. It was a brand new, green metallic, Mastercraft Stars and Stripes that skimmed the surface of the water as it flew into the wind. On a stifling hot Saturday afternoon he took me to Grand River near his home to do some water skiing. We had a blast together. As I went weaving in and out of the wake, catching air, the wind blowing in my face, I laughed out loud. After we got home we went for a long walk. It was like being together when I was a little girl.

Wayne was more than my big brother, he was my idol. As he sang, played piano and spoke in his easygoing masterful way people were drawn and enchanted by his charisma. He had always been the perfect child; his music had filled our home and our mother's heart. He was now a gifted preacher and had a beautiful family. He had become all our mother had hoped for, all she had dreamed. If in any way he had been a disappointment or broken her heart, it was long forgotten and paled in comparison to the grief and constant worry my life had become to her. Mom adored Wayne. We all did. But in his presence I still felt small. That afternoon, once again, I disappeared and was overshadowed. Being a baby sister is something you don't grow out of easily.

We had dinner as a family. Wayne and Sharon listened as Mom excitedly told them how well I was doing, how proud they were of me, my dad nodding dutifully in agreement. She showed them the booklet I had written and told of my plans to go back to school and become a doctor. She mentioned I was dating a young man in Victoria who was also at the university. I corrected her saying that Del and I were just friends and that we had only gone out on a couple of dates and I didn't really like him as I fumbled with my diamond and twirled it around, lining up the hearts just so. I had been told countless times by my mother that I needed to stop wearing my ring because I would never get a boyfriend if people thought I was engaged. But I didn't know how to decide to stop being in love. She said, yet again, that if I was expecting someone to be Don I was out of luck and then went on telling, in great detail, how this new young man, whom she had never met, and I were a perfect match. They all agreed I should at least move my engagement ring to my right hand. Choking back my food took every ounce of concentration I could muster. I felt sick to my stomach. I couldn't breathe.

When we went to church the next morning, I still felt ill. I was distracted. As I looked down at my diamond in its new spot, I tried to convince myself it was important to move it a little further from my heart so I could move forward with my life. I hadn't heard my brother preach since the day he baptized me when I was fourteen but I couldn't really hear what he was saying. The swirling eddy in my mind made his words crash around echoing off my skull like I was under water, drowning all over again. It was probably the usual stuff about how God is a loving father, full of mercy and compassion but also a just God who must punish sin. I knew about God's judgement. I had lots of sin in my life; I deserved His punishment.

I went back to Victoria on Labour Day Monday and moved into one of the new dorms on campus. I always liked the start of the new school year. Buying textbooks, pens and paper gave me a sense of excitement, a promise of new beginnings. Going back to school that fall was even more thrilling. I had a purpose; I was determined to become a doctor. I took six courses, some of which I had to talk my way into to get the prerequisites waved, so I was learning volumes of information at a rapid pace, always teetering on the brink of overload. I loved learning and because I had a goal I was able to keep focused during those long sleepless nights of cramming before midterm exams. I waited for the grades from those tests like my life depended on their results and when I realized I had done well, I was ecstatic. I went back to my dorm room but, instead of celebrating, I crawled into bed.

I couldn't sleep. I kept going over and over each question of every exam, answering them again and again, searching my mind to find the most perfect answer to tests already taken, already graded, already posted. No matter which way I turned, questions and answers tumbled over each other endlessly inside my head. My mind was roaring, revving in high gear. It would not shut off.

I went through the motions of being alive for a few days. I attended classes and tried to decode the noise coming out of my teachers' mouths. I methodically wrote down words to catch what had been said and then sat at my desk in the evening struggling to decipher those scrawls. The black lines and squiggles in my textbooks made no sense. My brain, although alert, had stopped working. I climbed into bed one chilly fall evening and as I lay there, exhausted and cold, tears started, slowly at first, but once they began there was no stopping them. I was cold then suddenly frozen. I couldn't move. I could barely breathe.

I yanked myself out of bed and began packing everything I owned into sturdy banana boxes. I piled them in the corner of my room and called a cab. I asked the taxi driver to take me to the nearest hospital. When I got to the Emergency Room, a nurse asked why I thought I needed to come to the hospital. I told her the only time I had felt like this was moments before I drank paint thinner three years before. She asked if I was having suicidal thoughts and I said no, I had never had thoughts, only feelings followed by actions. She looked at me, eyes widening and, quickly placing a name band on my wrist, told me to get into blue hospital pajamas. Later that night I was admitted to the fourth floor of the psychiatric hospital and put on close observation.

The Eric Martin Institute was not like the cloistered little unit at the Clarke. 4B was a large ward filled with about twenty-five patients who shared a common area with as many from the ward at the other end of the floor. I was sad and scared but mostly cold. That first morning, as I lay bunched up in my bed, I heard my name called over the PA telling me to report to the desk. When I got to the nursing station, a powerful looking middle-aged man stood towering above me. He introduced himself as Dr. Downe. In his hands, he held a thin blue binder with my last name written in block letters along its spine. He turned and walked briskly to the centre of the dining room and sat down at a table. I followed and took the seat across from him. I watched as he opened the chart and began to read.

I knew about charts. There would be intake notes from the psychiatrist who had spoken to me briefly in Emerge, giving his initial impressions. My vitals would be recorded and the nursing notes would likely say something about my sleep being fitful. I doubted the blood work had made it back and if it did the results would all be normal. I watched his face closely; we were summing up each other.

He closed the book and, placing it on the table, folded his hands and looked up. After a long pause he leaned forward. Forming his words slowly he asked why, "in God's name", a young woman would threaten to drink paint thinner. I tried to tell him I didn't say I was going to do it but rather I felt the same way as I had when I had done so as a teenager. He then asked sharply why I had done such a foolish thing. His question cut through my thoughts, splicing words, scattering them out of reach. After looking at the floor for a long while, I lifted my dead eyes to meet his. I quietly told him the truth. I didn't know.

He made it clear he wasn't interested in any nonsense. His favourite saying was, "You waste your time, you waste your life. Don't waste my time, don't waste my life," and with that curt statement after our short interview he got up and walked back to the nursing station. I sat in the dining room wishing the chair would swallow me whole.

When we met the next day, Dr. Downe told me he had called Toronto and had spoken with the two psychiatrists who had treated me as a teenager to get a clearer history. From what Arlette and Paul said, he was certain I was experiencing a delayed grief reaction and the stress of school had plummeted me into a severe depression. He told me I needed medicine because my brain chemistry was off balance. I didn't know what I needed. I just wanted to stop crying, something I was unable to do.

I hadn't told anyone where I was going; I just vanished, like I had from high school. Slowly friends found out and when they came to see me, I didn't know what to say. I had never told anyone about having anorexia as a teenager or being committed to a mental hospital after drinking paint thinner. I had left that life behind and started a new one hoping no one would ever find out. I didn't bother to fill in the gaps.

My friends supposed, along with my doctor, this breakdown was because Don had died and it was normal to feel sad after such a devastating experience. I hoped they were right but I was pretty sure I would never feel any different. They all believed I would get better with medicine. The doctor started me on antidepressants to dry up my tears, anti-anxiety medication so I wouldn't constantly feel like someone was about to die and many combinations of drugs to make me sleep. I took the pills. I felt less. Nothing seemed important. The sadness was more difficult to touch, but just as heavy. I'm not sure they will ever discover a medicine that can cure a broken heart.

I didn't know what was wrong or how to fix anything. There were too many things I didn't know how to talk about, stories I had never been brave enough to tell anyone, not even myself. I believed dying was the only way out but I wasn't even brave enough for that. So I cried for a whole year and spent most of my days wishing I wasn't breathing.

The Return Period

After an entire year being hopelessly sad and taking medication that never adequately masked my grief, I had had enough. My broken heart was still beating but each rhythmic pulse only made me aware how much it ached. I cried all the time and when I stopped, I felt guilty. I was too frightened to live and too scared to die but walking around lifeless and dead was unbearable. After leaving the hospital, I attended a psychiatric outpatient program, which only served as a daily reminder of how bleak my life had become.

In mid-December, my mom flew to Victoria to collect me and my stuff and I went back to Toronto for the holidays. In my stocking that Christmas morning, there was a packet of information about Crystal Springs Institute, a Christian School. I opened it to find an acceptance letter and, attached to it, a one-way airline ticket to Texas. Wayne had heard of a discipleship training course and he and Mom both agreed it was the perfect solution, a place for me to turn my life around. I didn't know what else to do so I packed a suitcase, boarded a plane and headed south the first week of January 1980.

When I arrived in Dallas, I was met by a man holding a sign that read "Agape Force" and was loaded into a brown van along with six other nervous people about my age. We drove 88 miles east and arrived at the ranch just before dinner. We were stopped at a gatehouse and a man wearing a uniform emerged from his tiny hut with a clipboard and chatted to the driver. He popped his head through the window, smiled and, in a deep southern drawl, welcomed us to Agapeland. The gate was raised then lowered behind us.

The 400 acre compound was headquarters for a Christian ministry called The Agape Force which had as its subtitle on all correspondence "God's love is the greatest power in the universe". I had read the blurb in the package stating that the goal of this interdenominational group was "the discipleship, training and deployment of young Christians to work within inner city missions". I had no idea what that meant or what I was doing there. I was just sad and mad. Sad for all the obvious reasons but mad at myself, the world and even secretly at God for reasons I couldn't exactly pinpoint.

It was a beautiful campus, mainly flat, with a few rolling hills that had several buildings scattered over the property. The large cafeteria, where students ate their meals along with those on staff comfortably sat 300 people. The spacious multipurpose room was perfect for meetings, classes and was where the community gathered. It had a fireplace centred on the southern wall surrounded by huge windows. From them you could see the back of the ranch dotted with barns, a couple of lakes to the left and horses grazing in the field near a large orchard.

Across from the cafeteria in the Old Town there was a long raised boardwalk with buildings streaming off of it. A daycare centre, a laundromat and a bookstore were on the right and to the left, a series of doors opened into classrooms used by the Prep School kids. Children from outside the community and those whose parents were on staff went to school there. Towards the front of the ranch, there was a twelve-bedroom hotel. It had a restaurant called Grublet's Hideaway that was open to the public on weekends. Up the hill from the cafeteria, beyond the motel where married couples lived, there was a large gymnasium. The student dorms were beside it and the accommodation for single staff was tucked in the trees further along the path.

The girls' dorm, although constructed in the same charming, rustic ranch style as the rest of the property, was an odd configuration of rooms. The washroom was a typical industrial style affair with several sinks in the centre surrounded by cubicles with toilets and the shower was one big room separated by thin vinyl curtains dividing eight stalls. But there were only two bedrooms for the students, each a long narrow barracks, with six bunks stacked three high where eighteen of us piled on top of each other.

The Agape Force liked schedules but took my love for them to another dimension. Our day started early. At 5:55am the light bulb, which hung directly over my head, was switched on, blasting brain cells to attention. The Team leader shrieked out the morning reveille, "Rise and Shine and give God the glory glory" and there was an immediate scramble. Being careful not to slam my head on the ceiling, I slid down the ladder, dressed quickly and grabbed my tennis shoes as we headed out the door en masse. We had just five minutes to be lined up in rows on the parking lot where we were marshalled through our morning exercise routine. We began by doing sit-ups on the concrete—great for streamlining the backbone—followed by thirty minutes of gruelling stretches. The session culminated with a cruel one mile run around the property. Limping back to the dorm, we took our three minute showers in a militaristic fashion: one minute of hot water, one minute with no water and forty-five seconds of hot water ending with fifteen seconds of cold where I plastered my body against the wall defiantly to avoid being chilled through. Dorm inspection insured that sleeping bags on each cot were neat and tidy and that all belongings stowed underneath the bottom bunk in our suitcases were folded precisely. This was not Bible College, it was Christian boot camp.

Breakfast was served in the cafeteria followed by quiet time. This half hour was set aside for individual prayer and scripture reading and then classes were held all morning. After lunch, work details were assigned and the afternoon was spent doing chores. The peach orchard needed pruning or picking depending on the season. There were barns to clean and gardens to tend. Kitchen duty, which included doing dishes and preparing dinner for 100 people, always needed a large crew of students and cleaning buildings throughout the ranch kept everyone busy. After dinner, study hall was held in the cafeteria. We were given time to read the book of the week, along with ten chapters from the Bible, to memorize the assigned scripture verses and prepare for the weekly Saturday morning test on class topics. Each night, I crawled up the ladder to my top bunk. When the lights went off at precisely 10:00pm I collapsed into a coma, completely exhausted.

I didn't like being there much more than I had liked being in hospital. The lack of privacy and the constant scheduling made me tight and testy. 4:00am was the earliest we were allowed to get up but because it was the only way I could get any time to myself, I decided to set my alarm. Prying my aching body off the thin, stiff mattress, I shimmied down the ladder and, after grabbing my backpack, headed to the laundromat to read and "pray". My prayers were consistently ones of petition: "God get me out of here".

I liked the school part, reading and learning. The first book we were assigned, called *The General Next to God*, chronicled the life of William Booth, the founder of The Salvation Army. His leadership style and vision of ministry was one the Agape Force admired and emulated. I wondered if our ridiculous daily routine was anything like the Officer's Training my parents had been forced to endure when they were my age.

We were required to read ten chapters from the Bible each day. I had heard most of the stories in Sunday School and memorized scriptures since I was tiny but had never read the Bible for myself. We worked our way through the New Testament and when done, started again. By the end of the first term we had read through all twenty-seven books three times.

Our classes were taught by teachers who explained how our faith and daily lives were meant to be interwoven, something I had never considered. I began to think about what I learned as a child and to grapple with what I had been taught growing up in various churches.

I had always considered myself a Christian. Since the night I was four, when I responded to the altar call after hearing my father's story about the lost lamb, I knew I was saved. As a born again believer, I had some idea what was required of me. I knew the rules and had tried to follow them but, of course, always sinned, missed the mark, fell short, failed. Backsliding was common enough and recommitting your life to the Lord was part of what happened every summer at camp when sermons about living a compromised life were preached. The guilt would make me raise my hand. With heads bowed, eyes closed and no one looking around, I'd be one of the first to slip from my seat and file down the aisle to join the mob at the front of the Tabernacle. As I knelt at the altar the counsellor, laying hands on my head, would pray. I always cried and again promised myself from then on I'd be pure in thought, word and deed. I was a typical Christian kid.

As I read scripture for myself and listened to what was supposed to happen in the Christian life, I realized obeying the law outwardly was not enough; following rules was not my ticket to heaven. An inner perfection was required; there had to be a change of heart. Instead of feeling relieved, I could barely breathe. I knew I could never measure up. I had tried and failed miserably over and over again. God knew everything about me. He saw my heart; there was no fooling Him. He was, no doubt, as disappointed with me as I was with myself. And although I had heard about His "Amazing Grace" I was convinced there wasn't enough of it to "save a wretch like me", there were after all unpardonable sins, things that could never be forgiven. And to make matters worse, I had questions.

I was afraid to ask most of them because I was sure they were not the kind of thing a Christian should be thinking and, even if I had been bold enough to raise my hand, I knew I wouldn't like the answers given.

I couldn't understand why an intelligent God would tell my parents to start a Group Home for juvenile delinquent boys where I was hurt so badly. That didn't seem even half smart. I didn't want to insult God or question His sovereignty, but I couldn't understand why He thought allowing Don to get smashed up by a logging truck was a good way to get my attention. It didn't make sense that God would trick me into loving someone then snatch him away to teach me a lesson. How a God of love could operate in these ways made no sense and hearing people say He made those choices for my own good was difficult to understand. The fact that His ways were higher than my ways and not to be questioned made me feel stiff and scared. I felt like a terrible failure, a bad Christian for not being able to just accept His will.

I was mad at God, although I wasn't brave enough to admit it, not even to myself and I certainly would have never voiced it aloud. The verse "God is love" had been engrained in me since I was a little girl. But rather than making me feel secure and deepening my trust, it frightened me. The well-known scripture "Perfect love casts out fear" haunted my mind. It's impossible to trust someone I don't understand especially if I believe He would intentionally hurt me. To think about God's actions and His inactions, the way He interacted with His creation, left me panicky, my perfect fear casting out all hope of love. I wasn't able to think about these things in the front of my mind. But my unasked and unanswered questions were a constant source of dis-ease that festered and fuelled my anxiety.

I wanted to be a Christian. Even though many things made little sense to my mind and created conflict in my heart, I intended to follow and obey God's laws and live my life the way I knew I should. So I tucked these thoughts tightly, stuffing sadness in between the fear, in the back of my head where I had learned to keep everything secret and separate.

I stopped asking myself hard questions and focused on enjoying the good things, music and friendships found within Christian community. There were more moments of comfort, sometimes bordering on joy, but just beneath the surface shards of sadness and fear poked through.

The school had a rule that students were to have no special relationships. That was fine with me. After Don died, I tried dating. The whole idea seemed absurd. The awkwardness of trying to pretend I was fascinated in what a rather boring boy was saying was mind-numbing. I wasn't interested in feeling again and the thought of anyone ever taking Don's place in my heart felt like treason. In some ways, it was as if I died in that car accident but, as a punishment, I was left inside my body and forced to lug it around. It worried my mother. She thought I was looking for Don and would never be satisfied with my illusion of his perfection. Perhaps it was true. Don had given me an experience of love to measure life by and I decided that I'd rather be single for the rest of my life than settle for less.

When we began our second session, our group was small. Because we took all our classes together, worked side by side and ate our meals in the cafeteria, we got to know everyone. Food was doled out in fairly equal proportions; the guys were starving while the girls were ballooning on Miss Charlotte's biscuits and gravy. I was a picky eater and grits and fried rabbit were scary fare, so I gladly shared mine with the guys at my table. Alan and I became food friends first. As he flashed his dimples and gladly gobbled up my leftovers, we talked. He intrigued me. Alan hadn't grown up in the church yet seemed able to grasp some of the basics of the Christian faith crisply and clearly. He didn't get muddled in his mind or rattled by rules. Nothing was complicated but refreshingly new and exciting seen through his eyes. I liked that.

On a sunny day in May, our class was given an unexpected free afternoon off the ranch. We loaded into cars and headed to town. Many of the girls went shopping while the guys tossed a football around at a nearby park but Alan and I sat in the parking lot of a mall and played backgammon for hours in the sweltering sun. At first it was just fun, teasing each other with winner takes all, but then I began to notice something. The same rush of heat, beginning in my chest, rose to my face and flooded out my eyes. When he looked at me,

I knew he was feeling the same way. From that day on, whenever our eyes met, we quickly turned away. Special relationships were not allowed. Dating was against the rules.

After finishing the school term, our entire class signed up for the internship program. The no dating rule still stood but there wouldn't have been time for it anyway. At the end of June, our group was divided and disbursed off the ranch for the summer outreach program. Our van, piled high with seven girls' belongings, travelled caravan-style with the guys' team and headed to Virginia where, as promised, we were introduced to inner city missions. We joined others from our ministry to help with street evangelism, work in the kid's program and sell records. The Agape Force produced children's music and selling *Music Machine* and *Bullfrogs and Butterflies* door to door was the way we buttered our bread and kept the machines of ministry moving.

In the fall, I was sent back to the ranch to work in the bookstore. Not being in school had many advantages. In the staff dorm, there were just six to a room and bunk beds were stacked only as double-deckers. Showers were not timed and reading in bed was allowed. The schedule was more flexible and, other than working all day, doing house chores, attending Sunday morning, evening and midweek services and volunteering, my time was my own.

In January, we had a conference. Teams from all over the country came back to the ranch to report and be given their new ministry assignments. At the conference, there were to be many changes; rumours rippled, everyone was anxious. I was scheduled for a meeting Thursday afternoon. I knew I could be sent anywhere, perhaps to join the Canadian team.

When I entered the room, my team leader introduced me to the principal from the Prep School. He handed me a list of student names and a pile of books. I was told, starting Monday, I would be teaching 7th, 8th and 9th grade Science. Four teenage boys would be my homeroom class and I would be responsible to oversee their education for the winter term. Then he nonchalantly asked if I had any questions. I stood there stunned. I had not completed my formal education and had only taught Sunday School as a young teenager. I hated boys and science was not my favourite subject. No, of course, I hadn't any questions. After carting the stack of books back to my room, I climbed to my top bunk and immediately started studying.

During one of our large evening gatherings at that conference, there was good news though. The leader of our community announced the internship program had been scrapped and said that those who wished could join the ministry, becoming staff with all rights and privileges, effective immediately. From the far corner of the room, Alan winked at me. That weekend, we went out on our first four-hour date and, when he kissed me behind the back barn and told me he loved me, I knew we would be together forever.

Alan's team returned to Virginia while I stayed on the ranch and taught school. Daily letters flew back and forth and, one night during our allotted once a week phone date, he asked me to marry him. I hung up, jittery and dazed, went back to my room, climbed to my top bunk and laughed into my pillow. Although it wasn't the most well-thought-out or romantic proposal, I didn't care and immediately allowed myself to dream of our life together.

Only a few days later at a weekly community meeting, the rules for new staff were clarified. There had been a misunderstanding: special relationships were not part of the package deal and dating for new staff needed to be postponed until one full year after completing school. I sat wide-eyed, gulped in silence and was relieved I hadn't told anyone Alan had already proposed. For the next four months, letters and phone calls ceased. I was beginning to hate rules.

At the June conference, Alan and I were finally officially on staff and able to date. When he slipped a diamond ring on my finger, I stared at the new promise of hope and breathed in deeply. We announced our engagement and excitedly began making plans for our wedding before anyone could change the rules. I wasn't scared and never imagined Alan would get smashed up by a logging truck. I fully believed this was a different time and I was ready to embrace our new life together. Alan was assigned to work on the ranch and in the fall I started teaching preschool, a more comfortable fit. My little group of four-year-olds were a constant source of joy to my life.

Once engaged, dating in the ministry was bumped up to two, four-hour time slots a week. But even if we had the money to leave the ranch, travelling to the nearest town ate up at least half our time together, so we spent most of our dates talking for hours, staring into each other's eyes and trying not to kiss too much. I told Alan about my life. I was honest about my struggle with anorexia as a teenager and the depression I experienced after Don's death. Alan held me as I spoke of the sadness and cried along with me. It didn't seem to matter to him that my life had not been perfect. He said he loved me and always assured me he believed the pain I had been through spoke more of my strength than anything else. What I experienced most in his presence was safety. I felt loved, accepted, open and free and, for the first time in years, deeply at peace.

Alan and I were married on a warm day in the middle of March because, in Texas, the sun rarely goes away and when you are teaching preschool, Spring Break is a perfect week for a honeymoon. It was a big wedding. All the children from my preschool class and their parents, the staff and students from the ministry and everyone from our church were invited to join us. Our families gathered; Alan's from Colorado, mine from Canada. My brother performed the ceremony, where we naively promised to love and cherish each other for better or worse, richer or poorer, in sickness and in health. My little niece Bethany was my flower girl and the rings were toted down the aisle by my sister's oldest son, my brother's namesake, Wayne. I was twenty-four when we slipped golden bands on each other's fingers and said our vows, sealing our promise with the words, "This ring I have chosen as a continual symbol of my love, devotion and consecration to you. Its presence will remind you that next to God I will cherish only you." It was a fun and joyful celebration, a start of a new life. We went to Colorado to ski and spent the days and nights being in love with life and each other.

We didn't have what some may consider a typical courtship but our love unfolded gently after we were married. Our first year was one continuous date, a daily discovery of each other. For the first few months we lived in one of the motel rooms on the ranch and were elated by such expansive privacy. On Saturday evenings, rather than eating in the cafeteria, we cooked hamburgers on our little Webber-go-anywhere and watched Barney Miller, squinting at our twelve inch black-and-white TV screen as we sat propped up on our waterbed eating popcorn. We laughed and talked and every morning awoke to the wonder of being together, sinking deeply into the mystery and comfort of being one.

We didn't have a lot of money so we had to be creative. We found many good deals to stretch a dollar and having fun was the adventure. We explored all the nooks and crannies of our 400 acre property and sometimes packed our lunch and went into town. We'd spend all Saturday afternoon at the State Park, reading and cooling off in the lake during the blazing hot summer where temperatures soared well over one hundred degrees, and then stop for a Frosty from Wendy's on the way home.

Tyler Texas prides itself on being the Rose Capital of the World. For a dollar a dozen, with a bunch thrown in for free if you bought twelve, a few bucks could be exchanged for an extravagant expression of love. To celebrate my birthday, Alan surprised me. When I opened the door to our little room, the whole place, glowing in soft candlelight with music from Chariots of Fire gently playing in the background, was strewn with yellow roses. Bouquets of them, arranged elegantly in huge glass vases and then trails of petals were scattered throughout gracefully, adorned our bed and bathroom. I had never seen anything so stunning, a gift created just for me. Alan kissed me gently and I was again overwhelmed by his love. It wasn't until the middle of the night when, in the midst of a full blown asthma attack and while we were opening windows and turfing all 156 beautiful flowers out of the room, I had to tell him I was allergic to roses. We had so much to learn about each other.

Before we were married Alan had told me that he loved sports. He had been captain of his high school football team. By all the pictures in his mother's photo album the year they won the State Championship, I could tell it was a big deal. But being a Canadian girl who had been solely immersed in band and choir, I couldn't fully appreciate what it all meant or how sports would shape our life.

In the fall of our first year, I was introduced to football season. On a warm sunny Sunday afternoon, Alan, donning his Bronco jersey, plopped himself in front of the TV to watch his team challenge the Dallas Cowboys. I had never watched football before and settled in beside him, eager to share his passion.

First, there was the pregame show where bands and cheerleaders riled up the crowd. Players were interviewed, microphones shoved in faces, shouting frenetically above the clamor of a packed stadium. Announcers talked enthusiastically, bantering back and forth about what they thought would happen, reviewing every game of the previous season, showing highlights with each play repeated again in slow motion, just in case you missed it. Half the afternoon was over and the game was yet to begin.

After the kickoff, I watched as grown men clobbered and sent each other flying, landing in piles. They intermittently kicked and threw the ball while men in striped shirts blew whistles and waved their hands frantically. Each catch was replayed several times from different angles; the camera backing up zoomed in, frame by frame slow motion. Then diagrams were drawn explaining what we had seen clearly only moments early. I pestered Alan non-stop, asking what was happening, thinking that if only I knew the rules, I might understand why people would spend a whole free Sunday afternoon trapped inside watching sports.

Downs, he explained, were tries, each team was given four downs to move the ball ten yards. If they managed to do so without the other team swiping it, they got four more tries. That was simple enough to understand but there were a myriad of other rules that caused all the fuss and which were not as easy to remember. The whole point was to get the ball to the end zone. When that happened the crowd erupted and Alan, standing to his feet, cheered or booed loudly along with them. For a couple of hours, I was enormously patient but, growing more fidgety, finally asked how much longer it would be. Alan told me there were only fifteen minutes left in the game. I learned that football time was different than real time but later discovered it was nothing compared to basketball time.

That fall we moved into a tiny two-bedroom trailer at the back of the ranch and shared it with another couple. Don and Ame were easy to get along with and having our own kitchen made it feel more like a home. Although Alan and I ate in the cafeteria most often, it gave us an option to eat on our own. I loved to bake.

In early spring, we began digging our first garden. We enjoyed working together and were delighted to watch green beans burst out of the brick-red soil. Alan worked in the orchard as part of his job and, at the end of each day, he gathered peaches that could not be sold at market and brought them home. I turned them into pies, cobblers, breads and jams, always looking for new ways to prepare and preserve them. Each evening, Alan, brimming with pride, presented me with The Peach of the Day, the biggest, juiciest, most perfect one he could find. "It was fair," he said, "a well-documented principle of gleaning, clearly laid out in scripture". We took that forbidden fruit and, after buzzing it up in the blender with a bit of honey, we sat on our front steps sipping our smoothie and talked about our day.

I taught at the preschool while Alan worked around the ranch. After seventeen months of marriage, our first son, Christopher John, was born. That August morning as I cradled the 6 lb. 2 oz. miracle of our love in my arms, I was breathless. I couldn't believe something so pure and innocent had burst from my body. The boundless blueness of his eyes drew me into a love so deep, one I had never known, and confirmed what I had believed all my life to be true: I loved being a mother.

Alan stepped into the role of being a dad as comfortably as he did every new challenge. He was a hands-on father who, right from the start, participated in even the mundane tasks of bathing and dressing our babies. He learned all the tricks and, after being squirted in the face a few times, realized he had to be quick while changing little boys' diapers. Each Friday evening, he got up throughout the night to give me a chance to sleep and always let me know how much he appreciated my work as a mom.

Right before Christopher's first birthday, we moved into a two bedroom place of our own at the front of the ranch. Life for our little family felt perfect. A year and a half later, Jonathan James was a gift to Alan on his 27th birthday. We had him at home and celebrated with cake and ice-cream, a birthday built for two. That night, as Jonathan and I gazed into each other's eyes, I fell in love all over again. I was surprised my heart had expanded and this love was just as full and fresh. I was more alive and at peace inside myself during those early years than I ever had been.

Alan had gone back to school when Christopher was a baby and continued to work full time on the ranch. Fitting in courses and studying made for long days and many short nights but because our family was most important, I never felt squished out. Time and money were scarce but we didn't mind. We were contented with our love and our little family gave us more wealth than we had imagined. Just before Christmas, the year "Duffer" was three and baby "Jojo" was learning to walk, Alan graduated with his degree in Computer Science.

Discontinuity

Life is always in a state of change. Sometimes the movements are so subtle it is difficult to detect but during those months everything was realigning. There had been a shift in the ministry and the ranch was sold so the focus could be on inner city missions. We were ready for a change, the timing was right; we wanted to raise our children living closer to family. We talked about moving to Colorado Springs, where Alan was raised, or Victoria, where I was sure God had done his finest handiwork creatively bringing mountains and seas together in one Eden-like place. Our life lay open before us, the choices abundant.

My parents were also exploring what they wanted in the new phase of their lives following my dad's retirement. Mom had taken a trip to Victoria to see my sister. Margaret and Peterjon had four children of their own and had settled on the west coast where the weather was mild and inviting. While visiting, Mom decided to put an offer on a house. She excitedly called Dad and told him to put their place, the old Group Home in Toronto, on the market since she was sick of winters. Within a couple of months, they moved into a big house on Beach Drive that had a suite downstairs. When we were trying to decide what to do, they generously offered us a place to stay while we got ourselves settled.

In January 1987, we packed up our lives and, with our two little boys in tow, moved into my parents' basement while Alan looked for work. We were hoping to live in Seattle, just a ferry trip away but when Alan was offered a job in Victoria, we decided to stay. We fell in love with the seaside city, joined a church and made lots of friends, friends who would be with us through more than we could imagine.

When we first moved into my parents' place, things went well. The house was perfectly designed for two families to live together. In the basement, the self-contained four bedroom suite made it possible to keep our lives comfortably separate. Christopher and Jonathan were allowed to knock on the door upstairs only after phoning ahead and asking if it was a good time for a visit and, when assured it was, would trundle upstairs and give big hugs and kisses.

The boys loved being with Grandma; she always greeted them with tea and scones. Most mornings after their yummy treat, they were bundled up and would set out on a long adventure with Grandpa. He took them to Sealand, Bowker Creek or Willow's Beach and they walked, tiny fingers curled around my dad's gigantic one, and searched the shores, gathering shells and sticks and beautiful pebbles. They hunted for endless hours because my father, for the first time in his life, had nothing but time and nowhere he would rather be than with his little buddies. They would return, squealing with delight, and eagerly show me all the treasures they had discovered to add to the growing collection that sat in a pail by the back door. It was comforting to have my folks upstairs and, once the privacy issues had been worked out, we relaxed and enjoyed one another.

We began attending Church of the Way. It was an interdenominational gathering of people who expressed their faith in a similar way as those in the Agape Force had, so we slipped right in. It was a vibrant community chock-full of young families. It was there we found a gregarious group of friends who were committed to doing life together. Because we all had at least a couple of kids, there were usually about a dozen children bundled together as we sat through May Day parades rain or shine, went on wagon rides to cut down Christmas trees, camped, skied, and celebrated birthdays, high days and holidays. These were friends who showed us they were committed to us and willing to be there literally through thick and thin.

Our families were friends but the women, of course, bonded as only women do; we became family. Every week, we gathered our brood of kids and met at each other's houses to have coffee and hold tightly to any sliver of sanity we could find. Between being pregnant and nursing, enduring sleepless nights with newborns while chasing toddlers all day long, we were all donkeys on an edge. We began calling ourselves the YaYa's and were, above all else, a force to be reckoned with. We talked and laughed, screamed and hooted, prayed and cried, sharing our hearts and lives with one another.

A few months after we moved to Victoria, I was visiting Vicki, one of my YaYa's, on a regular old day, doing what we often did, when my life erupted. Vicki had two kids the same age as mine and our children played together so often they may well have thought they all belonged to one big family. Later in the afternoon, we set aside our sewing project and stopped for tea. There was a new TV program on weekdays at 4:00pm that everyone was tuning in for. A young black woman with an afro was waltzing her way into the nation's heart. The new Oprah Winfrey Show was a talk forum where the host brazenly interviewed people and spoke candidly about everything. Nothing was off limits.

The topic that day was incest. Vicki and I listened as a woman told a secret she had kept all her life. As a child she had been molested by a family member and, as she recounted the story, the sadness and shame exploded from her heart for the whole world to witness.

During a commercial break, Vicki turned to me with tears flowing down her freckled face and asked if I could imagine such a terrible thing happening in a family. And from a place, buried so deeply in a corner of my mind I had all but forgotten it existed, I told her the truth: I could imagine such a terrible thing, because it had happened to me.

This was the first motion, the precursor to the quake that would cause the discontinuity between the memory plates of my life to collide and collapse my world around me.

After spending the afternoon with my new friend, I went home and made dinner. Our little family sat in the kitchen downstairs and ate together as usual. I cleared the table and washed supper dishes while Christopher and Jonathan played with Alan on the floor, rumbling and tumbling, the silliness of tiny boys and their dad, roughhousing that always seemed to border on dangerous. But they loved their nightly brawl.

When Alan heard me running water into the tub, he brought the boys

to the bathroom, carting Christopher on his back ~
his shoulders. He stripped them down and then plu
sudsy water. I scrubbed them, head to toe, as they
plopped bubbles on each other's heads. I wrapped C
sang to him until he was dry and then it was Jonath
them in their matching jammies and brushing their t
the covers in Christopher's big boy bed for a story.

I read *The Little Engine that Could* and of course another story, because one book is never enough. Jonathan fell asleep half way through. Lifting his limp body, I placed him gently into the crib and watched as his tummy moved in and out, the soft, even breathing of a sleeping cherub. I tucked his little white lamb under his arm and tousled his shock of dark wavy hair and kissed his forehead then lay back down beside Christopher. We sang a few songs and, as always, practiced adding and subtracting because he loved numbers. I asked him to tell me what his most favourite part of his day was. He liked playing with Brittany. The worst thing was that he had hurt his finger, which he lifted for me to see. I pecked his Peter Pointer and we prayed. I thanked God for friends and asked that Christopher's finger would heal as he slept and feel all better in the morning. After tucking the covers around him and smoothing back his little fair hair, I went into my room to lie down. Alan came and cuddled in behind me and asked, as he always did, how my day had gone.

Without editing the story in my mind or finding a good starting place, I blurted out that my brother had molested me from the time I was little and that the summer I was home between my first and second year university, he raped me.

Then there was an explosion. An eruption from the core of my being sent shock waves bursting throughout my body. Pictures began ricocheting in my head, feelings began shattering every cell of my body. Tears gushed out with deep long heaves and Alan held me tightly in his arms as we sobbed. We lay in the darkness for hours and every time I caught my breath and tried to say another word, the sadness and terror plunged me into blackness again. I felt as if I was drowning.

The next morning Alan came into the kitchen in a freshly pressed white shirt and a striped blue and grey tie. He reached out and tickled Christopher who was still in his pyjamas, sitting in his yellow booster seat and eating yogurt.

r smiled and took a big swig of apple juice from his Sippy- cup. As
lked by, he reached out and grabbed Jonathan's nose. Jojo flashed him
g grin, showing off his brand new baby teeth. He had been busily lining
up Cheerios on the tray of his highchair. He did this before meticulously
picking up each one, holding it high in the air, scrunching, and then flinging
it to the floor as he watched it bounce on the ground.

Alan came over to where I was sitting with my head hung low, fingers
curled around my cup of tea to absorb comfort. He put his hand on the back
of my neck and drew my head forward into his soft belly. He turned my face
up to his and gently kissed me on the forehead. He told me he loved me. Tears
welled up. I closed my eyes. I couldn't look at him. I bit down hard on my
lower lip, and then threw my eyes to the floor, holding my breath. He said he
was sorry but he had to go to work. I nodded and whispered I would be fine.
Swallowing hard, I began picking Cheerios off the floor.

There had just been a catastrophic event and yet I was the only one who
knew about it. Nothing was cancelled. There were no headline news bulletins
breaking in every few minutes announcing rescue missions or giving updates
on causalities. There was no information given for emergency evacuation
plans. No numbers were flashing on the screen, telling who to call for help
or where to register for crisis management. The whole world had collapsed
yet nothing had changed. There were little boys to dress, beds to be made
and diapers to change.

I was sitting on the edge of the bathtub watching as Jonathan looked
at the pictures in his book, legs dangling from his potty chair, strapped
to the toilet seat, when the phone rang. I knew it was my mother. It was
past 10:00am and she would be wondering why the boys hadn't called yet.
Christopher answered and, in his most grown up voice, told Grandma I was
waiting for Jojo to poop but he would be right up. Christopher came into the
bathroom and looked at me. Gently moving his little face in front of mine,
he asked if I had a cold and plucked a tissue from the box and handed it to
me. I smiled and told him I was fine, he could go on upstairs and Jojo and
I would be there shortly. Jonathan announced there were "no poops" and
began flailing, trying to get down. I wiped his bottom and put a diaper on
him. Potty training could wait.

I had to go upstairs. I had to have tea. I had to pretend the world was
still gently spinning on its axis while my life was violently gyrating on the

inside. If I didn't sit at the kitchen table and spread jam evenly on my scone and chatter endlessly about the weather, then life might really collapse on the outside as well.

I ran cold water in the sink and washed my face. Looking in the mirror, I was startled by the face staring back at me. I wondered who I was. Quickly, I brushed my hair, put on lipstick and headed to the back stairs where Jonathan was already making his way up. He was holding the rail, so proud he could do it all by himself. Turning his head every few seconds, he grinned and waited to be told he was such a big boy. Before I opened the door, the aroma of freshly baked scones floated into the air; I felt like I was going to throw up. I breezed into the kitchen and kissed my mom on her cheek and then went over to the table. Busily wiping jam off Christopher's face, I sat down beside him and, pulling Jonathan onto my lap, began buttering his scone, popping bites into his mouth.

Mom poured me a cup of tea then stopped and looked at my face. She asked if I was okay. I told her I hadn't slept well. I listened for the next five minutes as she chattered about what she called, the "fabulous herbal remedies that facilitated sleep and fortified immune systems so the frequency of colds could be diminished". She showed me papers purporting their potency and documenting the latest studies, supporting the Amway vitamins she had gotten for a decent price because they were still distributors although she claimed they weren't into it all that much. I held the pages in front of my eyes, pretending to make sense out of the black lines and squiggles. I couldn't read. I stared for what I hoped was the appropriate amount of time and nodded. I told her I would take the samples she had given me, promising to take them faithfully.

Luckily, my dad came in and the conversation turned to where he was taking the boys for their morning adventure. Christopher stuffed the last bite of scone into his mouth and took his plate over to the sink and said thank you to Grandma. I went downstairs with the boys and zipped them into their muddy-buddies and sat them on the stool to wiggle rubber boots onto their feet. After putting mittens on their hands and toques on their heads, I sent them out the door to wait by the back gate. When Grandpa opened the latch, they turned, waved goodbye and blew me a kiss. I went back into my own kitchen and stood at the sink and began to shake.

The feelings that had shattered every cell in my body were once again exploding inside, sending pictures shooting through my mind. Every time

I turned my head, images of being a little girl flashed to the front. The fear, the deep churning in my gut, the numbness, the half-formed thoughts void of words scrambled inside my skull. My heart was racing so fast I thought my chest was going to burst or collapse. I closed my eyes and held my breath. I needed to be quiet. I couldn't let Mom hear me cry.

I decided to have a bath while Dad was out with the boys. I cried while the water ran; rushing noise crashing over each wave of sobs. I was freezing. I lay back in the water, closed my eyes and soaked in warmth. Tears streamed down my face. I breathed in deeply. The world fell still.

Then, jerking and flailing, my heart jammed its way into my throat. My childhood fear of drowning, having my head plunged under water and held there until my lungs caved in, shot me upright, eyes wide open staring in the mirror. I jumped out of the tub, grabbed a towel and retched into the toilet. Crumpling into a heap on the hard tile floor, I lay there shaking, sobbing as quietly as I could.

I heard the creaking hinge of the back gate, little voices chattering and laughing outside the window. The back doorbell rang. Quickly I got up, yanked on my jeans and pulled a sweatshirt over my head and, tying my hair in a ponytail, answered the door with a smile. I sat on the back stairs with my two muddy little fellows and listened to their sweet voices. They told me tales of their wonderful morning trek as they gently offered up gifts, the treasures they had discovered at the beach.

In the weeks after telling Alan about my brother, I cried a lot. It was difficult living in the same house as Mom and not letting her know why I was so sad. She noticed, of course and, when she asked Alan about it, his heart literally stopped.

He was driving her to the hairdresser on his way to work, as he did each Friday morning. As they were travelling slowly up a side street in sleepy Oak Bay, my mom asked Alan a pointed question. She wanted to know what was going on. He didn't answer. It was then she noticed him veering into the middle of the road and, looking over, saw he was slumped forward. Grabbing the steering wheel, Mom was able to guide the car toward the side of the road before Alan's foot hit the gas pedal, sending them hurling into a telephone pole and then a tree before crashing to a stop. He was taken to the hospital by ambulance.

When I got there, he was lying on a gurney in a side room, with the curtains pulled around him, uninjured but embarrassed that he had fainted. As we were talking, his face grew frightened. Alarms sounded loudly. Nurses and doctors crowded in, squeezing me out into the hall. Through the crack in the curtains, I saw them surrounding Alan with paddles held high, ready to shock his heart. Moments later, after recovering his heart rhythm, he was whisked past me, down the corridor and gobbled up by an elevator. I was told he was being prepped for surgery to have a pacemaker put in to keep his heart beating. He was twenty-eight years old.

A couple of our new friends came and sat with me while I waited. The next day, when the scary part was over, a group of them arrived at the hospital with pizza in hand and we held the 4th of July party in the Coronary Care Unit. It was wonderful to know these people were willing to be there through tough times.

We were told by the doctors the cause of the incident was a faulty wiring system that had probably been flawed for years causing brief episodes of dizziness. We were assured Alan's pacemaker would kick in when his pulse went below 50 beats per minute. But I was more panicked than ever he would die and, once again, I would be forced to live alone in a world growing scarier each day. What was happening in our life was frightening enough to make anyone's heart stop.

A few weeks later, Wayne, Sharon and their two girls came for a holiday. The day before they arrived, Mom and I were downstairs making beds in the guest room when she asked, yet again, what was wrong. I couldn't hold the tears back any longer. They began flooding out, cascading down my cheeks. Through quivering gasps I told her that when I was a little girl Wayne started touching me. It ended the summer I was twenty-one.

There was silence, a silence so loud it split the room in half. As I looked up, I could see Mom's face erupt with fury. She told me I was a liar. She said she couldn't understand why I would make up such a cruel story that had the potential to ruin my brother's ministry. It was obvious I was sick again. She told me the doctors had been right all along and she had been warned from the time I was a teenager that I was unpredictable and had a serious mental illness. I tried to convince her I was telling the truth but she refused to even look at me.

When my brother arrived, we did all the ordinary things families do. We took in all the touristy sites of the city, had meals together then sat around the kitchen table talking for hours catching up on what everyone was doing. My brother's girls doted on their baby cousins and my boys loved them instantly. When my sister brought her four over, the eight of them ran around the backyard, darting through the sprinkler, and then sat on a blanket blowing bubbles in the sunshine and eating popsicles that drizzled down their arms.

One evening, after the kids were in bed, Mom and Dad, Wayne and Sharon and Alan and I were sitting in the living room upstairs and the bold self, the creation of my childhood terror, began to talk. The voice bravely told my brother I had already confessed about what had happened when we were growing up and about the afternoon I was twenty-one when we went waterskiing on the Grand River and later went for a walk.

Instantly, Wayne began crying and admitted it was true. He told everyone how awful he felt, and about the shame he felt over being involved in something so evil and about the guilt he had carried all his life. I felt nothing. I watched the conversation unfold from the corner of the room inside my head where I sat crouched like a tiny child. As an observer, completely detached, I listened. Everyone had their turn talking. But although I could hear words, I couldn't put the sentences together to make sense of what was being said. My brain was on the brink of disconnecting.

When Mom determined the conversation was over, she decided we should pray. I was sitting so far inside myself, I was only guessing at what was happening by watching everyone's faces. I imagine we prayed for God's mercy and forgiveness, all interspersed with scriptures and familiar religious language, but when it was over I didn't say anything, not even Amen. Afterwards, when my brother leaned forward in his chair and said he forgave me, I was relieved and grateful.

For the rest of their visit, we were just a regular old family going picnicking at Beacon Hill Park while the kids chased goats in the petting zoo. We watched the fireworks at Butchart Gardens and took pictures of the kids pushing each other in the blue wagon in the backyard. I had retreated deep inside myself as I had always done when life became too difficult. Being compliant on the outside was the only way to survive. My brave self carried on and did what she always did: what was expected. I was disconnected.

It wasn't until after Wayne and his family went back to their home and church that my life really began to unravel. The long-hidden and unspoken secret permeated my every thought and many conversations. Mom was angry. She told me she now understood why I had always been fraught with guilt and shame and my emotions had been so fragile. She talked about God's judgment, how, as a just and righteous father, God had to punish sin and now it was clearer to her why Don had been killed and my life had always been a struggle.

I agreed. In light of what I had done, I was guilty and understood I couldn't blame my brother. As Mom said, he had been seduced by me. I had drawn out an uncontrollable dark side of a vulnerable man; it was my fault. But what made my sin even more unforgivable was that Wayne was no ordinary man. He was a man of God and I had been used as what she called, "a tool of the enemy," to destroy his life. Because I had wanted everyone to know the truth, I had not only exposed my own evil but selfishly chosen to risk defaming my brother's character which could tear down his ministry, the very work of God.

Over the next several months, I could barely breathe. I cried a lot and I didn't want to live. There were days when I thought the sadness would swallow me whole and nights I prayed it would. Alan and I didn't know what to say to each other and every attempt he made to talk about what had happened caused me to dissolve deeper into despair. But, unlike other times when I was overwhelmed with grief, I had to keep moving. I had two beautiful little boys who loved music and dancing and building with Lego and by Christmas time I had found out I was pregnant with Micah. He was a gift that forced me to choose life because the miracle and blessing of life was once again growing inside of me.

I had few words to put around what I was feeling. I tried to do the things I had enjoyed before. Reading and sewing and being present to people were activities I continued to do but was unable to connect with. Enjoying life was beyond my capability. I did the necessary mundane, required stuff and managed to get everything done, sticking to my schedule. But I was hollowed out on the inside and becoming hollow on the outside too.

During this time, my sister asked a friend of hers who had a similar experience to talk with me. Mary had been abused by her father and had also struggled with anorexia for many years. She invited me to meet with her and a few other women who were all sorting through the painful issues of their pasts. Each week Mary, Karen, Nancy, Sandra, Rita and I gathered. The rules were simple: everyone had an opportunity to share and no one was to interrupt. Between the six of us, there was enough pain in the room to make the whole universe weep forever and, although we really didn't know what to do, we sat clustered in a circle and found comfort knowing we were connected.

Mom became sick again. Her blood pressure soared. The medication that had controlled it for years stopped working. She had tests and was sent to a cardiologist. He suggested that, because she was only sixty-eight years old, still young, and otherwise in good health, it was an ideal time to have her mitral valve repaired. Our GP, who knew nothing of what was happening in our family, tried to convince me this open-heart surgery was a simple procedure with little risk and that it held promising results for a much healthier and longer life for her. But I was terrified.

Mom and I were having tea one morning. The boys had already gone out for a walk when again I asked about the surgery. I told her I was fearful her recovery would be difficult because this was such an emotionally painful time for our family.

She held her Royal Albert china mug, the one I had given her as a gift many years before. Her thumb silently traced the gold cursive lettering outlining the word "Mother" arched over a bouquet of red roses, her favourite flower. Her vacant eyes stared out the window. With tears welling up, lip quivering, she glanced at me, then quickly turned away. When she finally spoke, it was just above a whisper. She said she would never recover. Then, looking straight at me, she told me she was going to die and when she did I would know I had literally broken her heart. Instantly the black velvet shroud suffocated me. I couldn't breathe. I knew I would be cut off, veiled in darkness forever.

I told her how sorry I was and promised to make it up to her. Through my sobs, I vowed never to speak again of what had happened and tried to convince her that our family could go back to normal. But my tears, she said, were too late. I had selfishly chosen to destroy our family.

On a warm sunny day in June 1988, I went to the hospital with Mom. We checked in with the receptionist early in the morning on the day of her operation. Mom had made a list of things I needed to remember to do while she was under the weather. We spoke about all the ordinary things nervous people talk about when they prefer to avoid the subject of their worry. The first hour was filled with the busy-ness of having blood work done, starting the IV and the quick, jovial exchange with the cardiovascular surgeon who went over the procedure and the post-surgical protocol she would have to follow.

Time went quickly. It was 10:00am when the porter came and I kissed her goodbye before they rolled her down the hallway toward the surgical suite. I went to the cafeteria to get something hot to drink. I looked down at the bag dangling helplessly from a string in the Styrofoam cup creating a murky brown "poothsue" and chuckled, knowing Mom would never consider this a cup of tea. But it was hot and it felt good slipping down the back of my throat, easing fear away. I settled myself and my six-month belly-full of baby into an uncomfortable chair in a small waiting room. Instead of reading the book I had brought with me, I mindlessly thumbed through the stack of outdated Reader's Digests to pass the hours.

The hands on the clock moved slowly. When the time went past the four hour mark and I hadn't heard anything, my own heart began beating so loudly in my head that it crowded out thoughts. I asked several times why it was taking so long but was told the doctor would talk to me when he had a moment.

Late in the afternoon, the surgeon rounded the corner and entered the waiting room. Everything stopped. The whole world fell silent. Time spread out. He sat down across from me and looked at the ground. He had a mask dangling around his neck and as he pulled his green cap from his head, he looked up, cleared his throat and softly said, "I'm sorry".

While those words were reverberating inside my skull, he told me the surgery had gone well and the repair had been simple and straight-forward, as he had predicted. The incision had been closed in short order and he was confident of a good outcome but, when the time came for her to be taken off the bypass machine, her heart refused to beat. He reopened the surgical site and meticulously went over his work along with another surgeon and, after looking at every detail, they concluded it was perfect. Yet her heart, even after being shocked many times, refused to establish a rhythm of its own. He couldn't get her off the heart-lung machine. I heard his explanation but was waiting for him to tell me what he was going to do and then again he whispered, "I'm sorry".

There was nothing else the doctors could do. My mom died the next day from surgical complications and unknown medical reasons but I knew the truth: she had died of a broken heart. I had killed her.

Our family gathered for Mom's funeral. My brother spoke and we all sang *It Is Well with My Soul* when in fact it wasn't. Funerals are often declarations of faith that contradict reality and defy all reason. The "peace like a river" spoken of throughout that old hymn was not attending my way. While "the sorrow like sea billows rolled" and raged and almost drowned me, my grief, wrapped in guilt, squeezed out all hope of calm.

A few weeks later, my dad went to Toronto to attend a class reunion of his Salvation Army Officers training session. While he was there, he became ill and had to return home. When Alan met him at the Vancouver airport, my dad was dizzy and disoriented. After the long ferry ride back to Vancouver Island, where he teetered in and out of consciousness, Alan made the decision to take him directly to the hospital. Alan called from the emergency room and told me the doctors had discovered my father had had a brain haemorrhage and needed surgery.

They drilled three burr holes into his skull to alleviate pressure in his head. I sat by his bedside for days and prayed. I couldn't imagine being responsible for killing my dad too. Slowly, he regained consciousness, fluttering his eyes and giving a feeble nod of his head to hint he was coming to. But the doctors were worried. He was difficult to rouse and when they spoke, he didn't respond verbally to their commands which they believed was a sign of brain damage, a disappointing but often inevitable outcome of the type of injury he had been treated for. One morning, Dad caught my eye while I was washing his face. I forced a smile and his face mirrored mine. His eyes responded and, as I leaned in, I was sure he was in there. When I spoke, he didn't answer. But it was then I noticed that the tight bandage on his head was covering his one good ear and once the nurse snipped the gauze away he perked up immediately and began talking.

When we brought him home, his recovery was slow. Dad needed help with everything. At first even getting him up, bathed, shaved and dressed for breakfast was a complicated and exhausting process. The boys sat with Grandpa at the kitchen table and patiently encouraged him to use a spoon and swallow each bite of porridge. The summer days were long. There were no walks to the beach to search for treasures, instead we huddled in the backyard under the shade of the tree and looked at books. We were all so sad.

Micah was born the first day of September of 1988. We brought him home from the hospital four hours later. He was a happy, healthy fellow with deep dimples like his dad. The nine and a half pound baby beluga with a voracious appetite nursed constantly and grew daily before our eyes. The busy-ness of life with a newborn and being up and down at night while caring for my dad all day was wearing. Jonathan, two and a half, was full of energy. He was our son who learned to run before he could walk and was always busy crashing toys, according to his big brother. Christopher had just turned five and was learning to read. He had always been mesmerized by numbers so I was feeling a bit inadequate and constantly challenged as our homeschooling days were launched.

The logistics of our life required a set routine to keep everything moving smoothly. On the outside, things seemed orderly. Pictures in our photo album show us celebrating Thanksgiving, Christmas and Easter with friends and family, every birthday captured with snapshots displaying homemade cakes with candles, complete with balloons and bunches of friends. The boys, in their matching Oshkosh overalls with clean faces and a tidy house in the background, all appear happy and healthy. But I was disappearing—on the inside and outside too.

I was unable to brEAThe. When I did either, breathe or eat, the feelings were too strong. When I held my breath and walked around in a low blood sugar daze, at least I was numb and could plod through each day doing the things required of a mother with three little boys and an ailing, aged father. The Christmas Micah was fifteen months old, I found out I was expecting again. I was nauseated and tired as usual but this pregnancy began much differently than the others. I was exhausted, sad and weighed eighty-two pounds.

My doctor, our next-door neighbour, knew nothing of my history but was aware of my mother's death and father's illness because he had treated our whole family for the three years we had lived in Victoria. After doing my initial prenatal exam, he gently but firmly confronted me with the seriousness of my physical condition. He cautiously mentioned that my sadness had become severe and suggested I talk to someone. I promised to start eating again for the baby's sake and went for counselling.

Rip Current

We had met Christopher Page and his wife Heather at a homeschooling meeting shortly after moving to Victoria. While talking for a few minutes, we realized we had more in common than each having a couple of children and wanting to educate them ourselves. As cities go, Victoria is small and the Christian community shrinks it down further so it's not uncommon to find your lives intertwined. But there were many colourful threads that wove our families together. We had mutual friends, they knew my sister and her family, and Christopher's father, the rector at St. Barnabas, had presided at Don's funeral. But the first time I really talked to Christopher it was quite by accident, which is the way most important conversations of my life have begun.

We started attending his small Anglican church after Mom died. St. Philip's was just a few blocks from my parents' house, a lively community and a hotbed for homeschoolers. I fell in love and found comfort in the ritual of liturgical worship. The message of grace, gently interwoven with scripture and folded into ancient prayers, gave my shattered soul a place to rest.

Perhaps it was my tears, which stubbornly pushed their way out against my will while kneeling at the communion rail as the chalice was brought to my lips or maybe it was the stark sight of me that caught his attention but, unlike others, Christopher not only noticed, he was unafraid to speak; he was unafraid to hear. And if he was scared by the sting of my life, he never made me feel his uneasiness and was able to push past his own sense of inadequacy to be present to my pain.

One Sunday morning, Christopher, like his father before him, stood in the narthex of the church like a mooring, shaking hands with parishioners to steady their faith as they filed out the door. When it was my turn, I gave the usual spiel about how I had enjoyed his sermon and asked how he was. He told me he was fine, but then, looking me directly in the eye, he said he could see I was not. Fighting back tears, I fumbled and finally agreed to meet with him a few days later before the midweek service.

Driving to the church Wednesday evening, I had no idea what I was going to say. I wanted to tell him the truth but at that moment the only sliver of it I knew was more than enough to make me want to die all over again.

Christopher met me at the front door and I followed him downstairs to his office, nestled away beside the nursery. He flicked on the light and, as he was taking off his jacket, invited me to have a seat. I settled into a chair and looked around.

The room was sparsely furnished, lined with bookshelves filled with interesting titles, some of which I recognized, others that I would come to know and love. The old green chair in which I was sitting was comfortable but threadbare, black strands worn through, most noticeably on the big arms, where others before me had, no doubt, sat, their fingers nervously searching for words they could not find on the surface of themselves. A desk stood across from where I was sitting. On it were tidy little piles stacked with papers, several books—dogged-eared and marked up lay open and dead centre—a family picture capturing Rachel and Naomi with their long braids, beautiful round faces and wide beaming smiles as their innocence peered out for all to see. Beyond the desk on the window ledge there was a sign with three simple words: Listen. Listen. Listen.

Christopher sat down and wheeled his chair around to face me and, leaning forward, asked if he could pray. I nodded and closed my eyes; tears had already begun slipping down my face. It was a gentle prayer, spoken softly, acknowledging the presence of God. Christopher asked that The Holy Spirit would comfort me and, as I found the courage to speak the truth, I would be set free.

Starting was the hardest part. I didn't know where to begin to tell the story, a tale so full of twists and turns, each corner grooved deeply with shame. Between the tears and halting gasps, I began to tell the story that had unravelled our life.

Every Wednesday evening from then on, before the midweek communion service, I sat in the green chair in Christopher's office and together we peeled back layers of pain. In the beginning, the main focus was on sorting through the guilt I carried around my mom's death. I believed I had killed her, that my sin and selfishness had broken her heart. I couldn't imagine being forgiven for everything I had done and didn't believe living was even a possibility.

Christopher was patient. He told me constantly that God loved me. And every time I found the strength to tell him another little piece of my story he took it, gently bathed it in grace and held it up to be healed in the light of God's mercy and truth. When I started to tell Christopher the stories that surrounded my life, the pain was visceral, as if my essence was being shredded from the inside out.

I don't know how old I was when Wayne began touching me. I don't know how often it happened. Children don't track time or store their past catalogued neatly in files in their heads but rather hold memory in each cell of their bodies and express them as feelings. Events that happen when we are small are often embedded in our mind through storytelling, the "remember when?" games families play to preserve and protect their history. Stories of painful, shameful things are not spoken of. They are not recounted or uttered aloud so they are lost to the mind but stored in the spirit and expressed by the body.

As I began to recall things, instead of solid whole stories, there were explosions of emotions from my gut with still shots, pictures whirling, ricocheting off the walls of my mind that all needed to be sorted and paired before they could be protected with words. Stories flooded out, detached isolated events, crisp pictures with raw jagged feelings.

We were living on Gothic Avenue. I had a
pixie cut. I must have been six.
My brother's lips were big and red.
He started tickling me. I laughed. Then it hurt.
I couldn't breathe.
It was happening again.
I crawled deep inside the safe place in the
corner of my head until it was over.

The yucky smell made me feel dirty.

I had to wash the stickiness off my pink baby doll
pajamas, trimmed with pretty white eyelet.

I was stained.

I knelt down at the side of my bed and prayed
that God would cleanse my filthy heart.

My mother was washing my hair as I lay naked in the tub.

My hair was longer, maybe I was eight.

Her upside-down face hovered over me, eyes searing, fully enraged.

She asked if I had been touching Wayne.

I closed my eyes to escape, heart racing, tears flooding out.

She grasped the nape of my neck and yanked me by the
hair, plunging my head under water. When she brought me
up, gasping for air, she told me to never do it again.

Then, forcing my head under once more,
she held me deep in the darkness.

My lungs began to collapse.

I knew I was drowning.

It was my fault.

I wanted to die.

I didn't deserve to breathe.

I was eleven.

Men were landing on the moon when he started
rubbing my leg under the blanket.

I was staying at my sister's old boyfriend's house. There was
no one else to take care of me. His wife's dark eyes were
glaring from across the room; she saw what he was doing.

Then naked, sprawled on their bed upstairs, I found out

there was a secret door that opened into a place so deep inside and it was through that hole my soul was snatched.

It hurt.

I lay perfectly still pretending to be asleep.

It happened over and over and over again.

I cried, but not too loudly.

As the stories barreled out, told between gasping, halting, torrents of tears, dozens of them infused with guilt and shame, they fractured the frame of my picture-perfect family and stripped away from my heart all supports, the many whom I had believed loved me. Every solid construct was shattered and after the soulquake I sat homeless, a refugee inside the ruins of my life.

There were stories about the church, the Group Home and betrayal by a doctor. There were tales from when I was tiny and more grown-up stories where I confused my value and worth and believed I was nothing more than a body to be used.

Telling the stories was not the most difficult part. Sorting light from darkness, sifting truth from lies was most challenging. Making sense of my mother, father, brother and sister, who I had become in our family and understanding how the shaping of my life had opened me up to such destructive choices was the real work of recovery. I didn't know who I was and I certainly didn't know who God was in the midst of it all.

After my meetings with Christopher, I gathered my fragmented self and made my way into the sanctuary upstairs. With a small gathering of people we celebrated a simple Eucharist and as the bread and wine, Christ's body and His blood, were received into mine, my soul began, tentatively at first, to accept nourishment again.

I had to restructure many of my beliefs. It took time to sift through what I had been taught, especially as it concerned my faith. Christopher Page created space for questions. The kind of God he spoke of was a welcome relief.

Rather than a dictator, quick to punish all who disobeyed His ridiculous rules that were impossible to keep, I learned of a divine presence whose essence was love. Religion often complicated things but God's laws were simple. Because of His intense desire for our good, He placed boundaries around people. These were not meant as barriers. All these so-called laws were just commonsense guidelines already written on our hearts directing us to live in harmony, within our natural design, so we flourished, stayed safe and didn't get hurt. Even when people did mess-up or make choices contrary to healthy living, God's response was always one of forgiveness, grace and open-armed embrace; His intention is to invite us into a life that is not just eternal but abundant.

The message I received did not make me lackadaisical and more prone to sin as I had been warned it would. "Greasy grace", as it had been termed by those who feared this doctrine of unconditional mercy, only helped me to relax in God's love as it wooed my heart toward better choices. But forgiveness was something I struggled with.

I had always been taught and fully believed that forgiveness was an obligation of my faith. Forgive and forget was the rule we lived and died by in our family and, although it wasn't found in scripture, the proverb had settled in my bones and had silenced me since I was small. I had always thought that forgiving meant I had to forget with both my mind and my feelings. I had to somehow find a way to erase the memory of what was done and carry on as if nothing had happened with no hard feelings towards the person who had harmed me.

I had been taught, as a Christian, forgiveness was not only required but a choice I needed to make yet I found getting my head and heart to cooperate really tough. My thoughts and feelings were at war and in that battle, truth, residing in my gut, always wins.

In the beginning, the thought of ever being able to forgive myself seemed unimaginable. I had always felt so guilty. From the time I was tiny, I believed I had caused my big brother to touch me. As a child, I thought, as all children do, the world revolved around me. I saw everyone's reactions as emanating from my actions. I believed I created wickedness in Wayne because I was bad. So when Mom told me in the months before her death that I was the one who needed to beg God's forgiveness because I had seduced Wayne, it confirmed what I had always known to be true about myself since I was a little girl. I reasoned I still felt guilty because some things were unforgivable.

One evening when I was particularly entrenched in my shame, Christopher reached for the frame that sat on his desk and handed me the picture of his two little girls. He asked me to look at their innocent faces and tell him what I thought they, as little girls, deserved. I took the image and, holding it in my hands, stared for a long time. They were cute, about six and eight years old, Naomi with her impish gleeful grin and Rachel with her more tentative and serious smile, both so open and trusting. As I gazed into their eyes, I glimpsed my young self.

For a brief moment, the innocence of the little girl I had been was reflected back to me. I had been open, trusting and vulnerable, not bad as I had always believed. I saw my size, how small I had been when my body had been stained by another. The tears, once again, began gushing out. But for the first time, I wept for the child within, for the pain she suffered and the shame she continued to carry. I didn't deserve to be treated as I had been. The sadness I felt for the little girl who had been me was so gut-wrenching that I thought I would drown. And then, immediately on the wave of sorrow, there was rage. The wrath that instantly surged was all-consuming and the anger I felt toward those who had wounded me crested like a rip current. I was terrified. I had enough fury to kill.

I never experienced intense feelings. At the first hint of uncomfortable emotions, I automatically launched into one of the many coping mechanisms created to keep them at bay. Throughout my life, scary emotions had often threatened to overwhelm me. Because my mind could only focus on one thought at a time, filling it with endless lists, rigorous rituals and secret goals was often distracting enough to help me disconnect and I could find temporary relief in the simple activity of obsessing about weight or calories. Being busy in mind often worked to make me feel safe and separate. On the continuum of dissociation, diversion is a familiar coping strategy that even emotionally healthy people use, distraction being a routine practice to deal with unpleasant feelings.

Pause and reflection is another common experience we all share when faced with dilemmas. When life became complicated, I was often able to escape deep within and huddle in the corner of my mind. There I sat and calmly observed the outside world until I could figure out what to do. It was a reprieve, where for a few minutes I remained safe, detached yet still aware.

But when the conflict between what was happening in my present and what I knew should be true was too great to reconcile, the collision between those two realities created a schism. It was impossible for my mind to hold together, so I separated. I sent out the bold self to face the dangerous world. Marian, my clever childhood invention, my mirror image, was far more capable of getting through tough things and having matter-of-fact conversations. That fractured part of me was practical and could think clearly because she kept feelings out of the equation. She was able to endure painful, shameful things and then somehow package those dreadful secrets, storing them safely in the back of my brain, out of reach, from my conscious self.

Marian worked for lots of things but when feelings became enormous or the two worlds kept colliding, especially as memories emerged, not eating and walking around in a low blood sugar daze, which numbed me through, became my only recourse, my drug of choice.

Christopher tried to convince me that emotions could not destroy me and that I could trust myself enough to feel. As the stories initially exploded out, I was immersed in the tidal wave of images and sensations; it was as if I was a tiny girl, drowning all over again, the terror and pain more vivid than in real time. With the barriers in my brain ripped wide open, I had nothing to shield me from the brute force of the trauma. But as I sat in Christopher's gentle presence and waited for the feelings to subside, I was always surprised to find myself still alive, safe in the arms of the big green chair. Often though, it was later, alone in the dark of night that things spoken in the light of day would replay in my mind. It was then, as I waited for the panic to recede, that I felt most in danger of disintegrating.

I didn't know what to do with the anger, so I used a tool I had once loved. I put words and feelings together and launched a letter writing campaign. All first drafts were destroyed, burned in the fireplace. Watching the flames as they licked around the edges consuming my words, I envisioned them ravaging the rage and pain. But the highly polished edited versions, pages filled with crisp words, clearly expressing my feelings, were sent to my brother, telling him of the damage his actions had caused. I wanted to know why he had hurt me and demanded proof he understood the depth of the consequences I had suffered as a result of his selfishness. Although he apologized many times, his responses always fell short and I was left holding the pages of his letter shaking with righteous indignation.

On an ordinary Wednesday evening as I sat in my usual spot, an extraordinary thing happened. I was angry again because of a response my brother had sent. The words in his letter were as close to perfect as anyone could expect, but still lacking. I don't know what he could have possibly said that would have let me know he understood the damage he had caused but I believed he wasn't truly repentant until he "got it", a prerequisite of my pardon.

I had learned that forgiving someone didn't mean what had happened was okay or that it diminished the depth of the wrong, but rather that forgiveness was extending mercy to one undeserving. I didn't know how I could ever forgive Wayne.

It is pretty easy to forgive someone if they take five bucks from you. They can pay you back or you can write off the expense. But if someone has stolen your innocence they can't return it and it is far too big a loss to simply absorb. I was caught. I wanted to forgive. I was sick of my anger and hated being stuck in the endless loop it had created. I wanted to let go and be at peace with myself and my brother but I didn't know how to move forward. In the quietness of that little office, nestled deep in the heart of my church, which had become my sanctuary, I asked God to show me how to forgive.

There weren't any words exactly but rather pictures and feelings that merged, aligning head and heart, cementing change. In the stillness, I became conscious that God saw my heart. I knew He was completely aware of the injustice and injury. I didn't have to tell Him anything or defend my point of view. He saw everything. He loved me. He completely understood.

Instead of feeling condemned, I believed God was deeply grieved by the pain I had suffered and was heartbroken that His precious gift of free will, given to us, the crown of his creation, had been used for evil rather than good.

I imagined myself as the little child Jesus gathered to himself and plunked on his knee telling the crowd it would be better if they drown than harm one so small. He was my defender. My heart was infused with a gentle sweet promise: only Jesus could mend my broken heart. No one else could. All the answers to my many questions were in His hands. I could trust Him because He loved me. I felt still. I was safe. I could breathe.

In that same moment, I became fully aware that it was from his fractured self that Wayne had wounded me, a place shattered by the pain of his own life by stories I may never know. But most clear to me was the truth that my brother, poverty-stricken, didn't hold the resources to repay me for what he had stolen from my life. I realized I had to stop looking to him for answers or to restore the brokenness of my life.

These weren't thoughts but a profound sense of knowing at my core. In the centre, in the stillness, in that deep place of prayer, there was a movement, as gentle as a breath, when heart and head merged, experience and thought aligned, fractures fused, shifting truth, allowing me to move toward forgiveness.

In the following weeks, as I turned my attention away from needing anything from Wayne and instead focused on God's promises to fix my life, I experienced the first fluttering of freedom. The anger that had roiled and ravaged and paralysed me for months lost its grip and allowed me to rest quietly and to find peace. It was a process, an intentional commitment, a practice of persuading my heart into faith but from that moment on I no longer looked to my brother for healing.

After the fury subsided, I was able to make some practical decisions around my abusers' responsibility. I spoke with Judy Kyle, a counsellor at The Women's Sexual Assault Centre about what had happened when I was eleven. She went with me to make a police report. An investigation was started but, because there were no previous charges against my sister's old boyfriend who had molested me, my statement was just kept on file. I was relieved. I felt I had done my part to protect children from him.

Judy expressed concern about my brother as well. She told me that, statistically, it is rare for a perpetrator to only have one victim and said others may be at risk. Because Wayne was a pastor of a church, she believed he needed to be accountable to those over him. I mulled it over for many months before writing a letter to the elders of his denomination. I simply told them my story and left it up to them to do what they thought was best. They responded quickly, assuring me my brother would be evaluated and sent for counselling. Wayne resigned from the ministry and underwent treatment. We never talked about it. His healing is between him and God and that part is his story to tell or keep secret as he chooses.

Forgiveness when there is a clear victim and a definite perpetrator, although not easy, is simple. When I understood that the people who had injured me had done so out of their own wounds rather than their words or actions being statements about my value, it allowed for a more detached yet compassionate extending of mercy. But rarely is hurt wrapped in a neat and tidy package. Most of the deep pain I experienced happened within relationships where, even if unbalanced, the hurt went both ways. Before I could experience the benefits of forgiveness, I had to tease apart the tangled, intricately woven relationship in which the wounding had occurred and take ownership for the part I had played in the pain.

As a small child, I held no responsibility for being sexually abused. It is always up to the grown-ups to protect the young within their care. My brother, although not an adult, was eight years older than me and, as he grew, so did the measure of his responsibility as did mine.

I was twenty-one years old when the sexual abuse stopped. Throughout my life, it had been intermittent yet the effects followed me constantly. I never knew when my big brother, who swung me up on top his shoulders so I could see above the crowd at the Exhibition where he won a blue teddy bear from a silly pull-the-string game, would turn and become a perpetrator. I never saw or sensed a shift until it was too late and, even if I had, I wouldn't have known what to do about it.

As a small child, I learned ways to get through each episode. I crawled deeply inside myself and left my body, pretending I wasn't there. The pattern was so established that even when I was old enough that I could have asked for help or protected myself, I didn't see the point. I accepted it as it was, part of my life, and then promptly cordoned off those memories in the far back corner of my mind. I never thought about them again, which allowed me the freedom to get on with the business of practicing my times tables, learning my spelling words or skipping rope. Forgetting was an adaptive coping mechanism, freeing up space in my head so I wasn't bogged down with despair every moment of every day. But not remembering kept me from learning from the experiences. I never figured out better ways to deal with future encounters and was equally shocked by each new assault.

The afternoon I was visiting my brother before going back to university, I was caught by surprise again. Wayne was married, had a child and time had lapsed. We had been waterskiing, having a blast and then went for a walk.

By the time I saw his lips turn red it was too late. I disappeared inside and instinctively sent the brave self out to get through the inevitable event. Rape, although always violent and destructive, isn't necessarily vicious or physically painful. And then I did what I had learned to do so well: forget the whole thing so I could go back to university and study to become a doctor.

When I crumbled into a depression and was hospitalized a couple of months later, I didn't think to tell the psychiatrist about what had happened in the summer and, several years later when my brother performed our wedding ceremony, it posed no conflict for my mind. My compartmentalized brain had a completely separate spot for those memories.

When I did recall the details of that afternoon many years later in counselling, I found it so hard to understand and was filled with remorse and self-loathing. I wasn't a child. I had been a twenty-one year old woman. I was told it wasn't my fault and shown how I had arrived at a place of being so unable to defend myself but still I felt ashamed.

It was then that I realized forgiveness isn't entirely about assigning blame and absolving guilt but also includes sending the offense away. I had to forgive myself, the young women who didn't know what to do, who chose, for many good reasons, to let it happen rather than fighting back or even bothering to say, "No," which may have been enough to stop it. I developed a deep understanding for the young self who felt she had no other option. Forgiving her, sending away the wrongdoing, took time and each wave of compassionate letting go brought an increased experience of freedom.

But tragedies rarely happen in isolation. Earlier in that same summer when I was 21, I lived with Peter and his family. I felt so safe and loved. After Don died, I was left gasping for air and the person who comforted me most was Peter. I called him immediately and throughout the next year he was the one I turned to when my heart was broken. I loved him. He was my hero. He had been my pediatrician and had literally saved my life. I didn't notice Peter's fondness for me had changed until he climbed into my bed. I didn't know what to do but I knew what was expected. I didn't want to embarrass him by protesting or showing him my shock and sadness. As I lay alone in the dark later that night, my only thought was, "I should have known" and I hated myself even more. The next morning after I had packed my things and loaded them in the car, we drove in silence together.

His flower was an apology for betraying my trust. I never saw him again. It was as if Peter died that day, a grief with no funeral to mark the end of a relationship that had started by saving my life. I never told anyone until I blurted it out to Christopher one evening as I sat in the big green chair a dozen years later.

The process of forgiveness with Peter was still the same, though perhaps a bit more complex. I had to forgive myself for being naïve, for not knowing people are complicated and the heart can turn one kind of love into another in an instant without necessarily meaning to. I had to forgive myself for wounding a marriage. And too, I had to forgive Peter for hurting me deeply, for taking my innocent pure adoration and distorting it.

I spoke with Peter after I forgave him. Fifteen years had passed. I phoned him at his office and when the receptionist said he was busy, I gave her my name and told her to interrupt him. He picked up immediately and said he had been waiting all those years for my call. He told me how sorry he was and said he was totally responsible for betraying my trust. He said he had never before or since been disloyal to his wife and asked what I needed to bring closure. I told him I needed nothing other than the assurance this was not who he was, that what happened had been a one-time bad choice, not a pattern of abusing his power. He managed to convince me that was true. Some to this day say I was naïve, but I believed him.

Forgiving my mother was complicated. There were no conversations to bring closure, only endless monologues that played out in my mind as I sifted and sorted to make sense of our relationship. Mom had known about the abuse. When I was eight years old, she confronted me. While I was lying naked in the tub, she came in to wash my hair. I could feel her searing anger. She asked if I had been touching Wayne and when I started to cry she held my head under the water. Yanking my head up, I gasped for air. She told me to never do it again. Deep in the darkness, I didn't want to breathe ever again. I knew no adult was going to rescue me from what I was being forced to endure; shame and fear cemented in that moment creating an air-tight seal separating all memories from my conscious self.

I have no idea how she became aware or why she chose such a harsh approach to her little girl. I can only imagine the stories she was not brave enough to tell of her own growing up years. Woven deeply into the fabric of her straight-laced, holiness-focussed, rigid charismatic mindset were dark strands of tangled beliefs about God and His design for intimacy. Perhaps she had never had someone tenderly show her a picture of her young self. But those are only my musings, my mind's desperate attempt to make sense of what to me was so senseless.

My mother's inability to protect or empathize with me as a young child was difficult to understand. But her more deliberate choices to put me in harm's way were even more challenging to reconcile. Encouraging her prepubescent daughters to date young men who were much older and deliberately subjecting me to the harsh, dangerous environment of the Group Home was, and is still, beyond my understanding.

We had only a few fractured conversations following my disclosure of the abuse the year before she died. Mom said she had always known I was "that kind of a girl" and asked "what I expected of men anyway", her sharp words cutting to the marrow. Once, when I was trying to explain how deeply I had been hurt, she asked if I thought what I had experienced was more painful than what children growing up in concentration camps had endured, a curious analogy for my life.

In the end, though, forgiveness followed the same predictable pattern: acknowledging the truth, understanding the person who wounded me did so out of their own brokenness and turning to God to heal and restore. I had to give up my need for one last conversation and instead face the truth: in her unhealed broken state, my mom was incapable of mending those deep wounds she carved. I knew only God Himself was able to lovingly bind my soul and breathe life back into my spirit.

Forgiving my father was less difficult because our relationship was straightforward. When I was a little girl, I knew my dad loved me; his eyes lit up when I walked into the room. He was gentle and kind and always spoke softly. As I grew and the chaos caused our lives to unravel, I watched him skitter off to his office to read and study, working long hours to make ends meet. I never really blamed my dad. His inability to stand up to Mom and protect his family was just that, his helplessness; he was paralyzed by his fear. Perhaps he should have found a way to forge past her, but he didn't and I believe couldn't. Mom often said she had four children, as she looked at him with loathing. I always felt he, too, was only trying to survive. More than anything, I pitied him.

When I tried to talk to my dad about what had happened after Mom died, he cried and told me how sorry he was and said he hadn't known. He was torn and broken yet had little to say. He continued to show me love in the concrete ways he knew best. He was a good grandpa to my boys and always generous with his time and financial support.

Telling the truth, reframing and reclaiming; layer by layer the healing continued.

Tsunami

In September of 1990, Joshua tried to enter the world by the seat of his proverbial pants. After complaining to my doctor that the baby wasn't moving right, I was sent for an ultrasound. The grey and white fuzzy image confirmed he was a frank breech, positioned with his butt fully engaged, folded like a hairpin, legs flush against his face, head nestled so very uncomfortably under my rib cage. I didn't want a C-section so, a month before his due date, my doctor turned him. Ouch. A week later, my water broke on a busy Saturday afternoon while I was shopping in Woolco, the predecessor to Wal-Mart—every pregnant woman's dreaded nightmare. Because my labour didn't start, twenty-four hours later I was induced. Joshua launched like a rocket and flew into the world, shooting through the birth canal without a pause. He was bruised from the tip of his little head to his tummy and, after five days in the Neonatal Intensive Care Unit, the six and a half pound baby came home to be passed from the arms of one big brother to the next. A rough start for sure but Joshua thrived and grew, rounding out our not so little family.

My dad's health had improved during the years following his brain haemorrhage and, when Joshua was six months old, he sold the Beach Drive house. Alan and I wanted to set out on our own and my father needed to be free to travel. There was a world he wanted to explore, finding his life apart from Mom, venturing forth in a world he hadn't navigated alone for forty years. He did well. A couple of years later when he told me he was engaged, I was taken by surprise. He had met True as a young man in his Salvation Army Training Class a half century before. After they were both commissioned as Lieutenants, she was posted to Bermuda and later married, settling in Minnesota, while Dad was sent to the Canadian prairies where he met and married Mom. As Salvation Army couples, they kept in touch, sending Christmas cards through the years. After Mom's death, Dad looked True up while visiting his brother on the east coast. She had recently been widowed and they rekindled a friendship. Both just shy of eighty, they married quickly and True moved into our lives with grace and filled the role of grandmother to my boys with joy and lots of cookies.

Alan and I bought our first house on Craigmillar Avenue in the spring of 1991. We were delighted to finally have a place of our own. It was a comfortable home, in a quiet neighbourhood, nestled in the heart of Victoria on a quaint little street that, with all its winding, winsome curves, resembled a country lane. I fell in love with that tired, worn-down house the moment I saw it. I believed it was just waiting for someone to see its beauty beyond the hours of work and loads of money it would take to transform it into our home.

We were initiated into our new community before our car came to a complete stop on the day we moved in. We were besieged by two little girls with a bouquet of flowers—probably swiped from the nearby vacant lot—brimming with laughter and chattering non-stop about how much they liked boys, boldly proclaiming that they weren't at all offended by our bringing four into their midst.

Muffins, straight from the oven of the neighbour to the one side, appeared about the same time as a dozen kids. Hanging from our cherry tree and from the apple tree that straddled the fence, the little gypsies tried to sell us everything from beautifully hand-crafted bird houses to the never-ending stream of chocolate covered almonds, to rocks, not pretty shiny ones but rather the natural kind that could be used for paper weights or recipe card holders. One of the little girls led us into our new home and told us where the TV went; she had obviously been in the house many times.

As soon as we arrived, we stored our stuff in the unfinished basement and got to work. My YaYa's and their husbands rolled up their sleeves and together we stripped off layers of wallpaper, carted out carpet and painted the whole place from top to bottom. I have a picture of Shawna standing in her overalls and baseball cap directing Kevin and Danny as they tore down the wall between the small kitchen and tiny dining room so our family could all sit together at one table. I even managed to get a rare snapshot of Sandy-doll painting a door rather than her fingernails, head tilted glamorously for the camera, a picture of devoted friendship in purest form. Jim, donning his Hazmat suit, worked to free our home of asbestos, avoided the photo album but his image is forever framed in my mind. We had so much fun, a bunch of us working each evening. When done, we threw a big House Blessing party to celebrate. It was as beautiful a house as I had imagined it would be; sturdy, strong, a place of belonging, a comfortable home to grow up in.

We loved our neighbourhood. It had a park at the end of the street that was a hidden jewel, bursting with azaleas, rhododendrons, and an extravagant perennial garden surrounded by huge rocks to climb and hidden trails to explore. It was a whimsical land where my four hoodlums spent hours running wild with friends. It was a throwback to a gentler time, capturing an era all but forgotten but never far from a heart's dream. Somehow, even amid the distrusts displayed before us through our evening news, we neighbours still believed we could reach out beyond fears and fences to befriend one another. Borrowing eggs was still allowed and it was commonplace to take turns minding each other's kids while we slipped out to pick up milk.

Brenda, a retired neighbour across the way, was the community matriarch who often could be found refereeing a group of about a dozen kids assembled in her garden as they played croquet during long summer afternoons. She was my mentor who gently led me into the world of gardening and engendered confidence in my artist eye. She is responsible for the proper English accent I still use to this day to describe all botanicals. We shared countless afternoons sitting in one of her tiny outside rooms, having tea by her waterfall, where she calmly imparted her wisdom assuring me that children grow up and that it all comes out in the wash.

Our home was filled with fun and laughter and we shared it with our neighbours and friends. We liked celebrations and surrounded each holiday with wonderful traditions. Because of Alan's American heritage, we often doubled up. Canada Day was followed directly by our 4th of July barbecue where Brakefield Burgers, Al's famous pork roast sandwiches, were on the menu to commemorate Independence Day. Some of our half-breed friends joined us for American Thanksgiving as well, often crowding up to twenty people in our tiny house for a traditional turkey dinner with all the "fixins", my pumpkin-chiffon pie with a chocolate-nut-crust and Vicki's pecan pie ending off the festival. As the children grew and later brought friends who became spouses, we had to trade places, the adults in the kitchen while they sprawled out in the dining room.

Thanksgiving, segueing into Advent, allowed us to stretch the Yuletide season and savour its fullness. Rather than focusing solely on Christmas day, we lit candles on the Advent wreath every evening for four weeks before Christmas, each candle illuminating an aspect of the coming of Christ and, as the wreath grew brighter, so did the excitement. We shared many of our holidays with our church family and our wide circle of friends continued to be the base for our relationships. Our kids grew up knowing they belonged to a wide community and that they were deeply loved.

We homeschooled the boys in their early years and we all thrived, enjoying the simple delight of exploring learning with our home as the hub of their life. We played with numbers, did fantastic science experiments and read for hours on end. Each night, Alan and the boys explored the magical world of Narnia and, as they grew older, Tolkien's works filled with Hobbits and enchanted adventures were their nightly tales. Our homeschooling group gave our boys lots of opportunities to get together with other children and our neighbourhood ensured they were never short on friends. Our house was always packed with boys and the occasional brave girl, just for good measure.

In our house, there were more than just boys to be wary of. What are little boys made of?—Frogs and snails and puppy dog tails. My guys loved all God's creatures, great and small. We had the required pets: hamsters, gerbils, goldfish and even a dog named Hannah. She had seven puppies of her own, born in 1997, the year Princess Diana and Mother Teresa died. I remember the timing clearly because it was their faces that lined the floor behind the kitchen counter where the bundle of wrinkled black and white mutts peed and pooped for six weeks straight. But those were not the animals most adored in our house. My boys had a great passion for exotic creatures, the cold-blooded eerie kind like reptiles and snakes that got loose and showed up in the shower when I was least expecting it.

One day when my YaYa's had gathered to celebrate—whatever excuse we were using for a party that particular day—I decided to bring the newest member of our menagerie downstairs and introduce Billy-Bob-Joe to my friends. He was a quite cute, twelve inch baby iguana with scales the most gorgeous shimmering shade of lime green. The creature had topped Jonathan's Christmas wish-list the year he was turning twelve. As I entered the living room with the little reptile perched on the end of my hand, his head bobbing up and down, there was a blood-curdling scream that ended some five minutes later. Debbie, one of the more demonstrative in our group, ran from the house and stood in the middle of my front garden shrieking as she gyrated up and down, completely inconsolable. She didn't like animals. She especially didn't like Billy-Bob-Joe and has yet to forgive me for introducing them. But boys and slimy creatures were all I knew; they were my life.

A couple of years later, after the iguana had become full grown, Jonathan rushed into the house completely distraught and handed me the cold, stiff, motionless body of Billy-Bob-Joe. He had escaped out of a second story bedroom window, flung himself to the ground and been discovered in the backyard in the middle of winter. I had just taken a first-aid refresher course. Instinctively, I grabbed the creature and, placing my mouth over his entire nose and mouth, breathed air into his lungs. His chest expanded but still he lay in my arms limp and lifeless. I quickly ran to the bathroom, filled the tub with tepid water and, slowly adding warm to it, rubbed his body to try and stimulate life. With tearful boys hovering in the corner, the heroic effort seemed all for naught. Then, out of the blue, the lizard leapt to life and began thrashing. Startled, I jumped, screamed and slipped on the wet tile floor. Billy-Bob-Joe had been saved but it was a while before I saw the humour in the whole thing.

Life continued moving rapidly. With four busy boys, I had to multitask and could only process the pain of my life part-time while cooking dinner, folding laundry and picking up Lego. The playroom often became an apt metaphor for the chaos of my internal living space. Although I was certain everything had a place, a bin for each piece, I was constantly inundated with scattered unsortable stuff. Just when I would get almost tidied up, something or, more accurately, someone would sneak up from behind and capsize another load for me to rummage through. I was often overwhelmed.

My friends and family provided wonderful distractions to even out life in my ongoing search for balance. I needed the lighthearted extravagance of dinner cruises on our friends' boat, Masuda, and building snowmen with the boys, as well as the mundane focus I found in ironing shirts and folding socks as I tried to figure out how to reconstruct family from the chaos strewn around me.

It seemed to me Wayne wanted life as usual and when he came to Victoria both he and my dad were baffled that I was uncomfortable visiting with them. It was difficult trying to figure out the difference between forgiveness and fostering unhealthy relationships while learning to establish healthy boundaries.

Margaret had her own theory of why our family exploded and what was necessary to put the pieces together again. Because I was unable to mirror her experiences, she was hurt and withdrew. Her family moved to the mainland which, for the amount we saw them afterward, might as well have been another planet.

I continued seeing Christopher Page for counselling. We had been hashing through my past for a couple of years when he wrote me a letter in August of 1991. I kept it tucked inside my book, *The Courage to Heal* by Ellen Bass, and often unfolded the single-page, worn and tearstained paper to reread words of hope when I needed something tangible to hang onto as life threatened to slip from my grasp.

During times of deep darkness the words shed light and breathed life.

ST PHILIP'S CHURCH ANGLICAN CHURCH OF CANADA

August 1, 1991

Dear Muriel,

Last night again, I sat here and watched as you dredged the depths of your pain. It has often been a terrifying experience to stand with you on the edge of the abyss and peer over into the dark below.

But more than terrifying, it has been awe inspiring. You have demonstrated an enormous courage in facing the dark and difficult truths about your life. You have persevered despite the fear and panic which have so many times almost engulfed you.

Your determination to carry on with this process demonstrates that you, in fact, have an enormous will to live, to live whole, to live healthy. Despite all evidence to the contrary, you have a tremendous zeal to walk in the truth, to live in the light. It is the strength of this drive within you which made the years of living dead in the dark so difficult.

You have never quite been able to escape from the tug to be fully human, fully alive. This is due in large part to the grace of God, calling you on to life. But there is something else which has kept you alive. You may think this is crazy; but I believe that it is because of Marian Rose. She is the one who never gives up. She is the one who will not let you lie down and play dead. She is determined to live. But, she needs your permission.

Let Marian live. Don't drug her out of existence. Don't starve her into silence. Nurture her; be kind to her; love her. She has so much to give of spontaneity, energy, enthusiasm, creativity and zest for life. She has a sense of humour and of joy which you allow her to expose in bits but which she longs to share more fully.

I know she may not always be quite as tidy as you would like. She probably even enjoys play-do and if you make two colours she'll mix them together. But the freedom and the hope which she can bring into your life are worth the cost of things being perhaps a little unpredictable and occasionally confusing— better a little chaos on the outside, than total chaos within.

I have great admiration for the distance you have travelled. You have taught me a great deal. You have caused me to look in astonishment at the depth and riches of the human spirit I see within you. I see so many signs of the mysterious, gracious work of God in your life.

God has never let go of your hand. He does not, nor will he ever, give up on you. You are rooted in him for eternity. I pray that increasingly you may learn to trust him and to rest, confident in his mercy.

Every Blessing,

𝕮𝔭

⸻ ∞ ⸻

But less than a year after Christopher wrote those words, I began to give up. Again it was hard to breathe.

There wasn't really a clear beginning or a crisp ending but there was a certain death, stinging and filled with grief. At first, it was more of a feeling. I watched people in church looking at me, faces smiling but eyes darting, noticeably anxious. There were a few odd statements from a few odd people and out-of-place questions inquiring about why I was always at church before the midweek service talking to Christopher with the door closed. That's how the rumours began.

Within a matter of months, those quiet murmurings became the subject of loud arguments and before I could believe what was happening, Alan and I were called into a meeting downtown with the Bishop of the Anglican Church. The wardens from our church were there, pens poised to record every word. It was comforting to know that at least they believed my story. The Bishop asked lots of questions. He wanted to know why I was seeing Christopher for counselling and probed and prodded, wanting to know all about the subjects we discussed. He asked how I felt about Christopher and from the way he phrased his questions, the tone of his voice, the tilt of his head, it was obvious he had been told we were having an affair. I was devastated.

After the formal investigation, the Bishop's report was clear. He didn't believe there were grounds for the accusations nor any evidence of inappropriate behavior between Christopher and me. But our church was split. The majority didn't want to talk about it but those who did became embroiled in heated and lengthy debates about what actions should be taken. In the end the senior priest, who had championed the allegation of spiritual adultery, was sent up island to pastor a small parish and wait out his retirement. Christopher was allowed to remain rector of St. Philip's but the Bishop cautioned him against counselling. Of course, he could continue to visit the sick in hospital, pray with folks, supporting people with little problems. But those with serious difficulties were to be sent for professional therapy. The church was no place to bring such deep pain.

It may have only been a small ripple in the life of our church. Many remained unaware of the squall, some by choice. For me, it was a giant tsunami that stripped me to my core and sent me silently spiralling again. I was left in the centre of the chaos, once more, to sift through the rubble and pick up the pieces of my battered life.

It was difficult marching our four little boys into church each Sunday morning with rumours flying, people obviously uncomfortable in our presence. I thought I would feel better after the truth was spoken. But when everything settled back into a humdrum routine, rather than relief, I felt raw. The exhaustion and grief combined and sent my heart racing back into a dark place.

I continued to meet weekly with my Group, careful sifters of truth, my lifeline to sanity. I talked to a few professional counsellors but appointments had to be booked between piano lessons and baseball practices and nothing anyone said seemed to help anyway. I continually found myself living in two worlds and navigating between them was difficult.

I loved my life and hated it at the same time. I clung desperately to my good life, the one I worked so hard to create and maintain, the one with deep friendships bursting with delight and high bustling energetic experiences, watching the boys grow and my love for Alan expand. But with the barriers in my brain blown wide open, there was no longer any place to stuff the sadness. The thoughts that I once neatly packaged roamed freely in my head and wreaked havoc with my emotions. Life was slippery, often raw and stinging. I cried a lot.

My GP retired. The boys ranged in age from three to ten when we found another family physician. He was a younger fellow, kind-hearted and great with the kids but my sadness scared him. He convinced me to see a psychiatrist for an assessment. I dubbed her Dragon Lady soon after our first visit.

She sat stiffly across from me and asked pointed questions, gathering my history and poking hard at feelings I was trying desperately to guard against. Telling a story straight can feel sharp and painful, especially when the questions don't factor in soft moments of family and friendships, the cushioning comfort of love. After a thirty minute interview, she had made a firm diagnosis: I was clinically depressed. She told me my brain chemistry had gone whacky and the only thing that would fix it was medicine. Because she believed the depression was acute and needed immediate medical intervention, she felt hospitalization was necessary. The Eric Martin, the same hospital I had spent time in after Don's death, is where I landed in 1994, after a dozen years of wellness.

I was admitted to the fourth floor. Once again, I was cold and sad and huddled in bed. I couldn't make the tears stop. I tried to convince my psychiatrist I wasn't sick and that the sadness I was feeling was a response to real things happening in the present and the so-called free-floating anxiety was actually securely anchored to my immediate experience. She abruptly told me normal people didn't feel sad and scared all the time and it was obvious from my history I had had a psychiatric illness since I was fifteen years old. I told her I hadn't been treated since I was twenty-two years old and I even questioned the soundness of that diagnosis.

I was first given the diagnosis of Major Depressive Disorder a year and a half after Don's death. I had gotten my life back together and attended university for a year. In the summer I worked on the Eating Disorders Unit in Toronto and went back to school in the fall. After midterm exams I collapsed into a heap and was admitted to the hospital. The doctor had told me the unrelenting sadness, my inability to concentrate, accompanied by insomnia were indicators of a depressive episode. He believed the pressure of school had brought unresolved pain to the surface and I was experiencing a delayed grief reaction. But because of my psychiatric history and the severity of my symptoms, he concluded there were clear signs of mental illness and that the Clinical Depression had been triggered by typical life stressors.

But in the years of talking to Christopher, I had come to understand the deep despair was really a response to being betrayed by Peter and raped by my brother, events that took place within weeks of each other, stories I had locked away in the far corner of my head. I told my doctor I was still trying to make sense of everything and that processing my life was the source of my pain.

She didn't buy it. She admitted that having such a long remission was unusual but she believed I had been sick all along. She said I had managed to mask my sadness, keeping busy and dodging medical treatment but was, and had always been, mentally ill. According to her, I met all the diagnostic criteria clearly outlined in the DSM, *The Diagnostic and Statistical Manual of Mental Disorders.* She said there had been too many tears and that only medication would work to make me feel better. In her matter-of-fact way, she told me that if I was too stubborn to comply with treatment, my husband wouldn't be able to stand it much longer and he would likely leave me, taking the children, and I'd be left alone in my sickness. Her words lodged deeply in my heart and echoed through my spirit as she marched out of my room.

Lying alone in my bed, I began to sob. I was terrified. I couldn't imagine living without Alan and the boys and feared she was right. It was true, I cried a lot. I was often overwhelmed with fear. My sleep was disrupted. My energy was low, which made managing each day difficult. I felt sick. Being sick was certainly more honourable than being plain old lazy and sad. And I had to honestly ask myself how long Alan would put up with having such a pathetic wife who wept all the time. Although I thought there was a lot to cry about, I was tired of the tears and desperately wanted relief from the emotional pain.

Reluctantly, I went on the anti-depressants and anti-anxiety medication again. I swallowed a myriad of different pills prescribed to make me sleep. They never worked; my tears continued to stubbornly push their way through the stupor.

I was in the hospital for less than a week, but the self who was discharged was not the same person who had been admitted days earlier. A diagnosis of mental illness changes things. I had been told the depression was a lifelong condition. The illness may be manageable but further episodes were likely if I did not comply with treatment. Taking medication was essential and reducing stress, critical.

Teaching the boys at home became impossible. My life as a homeschooling mom came to an end. Christopher and Jonathan were enrolled at the school down the street and would begin in the fall. I still had the little boys at home and when Joshua was seven and all of the boys were in school full-time I went back to work. I loved being with little children and found great joy supporting children with special needs at a preschool but desperately missed watching the delight on my own boys' faces as they discovered and learned about their world. Homeschooling was one of the many dreams that died when I got sick.

The eating disorder was something I never talked about. Once I was back in the Mental Health system, it became a topic of discussion again.

After leaving The Clarke when I was eighteen years old, I vowed to never speak of it. Even when I was working for Paul Garfinkel as a summer student a couple of years later, I only ever referred to it in past tense and never mentioned my ongoing struggle. I decided that if I couldn't beat it, I would simply learn to live with it. I kept my weight at a minimally acceptable adult level and controlled it by balancing my eating and purging. No one noticed and because no one asked, I lived alone, trapped in the shameful secret.

I had always assumed that not eating and purging were just bad habits. I believed they could be modified with behavioral therapy and conquered by willpower. I thought that the reason those interventions hadn't worked for me was because I lacked self-discipline, my character fatally flawed beyond all hope. My new GP encouraged me to go to the Eating Disorders Program for counselling. I was skeptical.

Expecting the usual hard-edged program, I braced myself to endure being weighed weekly and was resigned to sitting through nutritional counselling where expectations for weight gain and management would be clearly laid out and monitored. I envisioned the monotony of filling out menus with my caloric requirements calculated according to my BMI. The thought of the whole thing made me terribly tired and was soaked in shame because I knew, although it may be a good program, it wouldn't work. I was hopeless. But the approach at the Eating Disorders Program was different. Peggy began by listening. She gently asked questions to unravel my story.

The onset of the eating disorder had been unusual. It hadn't started as a diet or a teenager's pursuit to look thinner. I had been oblivious to my weight before being admitted to The Hospital for Sick Children when I was fifteen.

When we started the Group Home, I had been a naturally lean and lithe adolescent girl in an era before anorexia was a common household word. While my mother was away, I decided to spend as much time away from the Group Home as possible to avoid the noise and confusion. Getting up early, leaving before breakfast without packing a lunch and returning home late in the evening after dinner had been efforts to make my life safer. I felt scared all the time. I didn't know that fear and hunger felt the same.

By the time my mom returned six weeks later, my weight had plummeted. I ate the dinner she had saved for me that evening, the first full meal I had in a long while. My body, unused to that volume of food, rejected it; I threw up for the first time. I can only imagine the trouble Dad got in for not being aware of my physical decline. When the boys complained to him that I was being too noisy, he stormed upstairs and told me he would break my guitar if I didn't put it away. I was at a breaking point, so I took off running. After

I was brought home by the policeman, Mom, realizing I was sick, took me to the hospital.

I don't know what the doctors thought. Children were not included in discussions about their care. After doing a physical examination they started an intravenous. I was not only emaciated but severely dehydrated as well. They ordered a pregnancy test and admitted me to the hospital.

The next morning, I was evaluated by a psychiatrist. The message I received during that admission was that if I didn't eat I couldn't go home. I don't remember thinking about it but in my frightened, fifteen-year-old brain that probably seemed like a good deal. I didn't want to go back to the Group Home. I stopped eating. After I was diagnosed with anorexia, it was made clear my privileges hinged on eating and gaining weight and, in that moment, sadness and stubbornness fused in my heart. During the first week in Sick Kids, I had been nauseated and the muscles in my stomach developed a pattern that made throwing up easy so when they began tube-feeding me, I continued deliberately emptying my stomach.

The eating disorder became entrenched during that first hospitalization. I began to correlate being skinny with safety. Not eating made me feel numb, a welcome relief to the sadness, fear and anger I was always trying to cover over with being a good girl.

During my late teenage years, the eating disorder became a way of having a say without talking. When life at home became unmanageable, I could stop eating and get a break by going back into the hospital. Although being sick presented its own set of problems, it was a trade-off I deemed valuable.

As the years passed, purging became my way of controlling my weight. I ate what I thought was expected of me so that I would appear to be behaving normally but then threw up to keep my body small. I had misguidedly believed that being little would keep me safe. Feeling tiny and contained gave me an illusion of control. I hated having such a nasty secret. I didn't understand it. But I didn't know what to do. When I tried to stop purging, I couldn't. I never wanted to go through treatment again so I kept that part of my life separate. I never told anyone.

After Mom died, I was distraught. And when Micah was a baby, the eating disorder became a public nuisance again. I was nursing a newborn, caring for Dad and chasing two little boys around. The grief made eating all but impossible and during that year my weight bottomed out again. But as it dropped, I found I didn't feel nearly as sad or scared. When my weight was at its lowest, there were no emotions at all. I started eating again when I found out I was pregnant with Joshua, but continued to purge for reasons that eluded me. The more I talked about the sexual abuse, the more I threw up, often going for days without eating. I knew it was a sick, disgusting habit, one I could not break.

Peggy, in her quiet voice, suggested the eating disorder may have been a friend to me throughout the years, a clever invention to preserve my life, something concrete I could count on when there was no one else to turn to. She explained not eating and the numbness it ensured had likely kept me safe from feelings that were too powerful for me to face when I was younger, acting as a buffer, shielding me from overwhelming feelings. She told me that the fact I had survived and even went on to create a good marriage, had emotionally healthy children and great friends convinced her I really wanted to live. But Peggy also believed that as an adult I was strong enough to protect myself and could learn healthier ways to manage difficult emotions.

When I realized Peggy didn't look at me as a terrible person who lacked discipline but rather saw I desperately wanted to live, the shame was replaced with hope. I was relieved and began to relax. I was able to tell her things about my eating habits I had never shared before.

At first I didn't see the connection. I had always been told the eating disorder had been an attention-seeking scheme, which was difficult for me to understand because of the great lengths I went to conceal it. I had been told it was all about control and yet I felt so out of control. Coming to understand that my emotions were attached to my eating patterns made more sense.

I had become separate from my body, unable to read the signals it was sending me. Most emotions, especially intense ones, were lumped together as dangerous or to be avoided. I couldn't distinguish tired from sad, hurt from angry and I had mistakenly interchanged words like full and fat for frightened and furious. Focusing on food diverted my mind, filling it with endless lists and secret goals. This worked to distract me from feelings that flooded in from seemingly nowhere.

Instead of judging, Peggy listened, and then helped me create strategies to give myself time to process my feelings without using food. I started to trust myself enough to feel.

I finally began to see how feelings and food were intertwined and I worked diligently to untangle them. I began to understand that my body was not the enemy I had always supposed but had truly been a friend trying to protect me and tell a story I was unable to speak aloud.

Although it was a long, arduous process filled with many failed attempts, I was encouraged to slow down the process of feelings, allowing them to be, without judging them. Peggy taught me to inhale deeply, centring my eating. I learned to brEAThe.

The despair of depression folded neatly into the perfect pockets of time that made up our family life together. Although the sadness was ongoing and unrelenting, the intensity of the misery waxed and waned as our life marched forward without skipping a beat. After being diagnosed with clinical depression, I wobbled back and forth. Adjusting to medication was challenging. Feeling numb allowed me to move through my days with fewer tears, but sadness was not the only emotion frozen. Laughter also shrivelled. Gone was the easy flow of feelings that made me know I was alive, free and encouraged me to fight. There were months, even whole years, when the depression was manageable but the ongoing struggle with mental illness made life difficult.

I had well times. Very well times. I spent many sunny summer days walking along the beach at Rathtrevor searching for treasures and building elaborate sandcastles with my children. There were bundles of clear winter afternoons when I raced Micah and Joshua down Westerly on Mount Washington. They'd leave me in a swirl of snow as they whipped in and out of trees, flying over little jumps, darting through trails where I certainly couldn't go because they were made for little guys who can ski faster than their moms. I tried to hold on to those times because, out of the whole of my life, it was the truth.

What was also the truth was I got sick, sometimes very sick. When I was able to be at home, my days consisted of putting on a brave face as I got the children ready for school. After they left, I'd steel myself and go downstairs to put on a load of laundry then crumple into bed and sob because I felt so useless, so powerless, so alone and so very ugly inside. I would look at the clock and bargain with myself about when to get up and sort the Loathsome Load, the white socks that all need to be paired according to wear and stain.

I tried to finish each task. I usually did but when I couldn't I'd scuttle back to bed and tell myself terrible stories about how I was such a burden to those I loved and lived with.

I'd set the table for dinner at 11:30am if I was up because I never knew when those perky moments would end and once again I'd be slammed down, glued to my bed, lying in the dark with no sound because everything hurt my mind.

I made a real effort to greet the boys after school with a snack and to listen to their stories. When I was really ill, they took turns lying beside me, telling what happened during recess and which teacher was cranky or what sports practice was scheduled for that evening. They brought back more than their tales. They brought back life itself. They would snuggle in, speak softly, rub my back tenderly and tell me I would get well again. They extended such grace into my self-loathing, light into my darkness and life into my dying sense of self-worth.

When I wasn't so brave and I needed to be in hospital, pictures of Alan and the boys sat on my night stand and, through trembling tears, I'd search each face desperately trying to draw strength to live just one more day. But the lies that wrenched my brain around would scream they would all be better off without me. I believed I was a terrible mother, doing the worst job in the world by allowing my children to see me sobbing over nothing, curled up in a hospital bed taking sedatives to calm the suicidal thoughts that ravaged my mind until the meds kicked in.

I wanted the best for my kids and feared my illness robbed them of that opportunity. I worried over how my illness impacted the boys and how they would cope with being tucked in over the phone when I was in hospital. I wondered how they would explain to their friends, and later to themselves, the drastic difference between the mother who was full of fun and made birthday surprises so special and the one who burst into tears during dinner because the chatter of healthy conversation was too big. I was concerned about how my kids would look back over their young lives, having been exposed to such pain they neither created nor could comfort, because depression is inconsolable.

I tried to educate my children about my illness. I wanted to assure them I was not simply unhappy about my life, especially with them, but my tears and intolerance for noise and confusion were part of my sickness. I wanted them to know it was okay to feel frustrated, even embarrassed, and encouraged them to talk those feelings out with someone who could help them make sense of the chaos. I agonized over how they would cope if my illness won out and they were left abandoned with all their hurt, fear and rage.

I often said cancer would be kinder because if I got too sick to live, it wouldn't be my fault. If my body was ill, I wouldn't have to put up with people who didn't understand depression telling me to go for a walk or to look on the brighter side of life. The truth is, in the grips of a severe depression, walking to the bathroom is a strategically planned maneuver between moments of despair and looking on the bright side of anything hurts the eyes. Depression is a difficult illness not only because it is so incapacitating but also because it targets your sense of self-worth and zeros in on your will to live with the sole intent to destroy. And it is, of course, a recurrent illness, which in laymen's terms means it will get you again when you're not looking.

The end of a long bout of depression was always a celebration of life that seemed as sweet as the fragrance of a spring rain. My boys' beautiful faces would emerge from the flat picture book image that sat faithfully as a reminder of the truth of my well self. My days once again blossomed with life and promise of happier times ahead.

My life continued to be a funny mix. Woven deeply into dark depressions were strands of pure light and joy that made up the fabric of our family life. I had a great husband and four wonderful sons; our life was extraordinary in an ordinary kind of way.

When the boys were young, we did everything together as a family. We liked to camp, ski, read and were involved in sports. Like their dad, my boys liked every kind of sport best and, as long as there was a competition with a clear winner and loser, they were ready to play. They had a sport for all seasons and many overlapped and conflicted: baseball, soccer, football, rugby, BMX racing and wrestling were all jostling for their turn on the calendar. In our home office, there was a whiteboard that tracked their activities, colour coded of course, to make sure each boy arrived at the right place with the appropriate gear. When our friend Paul renovated our house and finished the basement, we designed it to accommodate our growing family and our busy sports life.

The back door entry was a large tiled area. After whatever practice the boys came in from they could toss their shoes in their own basket, peel their filthy uniform from their body, stripping down to their skivvies and then make a mad dash for the shower. In the back hallway, there was a large sports cupboard crammed with hats, bats, balls, cleats and jock straps in every size, complete with ace bandages, slings, air casts and crutches.

We had our fair share of accidents throughout the years. Everything from bumps and bruises to cuts; some gashes were great gaping wounds that needed stitches, others were tiny nicks that sent blood spurting to the ceiling. We dealt with minor and not so minor concussions, sprains, torn ligaments, broken bones and dislocated shoulders. Sometimes, they needed surgery to bind their broken bodies together but often they just needed time, time and lots of physiotherapy to heal so they could get back at it, cruising for a bruising. But with four boys, what would you expect? Well, I hadn't expected it at all. Even after I realized braids and ballet were not going to be part of my experience, I still thought my life would have a heavy dose of piano, band and choir, all of which they were forced to try. But I was never able to convince my boys that music was a priority. They liked sports. And so I became a sports mom. I washed uniforms and watched as many events as possible, although many were viewed with my eyes half closed, not out of boredom, but from sheer terror.

In the summer, we got a break from organized sports. We went camping because boys like that sort of thing. Packing all our stuff, ordinarily neatly arranged in cupboards and drawers, and heading north answered some primitive yearning males apparently need to do on an annual basis. It always amazed me we could get a stove, grill, lamp, two chairs, three tents along with a week's supply of clothing groceries and often diapers into our minivan. But that was not all: we were prepared campers. Amid the teddy bears and sleeping bags, we also loaded up five bicycles equipped with two baby carriers so Alan and I could take turns toting the little guys to the bathroom in the middle of the night. By the time we rolled out of our driveway, we looked like kin to the Beverly Hillbillies.

People often honked and waved giving us the thumbs up sign. I never knew whether they were cheering us on or merely trying to console me. But when we would arrive at our campsite, much smaller than our patio, and set up the tents, a kind of gentle magic would unfold. Alan, starting a fire with wet wood, happily went about creating a gourmet dinner. The little boys played with slugs and shovelled dirt into their pails while the other two set out on their bikes to fetch water so I could at least have a cup of tea in the uncivilized place we were calling home. We ate our meals off the green melamine dishes my mom bought the year I was thirteen and then washed them in a tiny dishpan with just enough water.

In the evenings, we sat by the fire and roasted marshmallows to golden perfection, then stuffed them with pieces of a Caramilk bar before squeezing the goopy mess between graham crackers. After the gooey little faces were kissed and tucked snugly into their sleeping bags, Alan and I gazed into the night sky and played backgammon. Teasing each other with winner takes all, we rekindled the spark that ignited our courting days. All was well with the world. The pictures were great, snapshots capturing the wholeness and holiness of the moment. And so, each year, we repeated the same trip, exploring different campgrounds around Vancouver Island.

Every August, we visited Alan's family in Montana. His brother JB and his wife Susan graciously hosted a family reunion each year. We spent a week in their small cabin on Flathead Lake where twenty of us crowded together to eat meals and sleep, little bodies piled in heaps on the living room floor. But the real living was done down at the dock where space was abundant. Waterskiing, tubing, jumping off the rope swing and laying in the sun was the way we spent the afternoons with Aunts and Uncles and cousins—faces all looking like the same one, just squished a bit differently. After dinner, we sat on the deck and played Crib and Rummy with real cards. We told stories and listened to the Almost There Comedy Tour where Alan and his brothers made everyone howl with laughter because they most often forgot the crucial part or the punch line to their jokes. We had fun as one big family and cried every time we made the long trek to the top of the hill, where we hugged and kissed and said goodbye before cramming into our separate cars to spread out in different directions until the next year when we would be reunited and do it all over again.

In the fall, soccer and later football kept us busy. I loved Saturday mornings in the autumn. It was a welcome break from my busy week. Alan would take all four boys out in the rain and return home several hours later with a van load of soaking wet, filthy hooligans with their grassy cleats and the smell of damp earth wafting in through the basement door. I always had pancakes and bacon and a heaping bowl of scrambled eggs with cheese slathered with sour cream, ready to be devoured. From the time the boys were tiny, I made them clown pancakes, each one individually crafted to depict their face and hairstyle. By painstakingly drawing a face on the hot skillet with a turkey baster, waiting for it to brown and then covering it over with batter, I had the clowns ready for my clowns as they emerged from the shower. Saturday brunch was a family tradition.

We loved skiing as a family. I raced Joshua and Micah down Linton's Loop then, after meeting up with Alan and the big boys, we rode the lift together so we could do it all over again. That was winter at its best. A weekend skiing took about a week to prepare for and another for recovery. I was organized and was thankful that my system, although not foolproof, worked. Each boy had his own basket and all his gear went in it: jacket, ski pants, long underwear, shirt, mitts, toque, ski socks, neck warmer, goggles, season's pass and lip balm. When we got to the mountain, each boy got dressed and at the end of the day everything on his body went back in his own basket. When we got to the lodge, each boy had a turn with the dryer so that nothing was to be mixed up, which was a disaster waiting to happen when things mysteriously disappeared. I did have a secret stash of extras for emergencies but I had learned that being organized was the key to all family excursions. We loved our ski trips, having a blast out in the cold fresh air all day long, playing games by the fire in the evening and then having an early night with four tuckered out little guys and a couple of exhausted but very happy parents.

We spent most of our evenings during the spring at the baseball park where hotdogs from the concession stand became the sole source of food for weeks on end. Alan coached the boys from the time they swung their first bat in T-ball right through to the end where he paced along the sidelines as they pitched those nail-biting games in Midget as lanky teenagers.

I was sitting on a bleacher watching baseball one afternoon. The boys were all at the same park ranging in age from five to twelve. Another mom sitting beside me struck up a conversation. She was obviously new to the game so I was explaining the rules to her, rules that changed with every level so knowing for sure what was happening could be tricky. She told me her little boy was number 7 and asked me which kid was mine. I told her I didn't have one playing on the particular diamond where we were sitting but

I was plunked there because it gave me the best vantage point to see the three other games where my boys were scattered. I pointed to the left where Alan was warming up the older two, who thankfully were on the same team that year, cutting down on at least one game and two practices a week. Directly in front of us, just beyond the fence, Micah was half way through a Minor Boys game while Josh was up to bat in his T Ball game on the diamond to my right. She stopped eating her onion rings for a second and, mouth agape, looked at me as if I was out of my mind. If she only knew.

I loved baseball. I sat comfortably on my stadium seat in my usual spot behind the ump on the third base line with a sleeping bag and umbrella handy, always working a Sudoku puzzle during infield practice and ready to cheer when one of the boys whacked that ball to the fence. After the games were over, we piled into our minivan, often stopping to get an Icecap from Timmy's. Sometimes before heading home, they had to drop me off at the hospital because I had just been out on a pass.

Life never stood still. Besides juggling the responsibilities with my immediate family, I was also the only one living close to my father. Dad was almost eighty when he and True married in 1994. They had a couple of good years before he got sick. He was diagnosed with dementia and within weeks he was too disoriented to live at home. His mind, at first jumbled, quickly shattered until he was as unrecognizable to me as I to him.

He was placed in a locked facility designed specifically for elderly people, whose brains had been capsized, spilling tidy files, a life filled with precious memories, into jumbled heaps inside their heads. I visited most days but rarely did he know. He was often frightened, sure of one thing only, that he was being held prisoner, his captors bent on poisoning him. It was painful to watch.

In the beginning, he made lists, endless lists. On pieces of foolscap, columns of numbers neatly entered in margins with corresponding letters, in code of course, tracked the comings and goings in his frightening world. Imposing schedule on chaos seemed to ease his anxiety; I understood.

Reasoning with him made him wary that I too was part of the conspiracy, so instead I read his reports and thanked him for his diligent service keeping watch for the government. Sometimes, I was able to coax him into participating in an activity by convincing him someone had better oversee the baking of cookies to ensure the safety of his fellow prisoners. The lure of chocolate chips and a chance to sneak a wad of unbaked cookie dough worked their magic and he would fold into being a little boy again, allowing him a few moments free from his frenzy.

I came to visit one day and sat beside him as usual. Conversation of any kind had ended. Instead I sat quietly and rubbed his feet; it was the only thing that brought any comfort near the end. It had been months since Dad had shown any sign of recognizing me. But, as I nestled in comfortably beside him this day, he turned toward me and grinned. Face beaming, he raised his bony hand, pointed his finger and said, "I know who you are. You are Susan Smyslo's best friend." My heart jumped at the possibility of connecting with my dad for even a brief moment. Softly I said, "That's right. My name is Muriel and I am your daughter". His milky blue eyes squinted, searching my face intently, but then he shook his head, hung it low and told me sadly he didn't have any girls, only a son. I rubbed his feet with peppermint oil and when he fell asleep, I slipped out.

That year, True became ill and the doctors believed she had had a gallbladder attack. When they opened her up, they found cancer had eaten her insides. She died three days later. Our family had been blessed with six years with a beautiful woman who knew how to love little boys.

It's hard to say when Dad died because the self that was Dad and grandpa had been abandoned long before his body was laid to rest. My brother came for his funeral. When we buried our father in his Salvation Army uniform and Wayne sang *It is Well with My Soul* I believe it was. Although there has never been a rebuilding of a relationship between my brother and me, I have made peace in my heart with him. Margaret chose not to come. We haven't found our way through the pain back to being sisters.

Storm Patterns

When I was feeling well, I loved my life but when I was in the depths of a severe depression I could not connect to that well part of me even to draw strength or hope that I could ever feel better again. Alan somehow was always able to maintain a belief life would improve. The line from the old hymn *Great is Thy Faithfulness* sustained him many times. "Strength for today, bright hope for tomorrow" was the anthem that moved him forward. He always reminded me that we were a team and when my mood began to slip he gently came in and took over but the minute I was well enough I resumed my role without so much as a hiccup. I appreciated Alan's confidence in my well self and his supportive calm steady hand when I felt wobbly.

By 2001 I had tried everything. I was sent to The Mood Disorders Clinic in Vancouver and had an appointment with a psychiatrist, aptly named, Dr. Misri. She was a live-wire. She did the quickest intake I had ever seen, firing pointed questions and scribbling down my responses at lightning speed. By then my well-practiced answers were mundane. I didn't even cry when I told her things that normally made everyone wince. I was hopeful she may have some answers but, when I read her consult note, it was just the usual, full of doom and gloom.

She said her recommendations were few because, from what she could see all the pharmaceutical interventions had already been tried. She suggested perhaps having a radical hysterectomy may be helpful in alleviating the hormonal overlay of the symptoms. I was finished having kids and, because I was experiencing difficulty with irregular periods, she thought surgery would be worth a shot. Her diagnosis was clear and my prognosis was "not very encouraging given the length and severity of the symptoms." In layman's terms, it sucked. But the only treatment this specialist of specialists believed offered any hope of remission from my "refractory, rapid cycling, bipolar depression" was ECT, shock treatments. In her consult note she stated that she had discussed it with me but noted I was reluctant to see it as a treatment modality. They were such fine and fancy words to cleverly disguise the dismal truth that I was hopeless. I went back to the hospital in Victoria with Dr. Misri's recommendations in hand.

They had changed the name from EMI to EMP as if substituting the word Pavilion for Institute made any difference at all. The Eric Martin was the same grey building that sat in the shadow of the Royal Jubilee Hospital where I had spent several months being treated for depression the year after Don died. During the quarter of a century that followed, I had been in and out of the psychiatric facility many times and we were now both just an older, more rundown, version of ourselves.

The hospital had six floors. On the main floor there was the entrance into a lobby. No one ever sat on those vinyl couches and chairs or looked at the magazines fanned evenly on the fake wooden coffee tables. There was a pay telephone and a small gift shop. Just like in the foyer of any cheap hotel, plastic frames surrounded nondescript prints which hung on either side of a mirror reflecting the emptiness of the faces that entered and exited the elevator. Locked doors separated the interior from the outpatient offices which had to be accessed from another outside entrance. I heard there was a theatre tucked somewhere back inside but in the twenty-four years that I was in and out of the hospital, I never saw it.

The second floor is where I attended the day program after I was discharged when I was twenty-two. It had meeting rooms, an art therapy studio, a gym, and an outside roof garden like a regular old country club, but even with a fresh coat of paint the drabness of the place made it anything but charming. At the end of a long, hidden corridor, there was an area that was completely blocked off. That is where they took patients to have ECT. I never understood how anyone thought attaching a tidy little acronym could make shock treatments any less dreadful.

The sixth floor is where the day programs were held those last years I was in hospital. I never went to any of them. I was past rehabilitation. I came in for treatments, had my medications adjusted and was discharged a few weeks later until the next time. The fifth floor was a transitional unit for geriatric patients. When my dad was first diagnosed with dementia, he was held there until we were able to find a bed in the long term facility where he paced around endlessly, doing his final orbit of this planet. The fourth floor was divided into two wards. 4A was general psychiatry and 4B specialized in schizoaffective disorders. 3B, dubbed The Mood Disorders Unit, was where I eventually wound up when a bed was found in the cramped, overcrowded Mental Health system.

Hospitalizations could last anywhere from a few days to a few months, three to six weeks was typical. I knew how the system worked. There were rules and a predictable pattern I had watched repeat over and over again.

Days in hospital were long but evenings and nights, endless. Mornings brought a little of the outside world's energy with it. Nurses arrived just before 7:00am as night staff wearily slipped out the side door. Shift change was not a good time to interrupt: questions were always met with abruptness. It was best to let the staff settle into their routine and wait until after morning coffee break before asking for anything. A cranky nurse could translate into twelve miserable hours for everyone.

Breakfast and all other meals were announced over the PA, but bored patients often began lining up early, gripping grey plastic trays with great resolve, as if being first would help the food taste better. I always waited until everyone had gone through because I had learned the secret to getting what I wanted: being friendly to the kitchen staff. They couldn't change what was on the menu but fresh fruit, different salad dressings and specialty teas could be set aside for those who recognized how hard they worked and acknowledged how thankless their job was. So, until the line died down, I sat in the dayroom and waited and watched.

Area clinicians, those doctors who divvy up the patients on the ward and assume their care while in hospital, would begin drizzling in while breakfast was being served. Some would say hello but most often these psychiatrists just scurried by. They would find a seat behind the desk, grab a stash of charts and begin reading without acknowledging the patients. Because EMP wasn't a big teaching hospital, the doctors met with patients individually on weekdays instead of doing formal rounds. I liked to go first to get that part of the day over with. I believed it gave me a better chance of speaking with my doctor before he became bored or irritated, so I sat in the dayroom working at my computer or unscrambling letters in the Jumble, torn from the Diversions Section of the Times Colonist, waiting until I got the nod to follow my doctor into the Quiet Room where I preferred to meet.

I had several doctors throughout the years. Some I liked, some I didn't, most I tolerated. My last was a tall, good-looking Asian fellow, young and arrogant. He had learned to temper his air of superiority, at least around me. I reminded him on a fairly regular basis that I had been in psychiatry while his mother was still changing his diapers, an image meant to paint the portrait of being human, my effort at levelling. It bugged him. I knew it. And I didn't care.

Every morning when I was in hospital, he sat down, opened my chart and flipped right to the section where medications were documented. Mine was always a very long list. His suggestions were predictable: increase dosages, combine the current ones with an old drug and add something novel to the cocktail. New trial medications were always available from the pharmaceutical companies and I usually got to try them out. Nothing worked, at least not for very long. In the beginning, most seemed promising. My mood would brighten, giving me the boost I needed to manage for a few months but then, without warning, the darkness would creep in and any meager hope of sleep would be turfed out. My days as well as my nights would be filled with tears, my mind engaged in a constant battle with terrifying thoughts until, cowering beneath the barrage of terrible images and no longer able to stand the weight, I would surrender and come back into hospital.

Nothing was working. After going through Dr. Misri's recommendations my doctor decided having a hysterectomy was the first priority. I had the surgery. Having both my uterus and ovaries removed did stop the cyclical crankiness and the monthly migraine headaches that accompanied my PMS, which was great. I managed for a few months but remained as depressed as ever.

My dark mood made even daily functioning impossible. I was told that if I loved my family and wanted to get well, I would at least be willing explore all viable options and ECT was once again recommended. But I was more than reluctant, as Dr. Misri had stated in her consult summary, I was terrified.

I read countless articles and watched the teaching tape about Electroconvulsive Therapy a dozen or more times, trying to override the movie version of *One Flew over the Cuckoo's Nest* which had been seared into my memory. The doctors believed it was the only thing that could possibly jolt my depression and assured me the short-term memory loss, often associated with the seizures, were just tiny pockets of time that would best be forgotten anyway. I tried everything I could think of to make myself believe that having probes stuck to my scalp, then sending electricity surging through my brain to intentionally cause a convulsion was not a scary, risky thing to do but even after I agreed to have ECT and finally signed the papers, I was panicked.

I was admitted to the hospital again and scheduled to have my first shock treatment in August 2002. I was scared. My friends rallied together and made a schedule, signing up to take turns coming to the hospital to be with me. Each Monday, Wednesday and Friday morning, one of them sat with me in the waiting room until my name was called and was there when I woke up. Because the treatments required a general anesthetic, there was a chunk of time I would not be able to account for and they were there to keep track. Through the years, I had watched patients walk reluctantly from the ward and be returned in a wheelchair a couple of hours later. They would be plunked in the dining room and left to stare at their breakfast trays as they wobbled in and out of consciousness. I feared being abandoned in my lost stupor for everyone to see. I wanted to be tucked in bed, completely hidden from sight. And even though those patients were up by lunch time, walking around and talking, they always seemed flat and lifeless. By the time I actually resigned myself to having ECT, I had realized I was just that. I was beyond hope.

In the waiting room, I sat with my friend. Everyone had their own idea of how to keep the hands on the clock moving forward. We passed time by chatting about our kids or upcoming events and, when there was nothing left to say, I slogged away solving the morning crossword puzzle, my resolute but futile attempt to convince myself my brain was still working. The nurse would come and retake my blood pressure then start an IV in my arm. This was the portal for the anesthetic to be sent into my bloodstream, rendering me unconscious just before the treatment. Waiting was the hardest part. There were usually four or five other patients rigidly sitting on stiff chairs, all in varying degrees of terror. Every time the door to the waiting room opened, I jumped inside, dreading I was next.

When the doctor called my name that first morning, I followed along behind him and walked through the door into the treatment room. The nurse told me to climb up onto the gurney. Lying on my back, I stared up at the dots in the ceiling tile. With too many to count, my mind shifted gears, sending my eyes frantically darting around the room. Long deep quivers, beginning in my bones, pulsed through my body; I couldn't keep from shaking. The nurse put her hand on mine and told me there was nothing to worry about. My mind knew that, but my body didn't believe it for a moment. I tried not to breathe. On my left the anaesthesiologist was attaching the IV to the catheter in my arm while the nurse fiddled with the oxygen mask. She placed it firmly over my face and told me to breathe deeply. The medicine-like smell was forced into my lungs. My eyes screamed. The anesthesiologist nodded to the psychiatrist, standing at the head of the bed. Suddenly my mouth was filled with a strange acrid taste and tears silently streamed down the sides of my head.

When I woke up, the nurse, taking my blood pressure, told me I was in the recovery room and the treatment had gone well. After drinking the orange juice and taking a bite out of the muffin, I was wheeled back to the ward.

For the first batch of treatments, my friends were there both before and after. They wrote in a journal so every minute was accounted for. After making sure I changed from the hospital gown into my own pyjamas and was soundly asleep, they slipped out.

The shock treatments didn't hurt. Other than having a tender jaw and stiff neck from the convulsion which they soon eliminated by adding more muscle relaxants to the anesthetic, I felt okay. I even managed to continue working in the afternoons. My doctor was outraged when he learned what I was doing. He said I couldn't have a general anesthetic in the morning and work in the afternoon. I told him that if it came down to a choice, I would opt for teaching. Frustrated, but unable to change my mind, he shook his head in dismay. My co-workers Deborah and Betty came at noon and took me to the preschool for the afternoon class and returned me to the ward at the end of the day. I loved teaching and it was my desperate attempt to cling to the last vestiges of my well life as it unravelled and slipped from my grasp.

I was in the hospital for a couple of months and after eight treatments, my depression lifted and I was sent home. But within five weeks, I was as sad as ever. I was readmitted and told I should have had twelve treatments and then maintenance ECT once a month for the rest of my life. Because I was no longer as terrified, I agreed and signed up again, flippantly saying to my psychiatrist, "Let the fireworks begin". The second round didn't touch the depression. When I wasn't recovering from a treatment, I was curled up in my bed crying and waiting for the next. One set turned into two, then three, until one day I realized I had had sixty-one treatments during a span of just seven months. Yet I was still sick.

When the nurse came into my room to take my blood pressure one Friday morning, I told her I wasn't having any more and none of her cajoling could make me change my mind. My psychiatrist appeared on the ward unusually early that morning and tried to convince me the treatments might be successful, if only we continued. But I didn't believe him.

My doctor was unhappy about my decision and so, besides being a hopeless case, I was also dubbed as noncompliant, a label no psychiatric patient wants attached to their chart. But something inside me did shift after having ECT. I knew I had tried everything. I would always be sick and there was nothing I could do about it. I gave up.

Because I was unwilling to cooperate with my doctor's prescribed treatment, the only other choice he saw was to become more aggressive with medication. He declared all-out chemical warfare. Over the next two years I was in and out of the hospital several times trying all sorts of unconventional combinations of drugs, in very high dosages.

I didn't begin by taking handfuls of pills. It was a gradual introduction into the world of pharmaceuticals. At first I was given an antidepressant to dry up my tears and when I couldn't sleep there was a medication added to deal with the insomnia. I was uptight a lot, especially when in hospital because I was worried about how my family would cope with my illness, so drugs to help with anxiety were added to the mix. When the sadness and fear kept me awake, day and night, new drugs were tried. Over the dozen years of being treated for depression, I had made my way through the entire list of psychotropic medications in every conceivable combination, yet I was still sick.

The side effects of the medications were annoying. Mostly they were benign and just bothersome. The dry mouth, heartburn and constipation were constant as were the tremors, blurred vision and unsteady gait. They, along with weight gain and no libido were the most common side effects listed in the CPS, the *Compendium of Pharmaceuticals & Specialties*, the thick blue reference book that comes out annually cataloguing all medications by their brand and generic names. It has lots of interesting information about each drug if you are able to wade through the technical language and read the miniscule print, which I certainly couldn't do anymore.

In the beginning, I used to research every medication before agreeing to take it. I would consider the risk/benefit ratio and question the potential for interaction with the drugs I was already on and ask that it be titrated slowly so I could take as little as possible and, hopefully, keep the side effects to a minimum.

I took the common antidepressants, the older Tricyclics like Amitriptyline. They were very sedating but, because sleep was always an issue, they were good to have on board. The new whack of Selective Serotonin Reuptake Inhibitors (SSRI's), starting with the most popular Prozac, Paxil, Effexor and Zoloft, always seemed to begin with a bang but fizzled out in their effectiveness. Nardil and Parnate (known as MAOI's, another class of antidepressants) had some advantages but the dietary restrictions were such a nuisance. I had tried all the typical sleep medications, like Imovane which made my mouth taste like metal, and Serax, along with the other benzodiazepines which only worked for a short time before I had to take skyrocketing dosages. The rebound anxiety coming off them was worse than the fretfulness they were there to treat in the first place but they were a standby that always had to be managed. Antipsychotic medication was commonly used for sleep but Haldol and Chlorpromazine could have some pretty nasty side effects, stiffening my whole body into rigor, cranking my neck in the opposite direction from where my eyes were locked, staring at one spot on the ceiling. The newer drugs, like Olanzapine and Seroquel that were initially developed to treat schizophrenia were frequently used for bipolar depression as well but the weight gain with both of those drugs didn't exactly make them user-friendly.

Many medications had such uncomfortable and even life-threatening side effects that it wasn't uncommon to be taking prescriptions solely for damage control. But I no longer kept track. I didn't even know the current medications I was taking, let alone the dosages of the dozen or so different drugs I ingested daily. I knew I should pay attention and that it was important to be aware because sometimes the side effects could be dangerous.

One morning, I woke up and noticed my skin was tinged a funny colour. While brushing my teeth, I looked in the mirror and was startled to see I had matching neon yellow eyeballs as well. The Wellbutrin I was taking was immediately discontinued because the doctor thought my liver was unable to process the antidepressant properly. I felt better in a matter of weeks and the jaundice disappeared as my liver enzymes normalized. The doctor said I should be really thankful my body was resilient and I hadn't sustained permanent liver damage.

Another time, a routine blood test revealed my kidneys had silently gone on strike. After the ultrasound and other tests came back, the nephrologists told me I had to immediately go off the lithium prescribed to stabilize my mood. When I told him I was afraid to stop a medicine that was working, he said dialysis was something I should be far more frightened of. Fortunately my body forgave me again and my kidney function rebounded without lifelong consequences.

Sometimes it wasn't the drugs themselves that caused problems but, rather, that specialists treating me didn't see eye to eye on which medications should be used. In the months after I had ECT, I was scared because I realised I had forgotten so many things. While many memories were intact, I noticed that some very common things, like phone numbers of close friends I dialed all the time, were completely missing from my mind and, when I looked them up, they appeared entirely new to me. One day, while driving to the mall near my home, where I had lived for years, I became completely lost. Most disturbing to me was that, during regular conversations with friends and family, I was often baffled by the blanks I encountered when they talked about places we had been or things we had done together. All these things frightened me, so I talked to my psychiatrist. He quickly started me on a brand new medication saying it would help with the memory loss.

When there wasn't any improvement, I was sent for neuropsychological testing. During the initial consultation, the doctor asked me when I had been diagnosed with Alzheimer's. I stared blankly at her and swallowed hard. I didn't recall having been told I had dementia and was instantly panicked and quickly reasoned I must have been told and simply forgotten, a sure sign of the dreaded disease. I tried to explain the memory loss she was supposed to be evaluating had started after having ECT. She calmly told me the extensive memory lapses she had read about in the referral and the gaps I was reporting were unlikely due to the shock treatments. She then added that my psychiatrist had prescribed Aricept, a drug designed specifically and used exclusively for Alzheimer's disease. She must have seen the fear in my eyes because she swiftly assured me they were making headway with aggressive intervention and new treatments were being developed every day to stem the deterioration caused by early-on-set dementia. I was stunned, then terrified. I answered all her questions and did pages and pages of problems and when she concluded her testing, she determined I did not have dementia because the memory difficulty I was experiencing did not interfere with my ability to learn new information.

I was relieved but she was disturbed. She and my psychiatrist had an exchange of words about the appropriateness of using Aricept to treat memory loss associated with Electroconvulsive Therapy. After scanning the neuropsych report, my doctor leaned back in his chair and told me confidently that he was a far more skilled psychopharmacological physician and that "off label" or experimental use, was called for when all else had been tried. He insisted I keep taking the medication as prescribed. I discontinued it, which made him mad. I made up my mind to pay closer attention to the medications I was on but it wasn't long before I lost track again because the drugs dulled my mind and I simply couldn't make myself care anymore.

After a rather lengthy hospitalization a few months later, my mood had once again been stabilized. I was taking a complete cocktail of chemicals, meticulously measured and meted out. After I was discharged, I drove to London Drugs and then slipped into Starbucks to meet a couple of friends, have a latté and catch up on each other's lives while my prescription was being processed. When I went back to pick up my meds, the pharmacist said he was unable to fill them because my doctor had made some errors. He pointed specifically to the dosage of Seroquel and said 1000mg had been written where my doctor obviously meant 100mg. I told him I was certain I had been taking the higher dose but the pharmacist told me that amount was unheard of. I was miffed but knew that, out of my stash of drugs I had in my arsenal at home, I would be able to create some concoction so I could sleep that night.

The next day when I went back to pick up my medications, the pharmacist told me he had spoken to my psychiatrist and been assured the dosages written were correct. Then, leaning over the counter, he told me he was concerned. He said he was reluctant to fill the script and went on to say he was being put in a moral and ethical dilemma because he believed the combination could be lethal. I shrugged my shoulders and told him it was fine and that I wanted to take the medicines my doctor had prescribed so he gave me the whole lot, duly blister packed, and I walked out the door. Accidental overdose did not frighten me. Perhaps my death could be surrounded with a shred of dignity and not be directly an act of my own hand.

Landslide

By January 2005 the admission process had become a stale routine, except humiliation always has a freshness to it, sharp and stinging. After waiting in Emerge, a process that could take hours or days—which is why I had chosen to do that part unconscious I, the Psychiatric Emergency Response Team (PERT) nurse, along with my chart and a big white plastic bag with the words PERSONAL BELONGINGS stamped in bold letters, were loaded into a taxi. I was driven to the other side of the hospital grounds and herded through the blue haze of smokers who crowded around the front door to the psychiatric hospital.

Lisa was kind enough. As far as PERT nurses go, she was the best, so at least that day I could consider myself lucky. She had brought me a latté from Starbucks to make the transfer bearable. I had no idea how long I had been in Emerge or the details of this particular admission but it really didn't matter because my hospitalizations were becoming so close together that the misery just bled into one endless stream of sadness. The security guard, sitting in his glassed-in cubical watching sports, nodded as we walked through the front door. I didn't know what ward I was going to and hadn't asked because I needed to convince myself it didn't matter.

As Lisa and I walked toward the elevator, she reached into her pocket and took out her plastic pass key and veered left so, as I had guessed, I was going to PIC. The locked ward of the Psychiatric Intensive Care Unit was on the third floor. I didn't mind the eight-bed Step Down area but the secure side was always hard to get used to with cameras glaring at me from the corner of every room. We got onto the elevator, and as the doors closed, so did my eyes. I held my breath. I hated this part.

When we got off the elevator Lisa turned right and I followed behind her. She pressed the buzzer, swiped her key and we went in, the thick door thudding, then locking behind us. She walked toward the nursing station and I went and sat down in the small TV area across from the desk and stared blankly at the wall. I hated that my heart was pounding loudly in my chest. I hated that it still bugged me that I didn't know which ward I was going to. I hated that I cared. But mostly I hated that I was alive, again. So I sat dead still, my eyes peering out frantically from behind my face, solid as stone.

When Richard walked over and smiled, I was relieved. He was from the secure side, which was the bad news. But he was my favourite nurse, which almost made up for the disappointment. It always amazed me that this kind, gentle man, with a soft English accent, could come to work each day, bringing with him a thread of dignity and weave it into the lives of his patients. I could only lift my eyes up to meet his for a moment. I tried to make my stiff face form at least a half smile and then, slamming my eyes to the ground, I bit down hard on my bottom lip. I didn't want to cry. I followed Richard and waited as he unlocked the big door separating the two sides of the unit. We walked through the dayroom, past another nursing station, and I was shown to my room. Richard asked me, as he always did, if I needed anything to which I whispered, "no thank you". On the floor there was a mattress. I lay down and huddled beneath the cold blankets facing the wall. Richard left, closing the door behind him. Thankfully he did not lock it.

I hated lying in the eight-by-eight cell alone with my thoughts. Closing my eyes, I tried to drown out the noise inside my head. I always wished I could sleep but, unlike many patients with chronic depression, I was awake day and night and seldom got a break from the dark thoughts that elbowed their way around inside my mind. I didn't have a clue what time it was and I tried to make myself believe I didn't care, but I did.

Time is separated in many ways but most often those partitions are only my mind's effort to place events in categories or sequences to make sense of them. Past and present are all the same when it comes to the realm of feeling. It was a different time, yet the same frame. Lying in PIC as a middle-aged, married woman with four sons, a young adult on 4B after Don died or as a fifteen year old girl with ice coursing through my veins on 6C, all felt the same: grief overlaid with despair, pain laced with shame. I tried not to think. I forbade myself to feel. I shut my eyes and tried not to breathe.

A minute or hours later, whichever it was, Richard poked his head through the door and softly called my name, announcing it was lunch time. I got up because there was nothing else to do and any distraction was better than nothing. As I was going past him, he handed me a medicine cup piled with pills and I washed them back with water without looking. I made my way down the short grey corridor to have lunch. On this six-bed unit, it really didn't matter when you came out into the dayroom because there were no line-ups. No one ate together but, rather, sat at separate tables in the open area and, in their varying degrees of drugged stupor, mindlessly consumed what was on their trays. Rarely did patients talk. It was quiet except for the noise inside our heads.

Richard had put my tray on the small table in the far corner of the room. I appreciated his gesture of privacy. Facing away, I looked out the window at the backside of the hospital complex and ate my lunch. I was hungry. It is pretty hard to ruin an egg salad sandwich or a banana. When I finished, I separated my utensils to make the counting of them easier; it always struck me as odd that someone might be tempted to use a bread and butter knife to harm themselves. But PIC was always full, filled to the brim with six desperate people frantically determined to put an end to their suffering. After placing my tray on the cart, I looked through the glass partition to the nursing station and gently rapped on the window. Through the small opening, I asked Richard for tea, which was always stashed somewhere behind the desk, out of reach. He brought me a cup of hot water in a brown plastic mug, a tea bag and two single-serving-sized packets of milk with a stir stick. I took it back to my room, which was against the rules, sat propped against the wall and brought my trembling hands carefully to my mouth, sipping slowly.

I hated this part too. I had so many things to cancel. I needed to call Betty and Deborah and tell them I couldn't even teach the one day of preschool my work schedule had been whittled down to. I had made an appointment for Hannah but could reschedule it without too much embarrassment. I didn't have to tell the vet I was an irresponsible dog owner. I had promised to take the boys skiing but fortunately I had been smart enough to not give them a date. I had a dentist appointment soon but couldn't remember when. I sighed deeply. I needed my computer. It was the only reliable source of memory I had left.

I didn't feel like moving my stiff body, but knowing Richard was working and that he may not be there the next day, it was important for me to get as much of my stuff as possible. Once you had your things, they rarely were taken away but getting your nurse to agree to give you anything in PIC was the tricky part. The rules were tight and meant for patient safety but some staff went more by the book than others. Richard was by far the most lenient. I liked having my things. They made me feel like more of a person. I decided I would try and trade Richard my cup for my computer and, shaking my head, smirked at the absurdity of it all.

I looked up at the camera looking down at me and, gathering all my energy, pulled myself up from the mattress. My head whirled, I wobbled and was instantly woozy; it was probably my own fault, not worth complaining about. I went out to the nursing station and waited until Richard got off the phone and, when I caught his eye, he opened the glass. I thanked him for the tea and, after handing him my cup, asked if I could use my computer. He closed the window and I went and sat down at a table to wait. Demanding gets you nothing in life but, particularly in PIC, it is important to be a compliant patient.

When Richard walked through the door with the entire bag of personal belongings, my heart skipped a beat, there was a shred of hope of getting at least some of the things I wanted. He sat down across from me and pulled my little laptop from the bag. It was my most prized possession. I took it everywhere with me because it was full of information and held memories I no longer could store in my brain. He gave it to me but kept the cord, which was fair. Anything resembling a rope was considered dangerous. I was hoping I had remembered to charge the battery before I left home. Clothes were set aside. That was a given. Everyone in PIC wore blue hospital pyjamas; I'd learned not to care. I asked for my socks because my feet were always freezing and he gave them to me, a bonus.

Richard handed me my small red photo album which held thirty 4X6 pictures. He asked me how old my kids were. With just the mention of my family, the dam broke, sending tears cascading down my cheeks. I quickly wiped them away, flipped the album open to the last page and showed him the most recent picture. The boys were getting big; Christopher and Jonathan had both graduated and the little boys, Micah and Joshua, were in high school. Alan hadn't changed since the day we married over twenty years before. He was still kind, gentle and patient. Looking at their beautiful faces contrasted by the ugliness inside of me sped up the torrent of tears, my thoughts quickly travelling down the familiar trail: "I don't deserve such a loving family." "I am a terrible person." "They would all be better off without me." Then, barreling along at full speed, I slammed headlong into the dead end, "I have to die." The flood of hopelessness streamed down my face. I buried my face in my hands. Richard waited until he heard me inhale and breathe out slowly. He was used to these moments. We had, through the years, shared many of them. His presence absorbed my grief. He softly commented how the boys looked so much alike and favoured their dad. I wanted this to be true; I hoped my children escaped without getting any of me inside them.

I asked Richard for my brush. He winced. I said I would return it and he tossed it to me. I asked for my package of Frisks, a container of breath mints fortified with Ativan and he added it to my pile. Feeling lucky, I was going to stop but when he asked if I wanted my books, Walkman and CD's, I happily took them. He held up the ear buds, wires dangling and looked at me wide-eyed, it was a question and a statement all in one. I chuckled. He smiled and said he was going to trust me. I cocked my head to the side and feigned choking to death. We laughed, but both knew that nothing in the Psychiatric Intensive Care Unit was beyond possible. I thanked him and was truly grateful for small mercies found in a sometimes merciless place. Gathering my stuff, I wandered back to my room and stuffed my belongings into a pillowcase. There was no use advertising I had gotten away with breaking the rules again.

Aware the camera was recording my every move, I tried to lay still on the cold stiff mattress in PIC. I knew I would be on the locked unit for a few days and, if I compliantly took my medicine and didn't cry too much, I would be transferred to the open ward after a short stay in Step Down. My mind was whirling. I had only been there a few hours but already I couldn't stand it. The wrestling match inside my brain was contorting my thoughts. To break their hold, I bolted upright. Rummaging through the pillowcase, where I had stored my stash, I began frantically unpacking my computer.

I couldn't remember how I had ended up in hospital this time and was thankful at least some of my memories were safely stored in files I could still access. The doctors had assured me that only short term memory may be affected by ECT but in the two years following the shock treatments, I had discovered holes, great gaping chasms of time that I could no longer account for and it frightened me. I opened the lid to my computer, pressed the on button and waited for the Microsoft jingle to open up the oodles of files; Word documents that, like my brain, held many memories if only I could remember how to retrieve them.

I went first to my calendar and quickly scanned it to find out what appointments I needed to cancel and then read my notes from the previous few days. There was nothing new, just the usual whiny, bleak, account of another decent into the dark despair of depression. I droned on for a couple of paragraphs, reading nonsense like, "I can't continue to live like this" and then, obviously tired of myself, ended abruptly saying I was, "signing out for a few days". My best guess was that I decided to go to sleep, took a handful of pills and ended up scaring the life out of my family and friends once again. It wasn't a suicide attempt but, rather, my cowardly way of admitting that I was unable to manage. I could never explain or excuse such reckless, risky behaviour. The stark stupidity made me shake my head. I hated myself all over again.

I needed to document my days, making a distraction from the moment and a reference point, should this time be erased as well. I opened a new Word document. What would I call this one? It needed to have a date to create order and a catchy title giving me a hint for context. PIC had been used too many times, how about "05-01-PIC one last time.doc" and, although I knew it would never be true, it was a file name I had not yet used. It would do. I began to write.

There was a gentle rap on the door. Richard popped his head in and told me I had a visitor. I rolled my eyes and asked who could have possibly found me this soon. He said it was my minister. I saved the document I was working on, shoved my computer back inside the pillowcase and followed Richard to the day room. Christopher Page was standing by the nursing station, his blue windbreaker beaded with rain, holding his backpack in one hand and bicycle helmet in the other. He nodded his greeting. I looked directly into his eyes.

Although the grief of my life, which sat perched in the pit of my stomach ready to explode at any instant, welled up, I felt no shame. Christopher knew all of me.

We sat in the uncomfortable vinyl chairs in the Psychiatric Intensive Care Unit with our backs to the nursing station in an effort to create an illusion of privacy. He leaned forward. As we turned our faces toward each other, a comfortable grace, a stillness, hung between us. He asked how I was, which made me smile. I shrugged my shoulders, shook my head and then wiggling my eyebrows said, "I have a private room". We both chuckled. And then, I started to cry. Tears rolled down my cheeks. I didn't even bother to wipe them away. I looked at him and he held me for a moment, not with his arms, but with his eyes. We didn't talk much because there was nothing left to say. We had used up all the words, and then some, throughout the years.

Christopher's hospital visits were never very long but always long enough. Sometimes he brought communion, sometimes just the essence of it: grace. He always prayed before he left. His prayers were short and comfortable. For a brief moment I felt safe, my soul was calm.

After Richard buzzed the door to let Christopher out, I went back to my room to wait out the long afternoon. When I couldn't sleep being awake was painful, time stood still and in PIC there was really nothing to do in that void but think. Lying on the hard, stiff mattress in the Psychiatric Intensive Care Unit, I was again fighting back sadness. I closed my eyes but within minutes I was engaged in the familiar battle. The loops inside my brain, a well-worn path, a maze of messages, ran seamlessly into each other. "I am a horrible person." "Alan doesn't deserve the pain of my life." "I am a terrible mother." "The boys would be better off without me." "If I just die Alan will be free to get a real wife." They wrenched my brain around and sent me hurling down the dark spiral, erupting a rollercoaster of emotions and plunging me into a black pool of despair. I sat up to shift the thoughts. It was an unwinnable battle, a competition where I was always the loser. I was too tired for war.

I got up, made my way to the nursing station and rapped on the window. I asked Richard what drugs I had available to me. He grabbed my chart and read from the list a long litany of drugs I could have at the nurse's discretion and Chlorpromazine was among the more sedating options. I chose CPZ, the big guns, because I wanted to be asleep, or at least unconscious. He said I could have 50-100 mg so I asked for the whole whack and in liquid because it worked faster. I quickly tossed back the clear bitter medicine and chased it with orange juice then headed back to my room. Within a few minutes my head began to swirl. I closed my eyes and crawled into the deep crevices of my thickened brain.

I awoke with my head throbbing. I tried to open my eyes but the lids were made of solid rubber. Forcing them apart, I let in a sliver of light before they collapsed under the weight again. I held my fingers against the sockets and pushed in firmly, the whole eyeball ached. My lips were dry and my mouth was filled with a bitter stickiness. My head was mired in the familiar thick bog of a drugged sleep that required the rigorous exertion of concentrated effort to plow through to the other side of consciousness. If I hadn't had to use the bathroom, I would have drifted back into the murky fog forever. I sat up and leaned against the wall. My eyes refused to open. My bladder was going to explode. I had to get up.

After navigating my way cautiously down the hallway, slipping along the wall and steadying myself with my hands, I found the bathroom. The fluorescent light sliced through my head and the noise of the fan shattered my brain, making every neuron vibrate. I splashed cold water on my face to force myself to feel. Taking deliberate, small, even steps, I made my way into the day area and sat down in a chair facing the nursing station.

The clock said 6:45. I didn't know if it was morning or evening. I closed my eyes again and sat in silence. I heard a door open and glanced up. Richard was pulling a chair over beside me. Leaning forward, he asked how I was feeling. Cradling my head in my right hand, I opened my left eye just a crack. He was smiling and seemed quite delighted and went on to tell me that, after my minister left, I had slept all afternoon and he had saved my dinner because he hadn't wanted to awaken me. Throughout the years, my sleep had unravelled into a tangled mess and, as my depression had worsened, sleep had become something we guarded and celebrated even if it was a drug-induced stupor. My mouth was dry. It was hard to form words. I told him I was fine and I would eat later. I felt sick but couldn't complain since I had asked for the medication.

Richard said he would be working the next morning and asked if I needed anything before he left for the day. I told him if he had a spare head kicking around I could use one and he smiled. I watched as he walked into the nursing station and put on his jacket. Before leaving, he came out and said I had a few messages and handed me three pink slips. I thanked him and said good night, relieved that he would be on duty the next day.

My eyes were more blurry than usual. Holding the papers at arm's length, I could see the first one had the familiar scrawl of my psychiatrist on it, with "a.m." in the middle; I guessed he would be by in the morning. The second was a message to call Peggy at the Eating Disorders Program to reschedule our appointment. The last had Alan's name with his work number but I knew by now he would be home doing my job, making dinner and sorting out the mess I had once again left him in. I closed my eyes at the thought of having to face people again. I hated myself.

I went to the nursing station and rapped on the window. A nurse about my age, whom I had met before but who I hadn't yet attached a name to, came to the door and opened it just a crack. I asked for the phone but was told she didn't have time to monitor my call. Instantly filled with fury, I swallowed hard and asked in the most pleasant voice I could find that she let me know when it would be a more convenient time. I went back to my room.

Lying down, I turned my face toward the wall to shield it from the camera. I needed to be still. I needed to breathe. I knew how this game worked. If I didn't comply and appear calm and personable, the next twelve hours could be miserable. I hated that I was stuck on a locked ward and that everything I wanted or needed was at the mercy of a person I didn't know. I hated the way that nurse hid behind the door like her life was at risk by sharing the same air space with me. I hated that her one statement could make me so mad. But this was my fault.

The cranky nurse barged right into the middle of my thoughts holding a cup of water and another cup piled with pills. I swallowed the whole whack in one gulp. As she was walking out the door, I asked again if I could please make a short phone call when she was finished doing her evening meds. She didn't really answer but, because she hadn't said no, there was still a small sliver of hope I would be able to say goodnight to Alan. I got up and made my way into the dayroom. I was hungry.

There were leftover sandwiches on a plate and box of digestive cookies on the trolley that held a big blue thermos of water. I made myself a lukewarm cup of decaf tea, grabbed half a peanut butter sandwich and sat on a chair by the window and waited. I picked up a magazine and looked at the pictures. I couldn't read. My eyes were too blurry.

The nurse had finished doing her evening meds and, from my chair by the window in the dayroom, I watched as she scurried back into her protected glass cage. I was hoping she had not forgotten and would let me use the phone. I needed to talk to Alan and although I dreaded it, I knew the first phone call after being admitted was the most difficult.

I was always sure he would tell me he couldn't take it anymore, that I was too much and that I had crossed a line that was unforgiveable. I feared he was going to have to ask me to leave him alone forever and say he needed to take the boys for their protection and start a new life, which is what I knew I deserved. It never happened. Alan, truly gentle and kind, always assured me of his love and told me I would get better again. But as the years kept rolling on, it was getting harder to believe this, especially since I seemed to be getting sick more often and the well times were waning.

When the nurse came out and handed me the phone, I was relieved. She told me I had only five minutes because she was busy. In my mind's eye, I surveyed the six semi-comatose patients within her care, all securely restrained in their chemical straightjackets, but I wasn't up for an argument so I smiled, said thank you and told her I would be quick.

Micah answered on the second ring and with the lilt of his voice I could all but hear his grin, big dimples just like his dad's, as he smiled ear to ear. He nonchalantly asked how I was feeling and then rattled on about rugby tryouts and told me about his day, which was always full of fun and friends and a little short on school work. He called Josh to the phone who also quickly reviewed what he was up to, his training and cutting weight for the upcoming wrestling tournament. He then bellowed for his dad in a voice that was beginning to sound like it belonged to his big brothers. When Alan said, "Hi Hun," my throat got tight. He spoke softly and told me he loved me. He asked if I needed anything, to which there was never a good reply. Keeping my voice steady so he couldn't hear the tears and wouldn't have to worry, I said I was fine. He told me he was sorry he hadn't made it in to visit and promised to come by after work or the next evening. I said it was okay and that I knew his schedule was impossible. I saw the nurse staring at me and told him I had to go. He asked me as he always did in a playful voice, "Who loves you, baby girl?" I swallowed hard to stifle the tears and bravely said,

"You do." and slowly, keeping the quivering out of my words, I told him I loved him as well. When I hung up, the sadness exploded. I went back to my room and crawled beneath the cold covers and prayed the medication would give me just a few hours of relief.

When my depression was at its worst, I felt as if I never slept but rather that I drifted in and out and in-between different layers of consciousness. My distant memories and immediate thoughts were a murky maze, all funneling into a reservoir of sadness that sometimes faded to shades more real than imagined, more present than past.

As I lay awake in PIC in the early morning, I wasn't sure whether I had slept at all. I had been there just one very long day and a terrible night but time is seamless and senseless in the realm of feeling. The continuous retelling of the story in my head gave it an air of endless agony. Unfinished stories are the worst kind. They demand being retold again and again until they make sense and, when they don't, they need to be reiterated with slight variations in the hope that some secret will burst forth to contain or frame the chaos with meaning.

Richard arrived, knocking gently on my door, with medications in hand. I yanked myself upright and, leaning against the wall, opened my eyes ever so slightly. Richard handed me two cups and said good morning. I quickly gathered the array of brightly coloured capsules in my hand and washed them back with water. As he was walking out the door, I asked him if he thought I would be transferred to the open ward that day. He turned and smiled and told me I'd have to ask my doctor and then cheerfully announced breakfast was ready.

I lugged my leaden body to the dayroom and found my tray in its usual spot. The crossword from the Times Colonist lay neatly folded on the table with a pencil beside it. Although my eyes couldn't make out any of the words and my brain was far too foggy to figure out puzzles, I appreciated Richard's attempt to make my morning manageable.

As I was eating my muffin and staring out the window, I heard the mumbling of my doctor's voice as he stood in the doorway to the nursing station. I didn't bother to look over. As he walked towards the table where I was sitting, the crisp clicks of his polished shoes made my heart jump. He took the chair opposite me, opened my chart and leaned back. He was busily leafing through the pages, his dark eyes swiftly scanning, absorbing other people's impressions, their accounting of my past few days. I watched. I waited.

This was always an unpleasant conversation, the first exchange after an unexpected admission. I would have to explain once again that my mood had probably been deteriorating more rapidly than I was willing to admit to myself or talk to others about. In one brief moment of panic, I just couldn't stand it anymore and took a bunch of pills to stop the thoughts, to make time stand still, to go to sleep. I didn't pay close enough attention to the dosages and ended up in Emerge. He would respond by telling me of the danger I had put myself in and say he was going to document it as a suicide attempt. I would then roll my eyes and remind him that when I decided I was done we wouldn't be having a discussion. It was a useless, embarrassing and futile dialogue that frustrated us both and I dreaded it. But I knew it was my fault. I deserved his harsh judgment.

When my psychiatrist finally finished perusing my chart, he looked up. Our eyes met. Throwing his hands in the air, he asked what happened. But instead of defending myself I told him the truth; I said, "I'm dying".

As soon as the words slipped out of my mouth, I regretted the stark honesty of them and wanted to reel them right back in. That wasn't the thing to say if, in the next breath, I intended to ask to be transferred to the open ward. But the words had already been spoken aloud and there was no way to retrieve them or retract the tears spilling out. I told him through my sobs, in complete exasperation, that we had tried everything. All the medications, even ECT had failed, there was nothing left to do and I simply couldn't keep doing this. His chiseled stone face set with cold, glassy eyes stared right through me. He didn't even blink. He waited until I was done and then began scribbling feverishly in my chart. With the long scratch of his signature, he abruptly closed my file and told me he would see me again the next day. He got up and quickly disappeared into the nursing station.

I thought about throwing my tray against the wall, which sometimes other patients in PIC did for no apparent reason. Fortunately, I was able to contain my frustration and, instead, made my way back to my room and crawled beneath the cold covers clenching my fists. I turned my face away from the camera and tried to calm myself. Lying perfectly still, I made myself breathe very slowly, in then out, in then out, but the fear and the fury and the sheer futility of it all welled up inside and I gave in to weeping.

Moments later, Richard came into my room and handed me a cup of water and another with two tablets I didn't recognize. He told me my doctor had made some med changes and these were to help me settle. I thought about screaming but instead I took the drugs without even asking what they were. I didn't want to know. I didn't care anyways. It didn't matter. Richard asked me if I wanted some tea but his gentleness made the moment even worse. I thanked him and told him I needed to sleep and would have some later, then slithered down and pulled the blanket over my head.

If sleeping were possible it would have solved many problems but even with copious chemicals coursing through my blood stream, several designed specifically to deal with insomnia, I was rarely able to even doze. Instead, my mind, cruelly alert, combed over every past conversation and criticised every word I thought or spoke aloud and carefully constructed new dialogues for future scrutiny. For me, this was the definition of crazy.

I knew that if I wanted to get out of PIC and get home again I was going to have to organize my thoughts, exercise better control of my behavior and, especially, monitor and manage my words more carefully. But the truth was, I could only do that for so long before reality set in. The despair of my inside life would spilled out and I would once again find myself being candidly honest, saying stupid things like I was dying, which any sane doctor was going to hear and interpret as insanity. The response was predictable. My psychiatrist would increase the dosages of my medications, add more sedating drugs to the cocktail and keep me on the locked ward until he deemed my mood improved.

Thinking was another problem. It was difficult to keep my thoughts organized because my mind didn't work anymore. I blamed the medication. Many times, Alan and I had talked to the doctors suggesting I just go off everything to give my head a rest and clear the slate, but we were always told the severity of the depression would be unmanageable without the support of pharmaceuticals. The reasoning was that once the combination was tweaked, my brain chemicals would become more balanced and I would feel better, so I remained trapped. I knew this was no time to be even thinking about having such a conversation. All I could do was wait out the day, try to keep myself from disintegrating then try again to appear more calm and compliant the next time I talked to my doctor.

It took several days before I was able to convince my psychiatrist that I was well enough to be transferred to the open ward and a couple of weeks before I was stabilized on the new medication regime. I had been taking my meds regularly without any unexpected side-effects and was allowed to go out on short, accompanied passes with friends. When Deborah and Betty arrived on the ward Monday afternoon, I went over to Starbucks to visit with them.

I ordered a tall, sugar-fee vanilla, non-fat, extra hot latté and, while standing at the counter, we talked about our preschool kids. I missed working and was always glad when they included me in their weekly planning sessions because it made me feel as if I was part of the team, which we all tried to pretend was still true. Deborah became distracted by an old friend who cornered her into a conversation so, while she was chatting, Betty and I found a small table by the window.

We were sitting across from each other when my head exploded. Betty's face shattered, splintering into tiny shards in front of my eyes. I could barely breathe. Blinking to clear the image, staring straight ahead, eyes wide open, I forced myself to focus and piece the fragments back together. I could feel my heart in my head. My brain was throbbing. I thought I was going to throw up. As Betty's face slowly shifted back into alignment, I could see she was talking but the garbled sounds, the long extended words coming out of her mouth were hard to understand. I could tell she was trying to ask me if I was okay.

I told her I had a bad headache. We quickly left, walked across the street and headed toward the hospital. After getting onto the elevator, I gripped the handrails to steady myself. Stopping at the 3rd floor, I went straight to the nursing station and told my nurse I was sick, something was wrong. Gayle casually told me to go and sit in the dayroom but followed right behind and sat on the coffee table in front of me and asked what was happening. Again my head exploded. The room was wrenched sideways then jarred askew in the opposite direction. Gayle's face split apart, sending sharp slivers of light spinning away in long circular loops. I tried to talk but the words were trapped somewhere between my thoughts and tongue and only sounds tumbled out. Gayle was strapping a blood pressure cuff on my left arm while my doctor, who had suddenly appeared, was doing the same on my right side. Numbers that did not match were being exchanged between the two of them. Moments later paramedics were hoisting me onto a gurney, slamming an oxygen mask to my face and starting an IV in my arm. I was whisked down the hall. The elevator door opened then banged shut. As the outside doors parted, cold air hit my face and I was loaded into an ambulance. The siren screeched loudly. I took a deep breath. The fear melted. The world grew strangely quiet. I sank down. Then, sucked into the deep, I was swallowed by darkness.

Rebuilding

Rebuilding
1: a: to make extensive repairs to: reconstruct **<rebuild a war-torn city>**
  b: to restore to a previous state <rebuild inventories>
  2: to make extensive changes in: remodel *<rebuild society>*
3: to build again

Example of REBUILD
They tried to rebuild after the earthquake.

Sharp shrill sounds shatter the silence.

Then sinking, slithering down into the stupor, my mind slides with ease back into the darkness.

Cold water swooshes over my head. Gurgling, grabbing, gasping for air, I am drowning.

Again stillness, so cavernous calls and cradles me and I am beckoned back drifting once more into the deep.

Breaking through the solitude, high pitched, harsh blasts echo in my hollow head and ricochet off the walls of my skull.

I retreat. Pulling back. The separateness enshrouds me. All is empty. All is quiet.

The shrieking scrapes along the edge of my mind, razor-sharp it pierces, punctures, then ruptures, reaching down it hauls me up.

Aware of the icy water once more I open my eyes and through the murkiness my brain is forced to register shapes.

My mind scrambles to suture the fragments together, to make sense of the shards.

I am in a bathtub filled with freezing water. Two bright eyes staring at me. I close mine for a moment and the piercing explosions make me pry them apart again. The yelping and yapping are constant now and once more I am thrust to surface from the depths of my dream world.

Flailing I open my eyes. Pacing frantically back and forth Hannah, my ten year old black lab, is barking in my face forcing my brain awake. I let the water out of the tub and shivering, scramble for a towel. Lying on the hard tile floor I curl up between her paws and cuddle into the warm, soft comfort of my dog. She lays her head over my body and I breathe. In then Out. In then Out. I fall fast asleep again.

Breathe.

Breaking Ground

After watching faces shatter in front of my eyes, I was whisked away by ambulance over to the main building of the Royal Jubilee Hospital. I was immediately hooked up to a heart monitor. While blood was being drawn, a doctor, prying my eyelids back, shone a hot piercing white light into the back of my brain and asked questions I didn't have answers to. I was taken for a chest x-ray, a CT scan, an ultrasound of my neck and an echocardiogram and, in-between each test the gurney on which I lay was left stranded in hallways where I watched and waited and secretly worried. A Holter monitor was put on my chest. For 24 hours it recorded my heart rate to track its rhythm and decipher irregularities. The next day, I was transferred back to 3B of the Eric Martin Pavilion.

On Wednesday evening, a neurologist came into my room. He was a tall, clumsy fellow with the biggest feet I had ever seen. He spoke gruffly and quickly did a bunch of tests, poking, prodding, pinching and then jotting down his findings in my chart. While asking questions in rapid succession, he shone a light in the corner of the room and had me track my eyes to where he pointed, and then he tapped my wrists, elbows and knees with a rubber mallet. As its hard edge scraped across the soles of my feet, I recalled the name of the test from my second year neuropsychology course, which seemed to delight him. He stopped everything and enthusiastically launched into a long diatribe about Dr. Babinski's work and asked whether I had read his paper in the original language or merely the translation into English. If he had been looking at my pupils, at that moment I'm sure they would have registered great irregularities. Wide-eyed, I sat on the edge of my bed and waited for him to finish his harangue and tell me what he thought had been the cause of the scary events of the past few days.

He said that the tests were inconclusive, but it was his impression I had probably suffered a series of TIA's, transient ischemic attacks. He told me that symptoms vary but I had reported most of the usual tell-tale signs of a mini stroke: the temporary loss of vision, difficulty with receptive language as well as speaking, the weakness and tingling sensation on my right side and the lack of coordination noted by the attending physician during the initial testing period. He said having a TIA put me at greater risk of having a major stroke. He thought I was on too many medications and his recommendation would be that my drug profile be streamlined.

He left in the same harried and hurried manner in which he had come and done his neurological exam. After he disappeared from the ward, I went and sat in the dining room. I was scared. Although dying had never frightened me, the idea of having a stroke and being left with permanent brain damage was terrifying. That evening, although I was fearful, my thoughts seemed unusually clear and crisp, not bogged down in the cloudiness I had grown accustomed to. I realized all my medication had been withheld and I had now been without anything for well over 48 hours. My brain felt alive. I liked the way my mind was working, the logical tracking, the facility of feeling.

I phoned Alan and relayed what the neurologist had said and asked him to come and get me. I wanted to get out of there; I needed to be at home. He tried to speak calmly but I could feel the panic in his voice as he patiently told me all the reasons he simply couldn't do as I wished. He said it wasn't just because of the depression but I was now also medically unstable and had spent the last two and a half days having a battery of tests to find out if I had had a stroke, which had frightened him more than he had words for. I tried to convince him I needed to leave immediately and to stay off all medication. As I bawled and begged, he did everything he could to calm me down. He spoke softly and told me he was leaving early the next morning to take the boys to Port Alberni for a wrestling tournament and would be away for the whole weekend coaching so he couldn't be home to take care of me. He promised he would contact my doctor on Monday morning and together we would again talk seriously about going off the drugs.

I hung up the phone, exasperated, and immediately began calling friends. With my heart racing and my mind focused, I was certain of one thing: I was in imminent danger, I tried to persuade my friends to come and get me. All I could think was that if I didn't leave I was going to die or, worse, I'd be left a paraplegic after having a major stroke. I knew my only hope was staying off the medication and keeping my head clear but, as I talked and cried, it was obvious to everyone I was just panicked and needed to be settled down.

My nurse told me to get off the phone. After I hung up, we went and sat in the dayroom. Through my tears, I tried to explain the medication had never worked, the side-effects were impossible to live with and that they now had even become dangerous. I told her I was at risk of having a stroke, could possibly die and I needed to stay off all my medication. Then I told her I wanted to go home. With her eyes wide and face motionless, she stared. Then she spoke in a slow steady tone enunciating every word carefully and stated the obvious: my mind was unstable; I was clearly overreacting again.

Betty came after 10pm. She had called Alan after we spoke. Although she knew she couldn't take me home, she decided to come to the hospital because she could hear how frightened I was. The elevators were already locked but the staff made an exception and allowed her to come up to the ward to see me. We sat at a table in the far corner of the dining room. My nurse joined us and explained that I had had an upsetting few days but that the tests had come back showing there had been no permanent damage. She believed it was possible, in light of the neurologist's recommendations, that my psychiatrist may consider decreasing some of the dosages of my medications.

I was crying and trying to make them understand how serious this was. But as we were talking, out of the corner of my eye, I noticed a nurse from PIC had walked down the hallway and was standing at the nursing station talking to the ward clerk. Their eyes kept glancing towards me. I needed to settle down. I needed to be quiet. I needed to breathe. I could tell they were trying to negotiate my transfer back to the locked ward. I didn't want to become an involuntary patient again, which could happen at the first sign of a patient becoming agitated and labelled noncompliant. Immediately I stopped and, inhaling slowly, told my nurse I was tired and agreed I was making too big a deal out of what had happened. I said the best thing I could do was try and get some sleep, then talk to my doctor in the morning. I quietly said goodnight to Betty, thanked her for coming and went directly to my room. I crawled into bed and lay perfectly still.

My nurse appeared in my cubicle and said she was concerned because I was so upset. She asked if I thought spending the night in PIC might be a good idea. I told her I was tired and had just been scared and temporarily lost perspective. I promised to stay in bed and, when she returned a few minutes later with my night time medication, I took it without hesitation. After she left I quickly went into the bathroom and threw up, ensuring my stomach was entirely empty, then climbed back into bed.

That night as I lay awake, my mind mulled over my options. I knew I had a mental illness; that would not change. I would never live free of depression. I had a chemical imbalance and was doomed to a life of sadness and anxiety. Those were the facts. But I reasoned I would rather have my mind alert than dulled with drugs and decided that even if I did cry every day for the rest of my life it would be a better alternative to risking having my brain damaged by the side effects of medication. I became convinced I needed to keep my head and body clear of chemicals so I could continue to think. I knew I needed a plan but at that moment I had to be still. I needed to breathe.

Room checks were routine but my nurse was particularly cautious that night. Every hour, she shined the flashlight in my face and asked how I was feeling. If sleeping were even a remote possibility, it was ruled out for sure so in-between her rounds I impatiently, plotted and planned.

In the morning after her last check, knowing a shift change at 6:00am would create a bit of a bustle and give me a narrow window of opportunity, I got up. I asked my roommate, a young girl who constantly chatted on her cell phone, if I could make a call. I dialed the number to Blue Bird Taxi and asked to be met at the front door in five minutes. Then quietly, after gathering all my things and stuffing them into the big personal belongings bag, walked swiftly down the back corridor.

I knew the elevators would be unlocked but as I stepped in and turned around my nurse came around the corner and asked where I was going. Our eyes locked. I didn't answer. As the doors were sliding closed, I held my breath and closed my eyes. My heart was racing. When the elevator came to a stop on the main floor, I strode quickly across the foyer, passing the security guard's office where I heard the phone ring. I kept walking, straight out the front doors and slipped into the backseat of the idling taxi. It was dark and pouring with rain as we drove off towards home.

I had expected Alan to be gone by the time I got home but when the cab pulled up to the house our van was still in the driveway. I braced myself, walked up our front steps and, after unlocking the front door, quietly slipped into our bedroom. Alan was busily pulling things from drawers and stuffing them into his duffle bag. As I crawled into bed, I looked over at him and smiled. He looked up, startled, and was instantly mad. But beyond the facade of fury, the fear on his face was most obvious. I calmly told him I just needed a break because the mental hospital was making me crazy. He didn't laugh. He started telling me he had to be at the school in five minutes to pick up the wrestling team and he really didn't have time for this. Rarely did Alan become agitated but that morning he was clearly upset. I spoke softly and calmly assured him I was fine and would take my medication—neither of which was true—and said we could figure it out when he got home. I managed to convince him I would be okay and reminded him that his first responsibility was to our boys whom he couldn't disappoint by staying home. I cheerfully kissed him goodbye and wished them all good luck and was relieved when he finally walked out the door. I climbed back into bed dreading the next conversation.

The phone rang just after 8:00am. I knew it would be my psychiatrist and the second set of half-truths would have to be carefully crafted. He asked me in a contrived, overly calm voice what was going on. I told him I was tired and needed a break from the hospital and would appreciate having some time at home after the hectic week I had been through. Abruptly, he stated that he could certify me under the Mental Health Act, call the police and have me escorted back to the hospital immediately. I told him I was aware that he was well within his right to make me an involuntary patient if he believed me to be at risk but I assured him I was not suicidal and promised to immediately come back to the hospital if my mood began to deteriorate. I went on to reason that had I not had the unfortunate incident on Monday where my blood pressure went whacky it was possible I may have been discharged soon anyway.

He asked me what Alan thought and I told him he was concerned as well but had taken a few days off work, which was true yet a complete lie, a willful attempt to deceive. He had taken a couple of vacation days but I omitted the fact he was gone for the weekend and I would be home alone.

My doctor asked me what I was going to do about medications. I assured him I had enough on hand to make it through the weekend and asked him what he wanted me to take. I grabbed a pen and paper and, as he read off the list of a dozen or so drugs and their dosages and I relayed it back to him, I was even more certain I would never touch another psychotropic medication in my life. I promised that, when my case manager contacted me, I would set up a home visit. I told him I would call at the beginning of the week to make an appointment to see both of them at the Mood Disorders Clinic. My doctor paused and finally agreed but stated emphatically he would have to say in his discharge summary I had gone home AMA, against medical advice. I said I understood and thanked him for his concern. As I hung up the phone, I breathed a sigh of relief.

I called the church at 9:00am. Christopher answered and I told him of my plans to stay off my medication. There was a brief silence that seemed to extend into eternity. He asked me if I knew what day it was. My mind scrambled for a date but the truth was I had no idea even what month it was. I wondered for a second if this was his litmus test for sanity and I had just failed. He gently said, "Muriel, I am always amazed at the gracious hand of God and His impeccable timing in your life. Today is the first day of Lent," and then asked if I was going to give up psychiatry for Lent. We laughed and then I told him all my reasons: the medication was not working, the side effects were too severe but most of all because the drugs made me numb, dumb and dull, unable to feel or think. He ended our conversation with a short prayer asking God to keep me safe.

There were more phone calls to make that first morning. Friends whom I didn't want to worry when they discovered I was not at the hospital needed to know I was safely at home. I called Debbie, one of my YaYa's, and recounted the events of the previous few days and told her of my decision. She started to hoot and excitedly told me my group of friends had gotten together to pray because they knew how sick I was. She said at the end of their time together they had all agreed I needed to go off my medication but then laughed at the absurdity of trying to convince me it was a reasonable solution. Others had different reactions, some expressing deep concern. Meredith was particularly uncomfortable with my decision because of her nursing background and, although she was clear she could not condone what I was doing, she showed up at my front door and handed me a brown paper bag with Gastrolyte and Gravol and said I would probably need it as I detoxed.

It took 72 hours before my body began to react. I had last taken medication at noon on Monday and by Thursday at the same time I began to feel nauseous. The sharp headache that accompanied the vomiting and diarrhea was compounded by alternating chills and profuse sweating. My heart was racing and every muscle in my body ached. All the flu-like symptoms hit fast and furiously, making me unable to think, unable to move. I woke up from time to time, surfacing from dreadful nightmares, panicked and completely disoriented. I found myself in bed, in the bathtub and on the bare floor covered in vomit, Hannah at my side, constantly barking and beckoning me back to bed where she sat vigil. If I hadn't been so ill, I might well have decided to forget my determined stance and buckled back into taking my medication but it simply didn't occur to me. I was too sick.

By the time Alan came home with the boys on Sunday, I was sitting in the living room "clothed and in my right mind," an expression I had often heard my mom use that made me chuckle. She had snagged it from scripture and cleverly contorted it, then used it to convey her solidarity with sanity. But as I was moving about cautiously, I tried to appear calm and casual about my choice to discontinue medication. I didn't tell Alan what my days had been like while he was gone. I didn't want to admit, even to myself, how fragile I felt.

On Monday morning after Alan had gone to work and the boys were off to school, my case manager arrived on my doorstep. I only vaguely remembered our conversation and setting a time for his visit. I tried to hide my surprise at his arrival. Immediately, I invited him in and offered him a cup of tea. As we sat and talked, I nonchalantly told him I was doing as well as could be expected having just come home from the hospital. I promised to take things slowly and not plunge into too many commitments. It was a well-worn script we had practiced throughout the years that bored me but seemed to ease his anxiety. He asked which medications I needed so I gave him a feigned list of drugs to call into the pharmacy. He wanted to book an appointment with my doctor for later that week but I managed to have it pushed to the end of the next, citing all sorts of scheduling difficulties. I knew I needed more time. I wanted to feel sturdy when I told my psychiatrist that I had decided to discontinue treatment.

After he walked out the door, I went back to bed, crumpled into a heap and began to cry. I felt sick. I was still nauseous. My head hurt. And every muscle in my body was sore. Mostly, I was scared. I didn't know what I was going to do. I had made a decision out of desperation but didn't have a plan and I had no one to talk to. I couldn't let anyone know how sick and sad and scared I was.

That first week I was home from the hospital was tough. I was overwhelmed day and night and, because the line between the two was so thin and taut, I was fraying around the edges and feared unravelling completely. My mind was alert and revving in high gear, darting back and forth, feverishly trying to keep all my thoughts neatly organized while folding my feelings into tidy little packages already bursting at the seams. It was exhausting.

I climbed into bed at the end of each frazzled day no later than 10:00pm and instantly fell fast asleep but always awakened before midnight. After tossing and turning the rest of the night, I would finally allow myself to get up at 5:00am, fully exasperated, dreading the day ahead. On a good night, I was able to gather together five hours of broken sleep but often only an hour and a half and then I'd spend the rest of the long night, bolt awake, fending off fearful thoughts that grew larger in the dark. I believed in time my sleep would settle into a more normal routine but if I had known it would be five years before I could count on a decent night's sleep, I'm not sure I would have been brave enough to wait it out.

In the beginning, the mornings were full of the usual routine of getting the little boys off to school. Having just two kids at home made life simpler but I missed the older boys. Christopher lived only a few blocks away and came home to do laundry, check his mail and chat but he was developing a life of his own which was good and right and difficult all at the same time. Jonathan was attending Simon Fraser University on a wrestling scholarship and was rarely able to come home on weekends but had celebrated Christmas with us then rushed off to a tournament before New Year's day. From my chair in the living room, I watched as Josh and Micah sat at the table finishing up homework, bantering and bugging each other as brothers do. I was instantly overwhelmed with guilt. I knew, because of my depression, they had grown accustomed to a different way of living than I had dreamed for them and, although they seemed to take life in stride, I wanted to crumple into a heap, weeping, and beg their forgiveness. Instead, that morning I forced on a brave face and asked them if they wanted pancakes for breakfast. It had been a Saturday tradition since they were small but these big boys were more than happy to have a treat mid-week. As I was mixing the batter, I decided there was little I could do about the past but I was determined to make each day one I could be proud of. My only hope was, if I stuck it out, I may be able to string enough good days together to create a span of time that in the future I could look back on without regret. They were beyond the age when they needed me to make breakfast or pack their lunches but I did it anyway. Quartering apples, slathering them with peanut butter and sticking them back together was one of the small ways I tried to make up for the losses we had all suffered.

After they left for school, I sat with the newspaper sprawled before me. It was big and fat and it scared me to bits. My eyes were no longer blurry and, because reading was a possibility again, I forced myself to scan the top stories and gather information about the world and town I lived in. I tore the Diversion page from the Life Section and settled in each morning to do the daily crossword, Jumble and Sudoku puzzle. I couldn't remember how to make the numbers in those nine, three by three squares line up and had to teach myself how to do Sudokus all over again. At first I was mad then sad but I realized my only option was to relearn what I had forgotten or stay stuck in my loss. Unscrambling the letters in the Jumble, something I had always done quickly, took a very long time but the clues for the crossword seemed an utter mystery. Everyday, random bits of knowledge, once easily accessible, eluded me. The trails to their whereabouts stored in my brain were, at best, blocked or had been entirely burned away, which is what I feared had happened. I completed as much of the puzzle as I could, then, sitting at the computer in the office, I worked painstakingly, looking up answers and reading about common things I had once known and somehow forgotten. I was frustrated and frightened and wondered if I would ever be able to make my brain work again. I often cried and couldn't believe what had become of my once sharp mind. I berated myself for the stupid choices I had made out of desperation.

I had always made a practice of reading scripture in the morning, usually in a hodgepodge sort of fashion. Because I was uncertain whether I had any memory gaps, I decided to read my Bible from cover to cover. Then, focusing on the New Testament, I read it in its entirety each month, complete books at one sitting, often aloud until the words felt familiar once again.

The sadness and fear that combined, then erupted, on a daily basis was wearing. Although they were an abiding conglomeration of feelings, they flowed in waves. Some feelings had such great force, crashing in from seemingly nowhere, that they were powerful enough to send me reeling for hours on end. Conversations with Alan or friends, where I would realize I had a lapse in my memory, were most painful. Listening to stories of events we had shared, occasions I had been present for, yet had no recollection of, made me aware that big pieces of my past were missing.

I felt stupid, sad, frightened and furious and those feelings chased each other around in an endless loop. I didn't know any way to retrieve those memories, unlocking them from my head. Most disturbing was the underlying fear: I didn't know what I didn't know. My former life lay fractured and fragmented, my very self shattered. I was unsure about almost everything. Often the simplest things seemed most complicated and had the power to catapult me into a spin, memories taken for granted that only showed up missing when I needed them most.

On a Friday afternoon I drove to my doctor's office. I had been home and off medication for just over a week and had called to make an appointment. I was hoping to see my GP before he received my discharge summary and read my psychiatrist's rendition of how the most recent hospitalization had unfolded, exploded and suddenly collapsed. I wanted to be the one to tell him why I had chosen to go off medication. His office was on Oak Bay Avenue. Nearly everyone who lives in Victoria is familiar with that major road. It was a section of town where I had lived for several years and I had been to the clinic on countless occasions but, just to be safe, I wrote down the address and stuck the paper on the passenger seat beside me.

I left in plenty of time and started driving the familiar route. After twenty minutes, I realized I didn't know where I was. I pulled over to the side of the road on a little dead-end street and screamed out loud. Pounding my fists, I buried my head in the steering wheel and began to cry. I was completely turned around, hopelessly lost. I couldn't remember how the city of Victoria was laid out, how the streets connected, in a town I had lived in for over eighteen years. It was as if the entire map had been erased from my brain.

After waiting for the panic to subside, I gathered myself together and, through my tears, grabbed the map book from the glove compartment. My hands were shaking as I fumbled through the pages to look up my doctor's address. After pinpointing his office, I drove around slowly, searching street signs and found names that, although they correlated, didn't ring a bell but were there on the map. After finally reorienting myself, I arrived at his office uncharacteristically late and in a complete spin.

By the time my doctor came into the examining room, I had managed to collect my thoughts and was prepared to launch into my well-practiced, carefully crafted speech, clearly outlining and defending my position. He sat down and jokingly asked how I had managed to escape. I closed my eyes, hung my head and sighed deeply. He had obviously already heard I had gone AWOL and discharged myself from the hospital against medical advice. All the precisely chosen words disintegrated and, in my frenzy, I blurted out that I had made a decision to go off my medication. With the words filling then vibrating in the empty space, I sat, eyes staring straight ahead, perched stiffly on the edge of my seat but cringing inside, dreading his response. He leaned back comfortably in his chair and, after glancing through a few pages in my chart, said tapering down on my meds seemed like a reasonable request considering the neurologist's report but cautioned me it would have to be a very slow process requiring a lot of patience.

When I told him I hadn't had anything in twelve days, his eyes widened. As he stared straight at me, I watched the words "twelve days" register in his brain. There was dead silence. My heart was racing. It was difficult to breathe. Then, shaking his head he asked how I was feeling. I started to cry, which I was trying desperately not to let happen, but the truth was I felt awful.

He didn't appear angry but told me clearly what I had done could have been disastrous. He said abruptly discontinuing multiple medications at such high dosages could have caused a litany of side effects which he proceeded to rattle off. He told me that, frankly, he was surprised to see me sitting in front of him. I fumbled and tried to explain I didn't feel as if I had any other choice. Every time I asked for my drugs to be decreased, I had been told it wasn't something to even consider and, even if we managed to reduce one medication, there was always another nipping at its heels ready to be added to the mix as an augmentation strategy. The side effects of the chemical stew were becoming impossible to live with and, I believed, even unsafe. I tried to describe how debilitating my memory loss was and recounted the most recent example of getting lost on the way to his office. I told him many things were missing from my head and that I really didn't even remember him becoming my doctor. With that, he slammed my chart closed and stormed out of the room.

I was stunned. I swallowed hard. Heart hammering in my chest, mind darting back and forth, I tried to figure out what to do next. I had obviously just infuriated the one doctor who could possibly be an ally. I drew a deep breath and, through pursed lips, exhaled slowly. Seconds later, there was a loud rap on the door and bursting through, with my chart tucked under his arm and his other outstretched, my doctor shook my hand and said, "Hello. My name is Kevin Wylie. I am your primary physician." He took his seat, opened my file and said with a grin, "Now you can remember meeting me." We laughed and resumed our conversation.

He was concerned and asked if he could do a physical. After listening to my heart, looking into my eyes and taking my blood pressure, he handed me a lab requisition with almost every box ticked off. He asked me to make an appointment to see him on Monday morning. I agreed and was relieved he was still willing to be my doctor.

Laying Foundation

On a dreary February morning, a couple of weeks after going off my medication, I sat on my front steps, tying the laces of my running shoes. My body hurt. Besides the headache and nausea which were subsiding, every muscle attached to my skeleton throbbed and pulsed with pain. I was weary and sluggish and felt like a lump, yet my mind was revving and wanted desperately to run away. I decided to go for a walk. I stood up and then braced myself before forcing my body forward.

I started off slowly, heading toward Playfair Park then followed the side trail that leads to Cedar Hill Golf Course. It is a well-worn track, quiet and, other than a few folks walking their dogs, I was alone, thinking my dreadful thoughts.

The hills were steeper than I remembered. After struggling up a few, I decided to cross midway. Taking the walkway toward the club house, I headed home. I was plodding slowly towards King's Pond, mouth dry and heart thumping loudly in my ears, when my hands began to tingle and my face grew numb. My knees buckled, sending me flying face first to the ground. I got up and quickly brushed the wood chips off then staggered forward a few more feet before the world coned in from the sides and collapsed around me.

I opened my eyes to find a woman squatting beside me, rubbing my back briskly and speaking in a high-pitched panicked voice. When I realized what had happened, I scrambled but was unable to yank myself to my feet. She helped me up. Still trembling and completely flustered, I quickly thanked her and told her I must have slipped but was just fine. She insisted on driving me home. As we were getting into her car, she told me she wanted to take me to the hospital because she had been watching me from her deck as I staggered around the golf course and she was concerned that I was unwell. I made up a story about having the flu and told her I thought I had gotten over the dizzy part and had gone out for a walk because I was too bored to lie in bed any longer. I managed to convince her to take me home. When she pulled into my driveway, she made me promise to call my doctor, which I vowed to do right away. I thanked her again and strode up the stairs with enough enthusiasm to give her the confidence to leave me alone. I turned and waved good-bye with the best smile I could find and watched as she drove off. That had been a disaster.

Sitting in my living room, my face buried in my hands, I started to cry. Not only did I feel weak and nauseous, I was scared. My body was tired, lethargic and out of shape to be sure but I was sick and didn't know what to do. I knew that in order to get well I needed to have a plan to build up my strength.

Soon after, Deborah and I started walking. We wanted to spend some time together so, instead of meeting for tea, we decided to combine our visits with a brisk jaunt around the same chip trail where I had fainted just weeks before. I thought it best to have a friend along as I tested my endurance and gained confidence. Each Monday, Wednesday and Saturday, we committed ourselves to following a program designed to take people from walking, to running 10K in just thirteen weeks. It was a well-laid out regime that systematically increases endurance in graduated and manageable stages. Well, that's what the book said anyway. I found it difficult, demanding and downright gruelling. We started out slowly, diligently following the instructions for each training session. In the beginning, we ran only 30 seconds and walked for four and a half minutes and repeated the sequence seven or eight times like the manual said. I groaned and complained miserably throughout each set, certain I would never make it. I was sure it was designed deliberately to make me cranky, secretly dubbing it the Purgatory Program. The part I liked was the satisfaction of scratching "exercise" off my to-do list, which is the only thing I did with vigor and enthusiasm. But by about week eight or nine, we were actually able to run five minutes at a time separated by one minute intervals of walking and, in October, we ran together in the Victoria 8K road race with a bunch of other, much crazier people who opted for marathons.

I didn't like running but I did like the way it made me feel. When I ran, the panic inside was almost overridden by the hammering of my heart in my head and the pure exhaustion that followed each session. After Deborah and I finished the training portion, we maintained our schedule of getting together twice during the week to run for thirty minutes and every Saturday morning we completed the 10K loop around Elk Lake. For two years, Deborah and I laughed and cried our way around countless trails in Victoria. We tore through the wooded paths, getting tangled in brambles, and along the oceanside with wind in our faces. We ran on hot sunny days of summer with sweat dripping off our backs and the cold autumn and spring rains soaked us to the skin. We even trudged through snow, slipping on ice but as we ran and chatted we chased fears away. Our hearts and bodies grew strong.

After I had been off my medication for a couple of months, the Recreational Therapist from the hospital called. She told me about a study being done to observe the effects of exercise on mood. The study was a combined effort by the hospital and University of Victoria to follow patients with a history of severe depression. The patients would be set up on a rigorous exercise regime while their mood was monitored to see if their symptoms improved with physical activity. After briefly outlining the commitment, Colleen asked if I would like to sign up. The timing was interesting. Deborah and I had just begun our walk/run program and I was in need of getting my body fit but I was no longer a patient at the Mood Disorders Clinic. I was in my psychiatrist's bad books after discontinuing my drug therapy. Colleen assured me the study was an independent research program and that taking medication or following other recommended treatment wasn't required, so I agreed.

On a Tuesday afternoon in April, I found my way to the McKinnon building where a small group of patients were introduced to staff from the university. We met in a classroom and were given all the information about the eight week study then asked to take an initial paper and pencil test, assessing our mood. We were shown how to fill out the logs, which consisted of a quick survey to be completed at the beginning and end of each session and then a written journal documenting how we felt throughout the weeks. We were all weighed and measured then run through some basic assessments for physical strength, endurance and agility.

I think I failed on all counts. Filling out the questionnaire, I realized how sad and anxious I was, certainly ranking very high on the depression index. As far as the fitness part, my weight was the only thing I scored high on. Even basic tasks, like standing on one leg with my eyes closed, lifting weights or touching my toes were completely undoable. When I ran on the treadmill, I bailed before a minute and stood to the side clutching my gut, gasping for air.

We moved from the comfortable classroom into a large gym rife with testosterone oozing from young men who were sweating profusely and grunting loudly as they flexed their enormous muscles while they clanked away on all sorts of scary looking machines. I had never worked out in a gym. I was immediately overwhelmed by the lights and the noise but mostly by the fear that my body wouldn't be able to do anything asked of it and I would look like a fool. As a group, we were taken on a tour and shown every workout station. As the trainers demonstrated how each piece of equipment was used, they described in detail which muscle group they were designed to target. I took notes feverishly because everything looked the same to me: terrifying.

Every Tuesday and Thursday afternoon, I went to the gym. At first I dreaded going. I forgot from one session to the next how to use each machine and felt dumb standing before the monstrous steel contraptions trying to remember what it was and how to get my arms and legs loaded into each apparatus. It seemed a long time before I knew what a Lat machine was and which weight to set it at before I sat down, looked straight ahead and forced my arms to pull down firmly and release slowly to strengthen the muscles of my upper back. But eventually I got the hang of it. With an individual trainer designing a tailor-made program and always there to encourage me, my body began to grow strong.

I noticed my mood was considerably better at the end of a session than it had been at the beginning, although I attributed the shift to feeling proud of myself for enduring the torture or just plain being relieved it was over and I was free to drag my weary body home and soak its aching muscles in a hot bath. But by the end of the eight weeks, I was comfortable in the gym and easily moved from one station to the next without a glitch. I felt stronger in both body and mind and was beginning to trust both, but just a little.

When the program was transitioned to a local Recreation Centre, the four of us who had stuck it out continued exercising together. We were followed-up by one of the staff from the university, along with the Recreational Therapists from the hospital, for several months. I branched out to other workout times as well and Alan and I started exercising together, but I maintained the routine that had been established for me.

Exercising—walking, running and strength training—didn't eliminate the sadness or quell my anxiety but while engaged in the activities I was so focused that those feelings were manageable. When running, my mind was fixed on knocking off another kilometer and while counting reps as I lifted weights, the grief and fretfulness had no place to register in my mind. Yet when I was still, most especially at night when my head was open, the despair and fear crowded in and still ruled.

I cried a lot, usually when alone. I didn't want others to feel as worried as I did by the weight of the depression that never seemed to give me a break. I had a routine and stuck to it religiously. Besides running and working out and continually challenging my brain, I explored other ways to cope with my illness.

During the meeting with my psychiatrist the week after I got home, I admitted to him I had gone off my medication. He told me I had made an unwise choice, one he could not support. He said if I decided to follow adequate treatment protocol he would follow me again but, until I was willing to cooperate, he saw no point in seeing me. After walking out the door, I realized I had just been kicked out of the Mood Disorders Club, my membership revoked, until I was ready to follow the rules. I felt relieved and abandoned all at once but it only made sense. I read my doctor's discharge summary. In black-and-white, he stated it would be only a matter of time before the depression became unmanageable again and I would have to start at the beginning with drug therapy. He said he believed I would likely present to the Emergency Room after a suicide attempt or, what he feared most, completed suicide. Those were unpleasant words to read but I knew if I were honest, they were the truth.

Although I no longer had a psychiatrist, I did have other supports. A couple of months before I went off the medication, I had started meeting with Peggy at the Eating Disorders Program again. I hadn't seen her for years. After untying the knots in the back of my head where food and feelings had become a matted mess, I had learned how they were connected and was able to live my life free of the eating disordered thinking and behaviors. But after gaining a lot of weight as a side-effect of the Olanzapine my doctor had prescribed, I tried to diet and the old monsters reared their ugly heads. I was scared. I phoned from the hospital and when the receptionist told me Peggy was unavailable, my call was transferred to the nutritionist. When I heard Susan's voice, I started to cry. It was several minutes before I was able to talk and explain what was happening. During her lunch break, Sue cycled to the hospital and talked to me as she always did, gently. She calmly told me I would be okay and wasn't a failure and then explained that restricting my diet in any way could reignite old thought patterns but addressing them immediately could turn things around quickly. She set up a meeting with the nutritionist from the hospital to make meal plans and help me get back on track and when I was discharged she made an appointment for me at the Eating Disorders Program. I was grateful.

Peggy was only able to see me for a brief period to make sure my eating patterns were correctly established. Because of the extensive work we had done, my relapse was easily redirected. And although depression is often associated with eating disorders, I no longer met the criteria for their program. She wasn't able to see me for long-term counselling. I understood but felt completely alone trying to wade through the overwhelming feelings of the depression that continually surged through me. I felt lost in the thick darkness of my black mood but didn't have the energy or the interest to find a new therapist and start over again.

In the early spring, I attended a Cognitive Behavioral Therapy Group once a week. It was a short course offered through Mental Health. I hated being there. The material we covered had some information that was slightly interesting, old information with a bit of a new twist but I was impatient. I was sick to death of my depression and wasn't in the least interested in hearing about other people's struggles. I didn't want an experience; I was looking for answers, not exactly the attitude needed to foster good group dynamics. But I learned a few things.

I realized it was true, my feelings were directly related to what I was thinking. Even if those thoughts flashed across the screen of my mind at lightning-speed, I found if I was alert I could backspace, edit and push delete, to tidy up the script to make the story more accurate, diffusing some of its energy. But the messages behind many of the words that thundered through my mind still had power. I discovered that how I felt largely depended upon the story I chose to tell myself. I realized I could shift my experience, at least temporarily, by redirecting my thinking and creating another narrative. I set out to be aware of and control every thought that breezed through my brain and rewrite the scary chatter clogging my head.

I met with a couple of friends each week to share our writing but mostly to process our lives together. Karen and Mary had been part of the group I had been in during the years I first began sorting through my childhood mess. It was one of the only places I felt I could be completely honest about how difficult things were for me. Nothing scared them. They listened patiently as I tried to connect my thoughts and feelings and always cheered me on as I continued getting my body fit.

I started volunteering. There was a woman in our church who had cerebral palsy and was also deaf. Most Sundays she had an interpreter but occasionally she sat in the service and only watched because there was no one to sign for her. I had some basic sign language skills and worked to increase my vocabulary by practicing as I listened to the music on the Christian radio station each morning. One Sunday when Val's interpreter was away, I offered to help out. Each week after, I signed for the music part of the service. I loved dancing with my hands and made a great friend.

After three and a half months of rigorous exercise and eating well, I was physically much better. My weight had come down and stabilized; my body was stronger. Tying thoughts and feelings together helped me to redirect my mind and gave me a way to shift out of some destructive thought patterns. Relearning information, being active with friends and volunteering gave routine and meaning to my days but I was exhausted. I wasn't sleeping. Every day seemed like boot camp, a forced rigid schedule of pushing myself physically and mentally. I knew this way of living was not possible in the long term. I was running straight into a brick wall, heading fast and furiously towards burn out.

I had weekly appointments with my GP, who was stuck with my care after

I made the decision to discontinue treatment at the Mood Disorders Clinic. He was kind and patient and I was grateful he was there to check in with. He seemed pleased and relieved that physically I was doing much better. Even my thyroid function had kicked back in, my TSH levels completely normalized and all the other tests showed I was remarkably healthier.

My allergies, though, seemed even more bothersome. I wasn't sure whether it was because, in my non-drugged state, I was more aware of the discomfort or if being outside running was exposing me to more pollen than my body could handle, but my itchy eyes, ears and throat made my day-to-day life miserable. The swelling seemed to take over the inside of my brain as well causing pressure that made me feel as if my head would blow off. I tried taking various antihistamines but nothing even took the edge off the discomfort. At night, I sucked on ice to soothe my itchy soft palate and throat. My nose bled from the constant irritation of sneezing and coughing. Despite this, the depression was still the biggest concern and hiding the obvious sadness from my doctor was difficult.

I sat in his office one Monday afternoon. I told him I had been keeping up with my running and exercise program but when he asked how I was feeling, my face crumpled. My mood was as dark as it had ever been. Like a traffic cop inside my head, I stood dead centre in the freeway of my mind redirecting thoughts, rerouting emotions and diverting or converting scary stories all day and all night. My swollen head throbbed and I sneezed, sucking on ice to alleviate the urge to tear my throat out. I had been micro-managing my mind and keeping myself active and moving forward for over three months. I was sick, overwhelmed and thoroughly exhausted but mostly I was desperately depressed.

Dr. Wylie asked me to rate the depression from 0-10, a game we had played over the years—10 being a perfect score, a life of bliss, pure Nirvana; 0 meant dead as a doornail with 2 designated as hospital material. I said I didn't want to play. He asked me if I thought I was nearing a 2. I bit my lower lip, looked slightly to the left and stared at the ceiling, then took a deep breath. When our eyes met, the tears that had forced their way out were spilling down my cheeks. I decided to be honest then politely told him that if he was offering me a private room in PIC, I had to gratefully decline. His face became sober and he asked me if I would tell him if my mood turned black and I was seriously thinking of giving up for good. I paused for some time to think about how to answer his question, and then whispered, "No" slowly and clearly. I told him I was never going to take the psychiatric route for treating my illness and if the depression did become too much, I would deal with it myself. He sighed deeply and said I was putting him in an awkward position. I told him I was sorry but it was the truth. The bluntness of the conversation left us both squirming in our seats.

He asked me to make an appointment for later in the week and when I did come to the office he said he had given our last discussion a lot of thought. He told me he had recently attended a conference and heard an interesting fellow speak. He asked me if I would be willing to talk to this psychologist. I threw my head back, rolled my eyes and sighed deeply. I didn't want to talk to anyone.

Talking never helped. I had already talked about everything. There was nothing new to say. The only thing talking ever did was focus my attention on how sad I was, making it impossible to even pretend to live. The reason I was sad was because I had a mental illness. The only treatment for my kind of mental illness was medication. Medication didn't work for me. Even ECT had failed. There were no treatments I hadn't tried and, even if something new did become available, it wouldn't work. The only thing I could do was hang on until I just couldn't anymore and, at least, when I died people would be able to say, "Well she tried." Hopefully, they would find it in their hearts to forgive me. I doubted my children would ever be able to forgive me, which is why I was still running and working out and fending off the terrible thoughts that tracked me down and tormented my mind day and night.

I don't remember how much of that conversation was said out loud and how much stayed inside my own head but before I left his office I had agreed to see another doctor I knew could not help.

Framing

Before I went to see Allan Wade, I sent a letter, a big fat wordy consult note of my own, documenting the course of my illness and clearly outlining all the treatment strategies I had tried throughout the years. I explained I had chosen to stop drug therapy four months before because the side effects were too severe. I told him, although I clearly had a mental illness, I was not willing to take medication or have ECT again and did not see the point in hashing through historical hurts. I ended by assuring him I didn't expect anyone to fix my life but was willing to listen if he had anything new to add or was aware of ways to help me live more comfortably, which was the best I could hope for. I gave him an out. If, after reading my letter, he chose not to see me, I absolutely understood. I didn't want to waste time, his or mine. He booked an appointment for the same week.

I had to drive to Duncan to see him, a small town about an hour north of Victoria. I wasn't nervous but dreaded the thought of sitting across from yet another doctor. I had done everything to skip over the boring initial intake interview, the gathering of information where dozens of questions would be asked and I would be suckered into telling the sad tale of my pathetic life once again. I had long ago grown weary of my story and had no sympathy for the choices I had made and understood I was fully responsible for the mess I was currently in. I had, in my 3,000 word, single-spaced, 11 point font manuscript spelled out exactly how hopeless my life was. I couldn't imagine anyone having anything bright to say. There were no magic bullets for the treatment of clinical depression. Psychiatrists favoured drugs, psychologists liked to talk. Neither worked. But because my GP was willing to put up with me, I was willing to at least humour him and go to this one appointment, which I hoped wouldn't take too long.

I found a parking spot on Station Street outside his building. It didn't seem to have a time limit so, after sighing deeply and summoning my last strand of courage, I trudged up the stairs. Finding the office, I opened the door to a tiny waiting area and settled into a chair. The psychologist was on time, a good sign. When he ushered me into his room, I saw my letter sprawled on his desk. I took a seat. As he was walking towards his, without the regular formalities, he launched into a question, I remember it verbatim. "How would your life have been different if, at the age of fifteen, when you were first admitted to the hospital someone had said, 'Good for you, you got out of the Group Home' and then come along side of you and said they were going to help"?

I was startled. The question seemed out of context, a scenario snatched from so long ago and having very little to do with the illness I was currently struggling with, but he had piqued my interest. We talked for a long time. He asked interesting questions and, as he did, all the solid constructs in my head were picked up, turned over, shifted, sometimes ever so slightly, to catch the light falling on them differently to illuminate their shadows. But the answers they stirred were most surprising. I was cautious, intrigued and curious but mostly amused by some of the things that tumbled from my tongue that I said I believed. I glanced at my watch and saw we had gone over the hour mark and yet noticed he was not becoming restless. He didn't stretch or shuffle, the subtle cues to the session's end right before the more overt reaching for the appointment book and billing pad. When we finished, I felt done. After I got into the car, I realized I had been in his office for two and a half hours. I had a lot to think about.

He said many things during that long appointment, the most startling being that he didn't think I was sick. He told me he didn't believe I had ever been ill and, from what I had told him, he was certain I had been misunderstood from the beginning. The symptoms of sadness and anxiety I was currently experiencing were not, in his mind, indicative of a mental illness but were completely understandable given my current beliefs. What was most curious to me was how I felt inside. Instead of being frustrated, confused and more desperate, I was energized and encouraged and, as I drove home, hope grew.

The following week, I began to ask myself a question which became the theme of my life for a long time. "If I am not sick, why am I feeling _____?" If I am not sick, why do I feel disoriented in stores? If I am not sick why do I feel scared when I am just watching my boys play baseball? If I am not sick, why do I feel like dying? If I am not sick, why do I feel like crying all the time? If I couldn't blame these wild emotions on an illness, what did they mean? I wasn't sure I believed him. But it was a quirky notion that sent my mind darting in a different direction, asking myself tons of questions with unanticipated answers.

I had long ago stopped assuming my feelings had any real meaning. They were merely dangerous, not to be trusted, indicators of my illness. I had recently learned I could reroute emotions by forcing my mind to think different thoughts which, although helpful, required constant attention, a completely exhausting exercise that was bound to push me over the edge and make me certifiably insane. I had come to believe my emotions were invalid in and of themselves.

Until I started asking myself these questions, I believed what I had been told. I thought I felt disoriented in stores because my brain didn't work right, which was a symptom of depression. I felt scared doing routine activities like watching baseball because people who are depressed are easily overwhelmed by even the most benign things. I felt like dying because suicidal ideation is one of the most serious indicators that a depressive illness has become unmanageable and needs immediate medical intervention. Crying all the time was also a definable symptom of the illness, clearly laid out in the DSM, the big blue bible of psychiatry that doctors use to decipher a diagnosis and then proclaim their prognosis, clarifying who I was and what would become of me. All my emotions were just symptoms that gauged my illness, neurotransmitters gone haywire, brain chemicals whacked out of balance which could only be fixed by medication that hadn't worked and, since I wasn't willing to take any more, I was hooped.

I began to ask myself questions whenever I had a feeling, prefacing it by the clause, "If I am not sick why I am feeling _____ ?" so when I felt sad or scared or mad, instead of letting myself off the hook by saying it was a symptom of an illness, I forced myself to go past the well-worn answer, "Because I am depressed". I decided to pay attention and what I discovered was fascinating.

I noticed I was fairly comfortable in some small shops but big box stores, with little natural lighting, instantly made me edgy. Instead of fleeing for the door or fighting with myself, barreling past the discomfort while chiding myself for being ridiculous, I stood stock-still and observed what was happening. I noticed that the fluorescent bulbs made my eyes jump, forcing me to focus really hard. Choosing apples and oranges from a dozen or so varieties at varying prices in the middle of a strobe-light show was unsettling. Stores are filled with odors. Soaps and perfumed detergents and the smell of plastic used in many products and packaging, although only a slight annoyance to many, made my head feel swollen because of my allergies, slamming me with a splitting headache. Combine the headache and the flashing lights and it was easy to understand why I felt lost and disoriented in huge stores.

Watching baseball had always been something I enjoyed but now the once-loved activity was packed with stress. I knew it wasn't the game that made me uneasy or sitting outside in the bleachers that sent my heart racing but, as I sat still and paid attention, the source of the feelings came into focus. I was uncertain whether I could recall the names of the parents sitting beside me and wasn't sure which ones I knew from previous years because my memory was riddled with holes from ECT. This made me feel sad and ashamed, reminding me I was mentally ill. I was overwhelmed, not by baseball or other routine activities, but by the shame, fear and grief interwoven with the experiences, most especially and specifically the ones that reminded me I was sick.

When I slowed things down, I realized I felt like crying or dying all the time because I knew I had exhausted all treatment options for my incurable illness. The symptoms I had to deal with on a daily basis made living a dreadful burden, which scared me because I believed what I had been told: I would wake up dead one day. It is reasonable to feel sad, scared and anxious about your own impending death.

Most of my feelings circled back to the one fundamental truth I had based my life on, that I was mentally ill, a truth that was now up for grabs.

So when I took that out of the loop, I discovered my feelings really did have reasons for them. They did make sense. It sounded too simple to be true.

I was surprised I had forgotten to schedule another appointment at the end of our session and, when I called Allan Wade's office to rebook, he set up a meeting for the next week. I told him I had given serious thought to his novel theory that I was not sick. We talked about how my emotions kept circling back to my belief I was mentally ill and without it as a base or an excuse I was figuring out my feelings had reasons for which there were other possible logical explanations.

I told him that, although I really didn't like the idea of therapy, I was willing to commit to seeing him on a regular basis. He cocked his head to the side, eyes twinkling. The corner of his lips crinkled. Then, breaking into a broad smile he burst into bold laughter. I stared at him. His eyes still glimmering, he gently asked me why I thought I needed to see a doctor when I wasn't sick. The question startled me and made me smirk. He told me that as far as he was concerned I was perfectly healthy and went on to say that, if from time to time I had something I wanted to chat about, he would be happy to see me but he didn't think I needed therapy. He thought I needed to remain curious and continue to live my life. I was a little taken aback and then overwhelmingly relieved. I left his office skipping down the steps and when the sunshine hit my face, I smiled. I could breathe.

Over the next several years, I did a deep purging of words and scrapped labels from my vocabulary. "Depression" was the first to go; "sensitive" was the next. I had always been told and fully believed the word adequately described my personality and was a true statement about me. Sometimes, when people refer to another as sensitive they use it as a compliment to honour their delicate, tender heart but most often I experienced it as a criticism, a kinder way of saying I was touchy, moody and fragile, not to be messed with. I would watch people who had just dropped the "you are so sensitive bomb". Most often their placid smile was accompanied by a wide-eyed blank stare. But if I zoomed in on their pupils, still and glassy as stone, I could almost detect their eyes rolling in their mind as they heaved a deep sigh without a sound; sensitive people are a pain to deal with. As I thought and talked and pushed the word around, I decided the word "aware" was more accurate.

At first, it seemed more like semantics, a clever crafting of words to explore the subtleties of the same thing and perhaps that is what the conversation was at its core. Is there really a difference in stating, "I am a sensitive person" or saying, "I am an aware person"? Maybe not, but the simple substitution of one word for another revolutionised the way I perceived myself and changed the way I was able to respond to my world.

Rather than feeling fatally flawed, gimped, injured, a survivor at best, I came to honour that my life's experiences had demanded I become keenly aware of my environment and taught me the wisdom in remaining alert to not only the words but to the energy within the realm in which I lived. When a person walks into a room, he or she brings an essence into that space. The frequency can be low, soothing, gentle, sluggish or draining. High energy can be fun, vibrant, creative, leeching or intrusive. Many people interact with their world by listening to what is being stated verbally. Others have trained themselves to pick up on body language to gain more information and some of us, out of necessity, have grown in our awareness and are more perceptive of the nuances of energy, the subtleties of interaction. People have different ways of expressing this truth, some frillier or more scientific, but all I know for sure is I need to be responsible for the energy I bring into a space and accountable for what I allow into mine.

Coming to believe I was well, that there were reasons for my feelings and accepting my awareness as a gift, freed me to live my life with more hope and confidence. Allan Wade and I met from time to time to turn over and explore words together. We had interesting email exchanges and sometimes talked on the phone or over a cup of coffee, but on-going therapy was not what the doctor ordered. His diagnosis of my wellness was one I began to live into, my prognosis shifting instantly from dismal to excellent.

Moving In

The year I turned fifty, my life was in motion. The boys were grown and had all moved into lives of their own so Alan and I moved into our new life together. We sold our home, purchased a lot and built a house in Mill Bay, about half an hour north of Victoria. Everything had changed and I changed everything, not because I had to but because I could. Colours were most noticeable. In our new place instead of peaked-pastels with wishy-washy names like Peach Melba, which had graced every wall of our home before, I went for bold and vibrant. We painted the bedroom red,—not plum or mauve, Kiln Red was the name on the swatch from Benjamin Moore. We had fewer rooms and less square footage but everything was wide open with tall ceilings and big windows inviting the world inside.

Alan had to commute to work and I was in a brand new home where the completely stripped, half acre lot, was bellowing for gardens to be created. I wanted small, easy to maintain beds that burst with colour surrounding a couple of ponds, joined by a little brook, spilling over a waterfall where I could sit to read, watch birds and maybe even write again. We began attending a different church and meeting new people and exploring our community. I was alive and well and still not sleeping.

I had been off all medication for five years and spent my days enjoying feeling stable and confident, but nights were long. My body was tired yet my mind, wide awake, fretted in the dark. I went to bed each evening with a list of things I could not think about. Anything in the future was definitely not allowed. My mind, instantly worried, would become embroiled in creating endless to-do lists with unimaginable detail sucking me into a virtual vortex from which there was no escape. Events from the past, also a no-no, had a way of catapulting me into feelings of regret and shame as I remembered things I was powerless to do anything about, entrenching me in a quagmire of self-loathing or pity. I would try rolling over to change the channel but once my mind was stuck the only way to unglue it was to get up, which was difficult because I was exhausted. Once up, there was another list of things I could and could not do in the middle of the night. I had to hold my thoughts still to keep them from racing off the craggy high-cliff edges of my mind.

I still liked to tell myself frightening stories in the dark. I had learned to ignore most of the tales but the one most prominent and true was that, because of the state of hyper-vigilance that kept me alert day and night, I had to live a very small, contained life. I was able to relax more easily when my schedule was wide open. If I was still awake at 3:00am and had an appointment scheduled for early in the morning, it screamed trouble. Sitting bolt upright, perched on the edge of terror, watching my thoughts accelerate, careen around the steep corners and crash left me frantically wondering how I'd cope the next day. I feared it was useless to even try to go back to sleep and resigned myself to staying awake the rest of the night. I felt forced to live my life with care. I accepted the truth I would always have to just manage and went about my quiet life trying to remember to surrender, be grateful and accept where I was. It was a nice idea but often, inside, I was stomping my feet in a snit because it made me so mad to have come this far and still not be free.

A day following a dreadful night could be difficult. My head hurt, my eyes burned, lights flickered more than usual. My mind raced, making it harder to track my thoughts and keep them in their tidy places and, of course, I cried more easily. I had given up talking about my struggle with sleep as I had long before taken a vow of silence, refusing to discuss my ongoing difficulty with allergies. Everyone is an expert and has an aunt or second cousin who has found some miracle cure they feel compelled to share and then, because you have complained, feel forced to try. I was sick of having problems, so I kept mine to myself. I liked reading and the stillness of my days. I enjoyed walking by the ocean alone or spending quiet afternoons gardening or being with people I loved.

During these first few years in my new community, I made several good friends. Renee was fun and bright and shared my dry sense of humor. We hit it off instantly. She lent me a book with a corny name *Becoming the Person You Want to Be* which was completely juxtaposed to the message suggested in the title. In it, the author, Jim Richards, speaks from a biblical perspective and challenges the reader to begin to dream new dreams for their life, not by changing but, rather, by allowing themselves to be more fully who they already are, complete in Christ. I found it interesting and went on to read several more of his books that, curiously, took many of the principles I had learned as I had healed and interfaced them with my faith. So when Renee offered me a CD of his, I was more than happy to listen to it.

I was awake as usual that night and bored out of my mind so I stuck in my ear buds. A man with a heavy southern drawl began the thirty minute meditation with the words, "Peace, you are at peace" and continued to state biblical facts of our identity in Christ. He didn't say anything I hadn't heard before but I sunk down into the comfortable truths: I am a child of God, dearly loved, protected and provided for. God is for me, not against me. All He has is mine; all I am is His...—I woke up to Dr. Jim's voice as he deliberately calls listeners to alertness at the end of the meditation. I listened again and almost immediately went back to sleep only to be rudely awakened at the end of it. I wondered whether, if I spliced off the last part and ran a loop, I would be able to sleep forever. Renee's eyes smiled when I told her how I had drifted off into dreams. She offered me a meditation course she had of his, which appeared so instantly I swear it slipped from her sleeve and had been tucked up there for just the right moment.

It was fairly simple. Several CDs outlined the fundamentals of the Christian faith crisply and concisely and, other than the clarity and ease in which it was presented and his unswerving belief that God is good, there was nothing new or startling. The guided meditation gently directed me through a progressive relaxation exercise and, once I was fully at peace, created imagery that allowed me to envision the basic principle of my faith: Christ literally stepping into and becoming one with me. Instead of remaining a function of my thought alone, my emotions engaged with that truth. Peace flowed through my entire being.

I was challenged to look at where my thoughts were rooted and, rather than in my head, I began to see they were an out-flowing of my heart. My heart beliefs, although not necessarily true, are the creeds I live out of. So, instead of chasing my thoughts away or trying to corral the emotions they evoke, I spent time asking another very simple question, prefaced with the one belief that, as a Christian, I say I fully embrace: "With the fullness of Christ living in me, is that _____ true?" Is it true I am limited? Is it true I lack anything? My prayer time radically changed; petitions turned to praise. Instead of asking for healing, I leaned more fully into the truth that in Christ I am completely whole. Rather than pleading with God to come, I recognized His deep abiding presence. In exchange for asking for wisdom, I thanked Him that I have already been given the mind of Christ and, by gauging the level of peace I was experiencing, I made my decisions confidently.

During the days, I systematically combed over everything I had been taught about God and weighed it against the fundamental truth of His character, His love and goodness. I took apart concepts ingrained in me since childhood and challenged them. Does a God of love, who is truly good, wound me in order to heal me? Would a loving Father use guilt and shame to coerce me into compliance? Does anything, even my sin, have the power to separate me from the love of God? Is the essence of love unpredictable, difficult to understand, deliberately designing dilemmas to keeping me guessing and on my toes? And as I answered those questions, I fell in love with a God whose only goal is to express His love and be completely connected with His creation, settling my heart into a deep abiding peace.

When I went to bed at night, instead of fighting my thoughts, I considered deeply what was most true and called my mind to focus on the reality that Christ literally lives in and through me and, as I rested in that truth, I gently drifted off to sleep. If I awakened again, I relaxed my body, stilled my mind, quieted my soul and visualized His presence. In a matter of minutes I was able to surrender and sink into peace.

The world looks a lot friendlier when you are getting consistent, restorative sleep. Immediately, the fear I had carried in my belly dissolved and I was free to explore and ask more questions.

One Wednesday afternoon, I was sitting in Liz's living room. Five of us had been meeting regularly; I was the newcomer to the group. We call ourselves the Bags of Joy, Bags for short and, at our weekly Bagfests we talk and pray together. I made a joke about my memory and Liz instantly welled up with tears. Later, as we were praying, she said she knew God remembered all the events of my life and simply asked Him to unwrap those memories and give them to me as gifts. Cindy, Teresa and Renee agreed they could see the neurological pathways being rejuvenated and reconnected, giving me complete access to my past. It had never occurred to me to claim the healing that was mine, having the mind of Christ.

Each morning after, as I sat in my little away room and centred myself in prayer, I visualized the healing light gathering, mending, blending the tattered threads inside my head and weaving them once more into a complete tapestry of my life. Sometimes when I was done, I realized I had been sitting there for an hour in a time of complete stillness, empty of words but full of energy. There is no way to measure what memories have been restored but in conversations and everyday exchanges I am not encountering the blanks I once did. Jumbles, Sudoku and Crossword Puzzles are merely fun again. I believe my brain has healed.

In the springtime a couple of years ago, I was out in my garden, plucking weeds and hauling earth. I sat down in my zero-gravity chair near the pond to rest and breathed in deeply. The scent of freshly cut grass wafted up my nose; it smelled sweet. My eyes bolted open. I realized I wasn't experiencing my usual allergies, the spring hay-fever when my symptoms grew most out of control. I had noticed the sinus headaches and haunting heaviness I had learned to live with had lessened throughout the winter. That made sense since I had consciously created a more allergy-free environment. We didn't have animals; I had eliminated most carpet from our new house and only used cleaning products that were scent-free and eco-friendly. I refused to put myself in situations that made me sick, even if it meant having to excuse myself when a perfume was too strong or natural lavender was being processed. I liked feeling well and protected my newfound sense of health with great fervour. But being outside on a sunny day, inhaling the scent of spring bursting into bloom without the sneezy, itchy, watery-eyes or my nose pouring and throat swelling shut, was a complete miracle.

I don't know what has changed inside my body. Being at peace has caused many wars to cease. Perhaps it is a combination of things but what I feel most strongly is an ever-increasing alignment between my head and my heart that allows me to live my life wholly and holy. I am loved by God. Christ lives in me. I am fully alive. And now I can brEAThe.

Afterword

At Christmastime last year, I was standing in the foyer of The Royal Theatre in Victoria. I had just watched the matinee performance of the Nutcracker Suite. Laura, my soon-to-be daughter-in-law, asked a question. We had been talking about how children are shaped by the experiences they have had growing up in their families. I told her there were things my boys may not have completely understood about our family because there were many parts of my past I had not fully spoken of, details they simply may not know. She asked if I thought it would have been easier for them if I had told my boys the story of my life. I turned the question over many times.

It is hard to tell a story from beginning to end, most especially when the unfolding of it starts in the middle and works its way out from there. And where do you begin to tell an untidy tale so full of twists and turns?

So, for Christopher, Jonathan, Micah and Joshua, for Laura and all the other beautiful and brave women my boys will love, "I was fifteen when I ran away from home. I ran away for the same reasons most kids do: because I was hurt and angry but most of all sad...And now I can brEAThe".

Acknowledgments

Thank you Alan, love of my life, for bravely slogging through the many dark, dreary days we had to journey together in order to find healing. I admire the strength and courage it took to come home each Monday evening last year and listen to the retelling of those tales. Thank you for weeping with me as we waded through each story again and for always encouraging me to tell the truth.

I will be forever grateful to you Christopher Page, you were the first to listen and hear this story. Because of you I discovered my voice and have been freed to find words to place around the pain. I offer many thanks to you Mark Buchanan, for being my pastor and continually challenging me to share this untidy tale with others. I appreciate that you two spiritual mentors have given so generously of your time, reading through rough drafts and then offering your wisdom. Your encouragement and sharp pencils helped sculpt these scattered stories so they could be bound together into a book. Your lives have inspired me to walk in the truth and live in the light.

Thank you: Shawna, Marylou, Marita, Karen, Juliette and

her friend Diane for trudging through early drafts, giving me honest feedback and always cheering me on.

To my YaYa's, Group and other precious friends who lived this story alongside me: I owe you all garlands of gratitude. Because of your faithfulness we can now rejoice together safely, this side of the saga.

I'll always cherish the encouragement I received from you my dear Bags: Renee, Cindy, Teresa and Liz. You stood beside me steadfastly holding out a clear vision, seeing the end from the beginning. Because of you I wasn't left mired in the murkiness of the moment when my mind became muddled in the middle.

Thank you, Deborah, for patiently listening as I read and always being just an early morning phone call away.

Hugs and kisses to you Cindy, Lisa and Pat for working so diligently on the cover design and to Malleia for calming holding your breath as your Auntie snapped dozens of pictures of you underwater while Uncle Andy stood guard. In real life I pray you will always be free to breathe.

Deep thanks to you, Celia McLean, my editor and friend. Your questions, first piecing me through, prodded and pushed me to tell a more complete and straightforward story. I owe you buckets of gratitude for doing all the finicky work I so detest.

And to those of you who have taken the time to read this long tale: thanks for listening. May you pass on any nugget of hope that you have unearthed as you have sifted through my story. It is my prayer that you will embrace the courage within you to speak your own truth boldly so you too will experience the freedom that your heart desires and God Himself longs for you.

I belong to a speaking group called "The Bags of Joy". We are a fun group of women who study together and teach out of our varied and vast life experiences. Through laughter and tears we encourage and guide others to follow a God of grace so they too will be freed to live joyful, redeemed, peaceful and purpose-filled lives.

To connect or inquire about speaking engagements please visit us through:

Facebook: The Bags of Joy
Website: thebagsofjoy.com

Muriel Brake

250 - 733 - 2577

CPSIA information can be obtained at www.ICGtesting.com
Printed in the USA
LVOW082330030613

336733LV00001B/29/P